FREEDOM THROUGH
GRACE

FREEDOM THROUGH
GRACE

What people are saying about

"I can attest to Shannon's capabilities of consistently demonstrating the expertise, integrity, and professional competence in delivering technical excellence that our ministries absolutely depend upon week after week to maintain our professional standards of ministry performance."

Dave Dupree, Minister of Music, Shandon Baptist Church
Columbia, SC

"Shannon Ericsson and his team meets every challenge head-on with professional skill, expertise and determination to get the job done, and establish a testimony with the church staff of each ministry—we consider his work to be exemplary, across many projects over several years. His ministry program development, and technical systems programming, always produce excellent results on our many church projects."

Curtis Doss, McGehee, Nicholson, Burke Architects
Memphis, TN

"We are absolutely delighted and satisfied with the work that Shannon and Omega have provided First Assembly of God. Our church seats 5,000 people within our sanctuary and we really depend upon the quality technical systems, and ministry program consulting, that Shannon and his Omega team have provided for our ministry."

Larry Alverson, Minister of Administration, First Assembly
Grand Rapids, MI

"Shannon Ericsson has designed & implemented a new technical system for ministry in our large worship center. In addition, his ministry program consulting services and hands-on efforts have resulted in a much higher & more effective ministry performance level which has exceeded the objectives which we had established."

Robert Deal, First Baptist Church
Los Altos, CA

"The system that Shannon designed for our new 3,000 seat worship center is a joy for our ministry to work with. His ability to speak & teach very complex subjects to non-technical church volunteers, and then train them in high performance ministry, has exceeded our expectations.

Judi Jarmula, Media Services, Calvary Church
Naperville, IL

"Shannon Ericsson and Omega has been the technical ministry consultants on five of our projects, and our firm has been completely satisfied with the work effort and expertise of Shannon and his team, which has included design, specifications, ministry programming, and project management."

John Taylor, AIA, GBP Architects
Seattle, WA

FREEDOM THROUGH GRACE

Thriving More, Striving Less, and Thoroughly Enjoying Life
A Powerful Life-Action Plan Leading to More Peace & Freedom
Gods' Gift of Freedom

Capture It–Own It–Live It!

Fly Beyond Every Life Struggle and Feel your Spirit Soar

SHANNON ERICSSON

FREEDOM THROUGH GRACE
Fly Beyond Every Life Struggle and Feel your Spirit Soar

Copyright © 2022 by Shannon Ericsson
www.shannonericsson.com
All rights reserved.
ISBN: 979-8-9859204-0-6

SCRIPTURE CITATIONS:
NIV ® Copyright © 1973, 1978, 1984, 2011 by Biblica, Inc.
Scripture quotations marked "NIV", "New International Version", "Biblica", the "Biblica Circle Device" and "International Bible Society" are trademarks registered in the United States Patent and Trademark Office by Biblica, Inc. Used with permission. All rights reserved worldwide.

Scripture quotations marked "NASB" are taken from the New American Standard Bible®, Copyright © 1960, 1962, 1963, 1968, 1971, 1972, 1973, 1975, 1977, 1995 by The Lockman Foundation. Used by permission.

Scripture quotations marked "AMP" are taken from the Amplified® Bible, Copyright © 1954, 1958, 1962, 1964, 1965, 1987 by The Lockman Foundation. Used by permission.

Scripture quotations marked "RSV" or "NRSV" Revised Standard Version of the Bible, copyright © 1946, 1952 and 1971 National Council of the Churches of Christ in the United States of America. Used by permission.

Scripture quotations marked "HCSB"®, are taken from the Holman Christian Standard Bible®, Copyright © 1999, 2000, 2002, 2003, 2009 by Holman Bible Publishers. Used by permission. HCSB® is a federally registered trademark of Holman Bible Publishers.

Scripture quotations marked "NLT" are taken from the Holy Bible, New Living Translation, copyright © 1996, 2004, 2007 by Tyndale House Foundation. Used by permission of Tyndale House Publishers, Inc., Carol Stream, Illinois 60188. All rights reserved.

Scripture quotations marked "TLB" are taken from The Living Bible copyright © 1971. Used by permission of Tyndale House Publishers, Inc., Carol Stream, Illinois 60188. All rights reserved.

Scripture quotations marked "MSG" or "MESSAGE" are taken from The Message. Copyright 1993, 1994, 1995, 1996, 2000, 2001, 2002. Used by permission of NavPress Publishing Group.

Scripture quotations marked "KJV" are taken from the Holy Bible, King James Version (Public Domain).

Cover & Layout Design by William Alyea – Seven3Creative
No portion of this book may be reproduced in any form without permission from the publisher, except as permitted by U.S. copyright law. For permission contact: shannon@shannonericsson.com

FIRST EDITION

DISCLAIMER – TERMS OF USE

The author and publisher have used their best efforts to develop and prepare the Freedom Renewed Program©, within this book, prior to publishing. They make no representation or warranty with respect to the accuracy, applicability, fitness, or completeness of the contents of this book. This book contains the authors' opinions, ideas, and suggestions—it is strictly intended to be an informative, educational, and beneficial resource to the reader, and is sold with that understanding in place.

Every effort has been made to accurately represent this program and its potential benefit and value. However, there is no guarantee that anyone will actually improve their lifestyle in any way using the techniques, ideas and recommendations within these materials. Examples used in these materials are not to be interpreted as a promise or guarantee of anything. All self-help and personal improvement potential is entirely dependent on the person employing the books' program curriculum and course of study. Therefore, the author disclaims any warranties at all, *(expressed or implied)*, merchantability, or fitness for any particular purpose. The author shall in no event be held liable to any party for any direct, indirect, punitive, special, incidental or other consequential damages arising directly or indirectly from any use of this material, which is provided – *"as is"* – and without warranties.

The author has made every reasonable effort to ensure that the information in this book is accurate, however, it is not intended to render any personal, medical, health, or any other kind of professional services. The reader should consult competent medical, or other licensed professionals, before taking any kind of action, or drawing any inference, from opinions and suggestions made by the author in this book.

MEDICAL – HEALTH ADDENDUM

Abundant, and notable documentation, from competent researchers over many years has revealed that there are a number of Christians who are suffering the toxic effects of abusing drugs and alcohol in their bodies and their minds over a long period of time. Should the reader be one who falls into that category, the author encourages the reader to first seek out medical professionals who can provide effective therapy to de-toxify the body of the poisonous results of abusing booze and drugs, in particular. Having done that successfully, the reader will have put their body, mind and soul into a much better place to successfully take on the life challenge of acquiring authentic biblical freedom—a new found freedom from substance, and other abuse, that can result in a deep-rooted contentment and fulfillment from the Christian lifestyle.

FREEDOM THROUGH GRACE

TABLE OF CONTENTS

BOOK 1
FREEDOM THROUGH GRACE

Table of Contents 9

Foreward... 11

Preface 13

Acknowledgement 15

Introduction.. 17

PART 1
CHALLENGING THE STATUS QUO

Challenge 35

Pathways 85

PART 2
BELIEVE GOD BEFORE YOU CAN OBEY GOD

Faith.. 111

Firm Faith... 147

Faithfulness.. 175

ADDENDUM 1
EVIDENCE FOR THE CHRISTIAN FAITH

The Evdence for the Christian faith 189

PART 3
FREEDOM STRATEGY & LIFE ACTION PLAN

Lifecycles.. 195

Obedience through Faith... 229

Freedom Tactics 253

Freedom through Grace 277

BIBLIOGRAPHY *(A Partial Reference List By Relevance)* 316

FREEDOM THROUGH GRACE

FOREWARD

How do you thank someone for rescuing you from your own ignorance? I am now 60 years old, but at the age of eleven I gained what I call, "The scars of ignorance." I had always been curious of fire, but I did not know its dangers, nor was I aware of the deadly combination of fire and gasoline. You see, my dad used to grill on those old round charcoal grills, and he used charcoal lighter to enhance the flame. Charcoal lighter, or gasoline – who knew the difference? Not me, I was ignorant to the difference. Well, one hot day in May, a five gallon can of gas and a small fire turned into a major explosion—stop-drop and roll—followed by a really fast ride to the hospital by my neighbor, a year's recovery from third degree burns over half my body, and a lifetime of internal and external scars. Why did that happen? Ignorance! Turns out, what you don't know can hurt you. As I entered into adult life, I was a long way from that day in May, and my physical scars have healed, but the impact of those internal ones rise up often to interrupt my life and my thinking. If anyone ever needed to be delivered from the bondage of their own thoughts, it was me.

I first met Shannon in a project at our church in 2001 of which I was again, ignorant. How to put sound in a rather unusual building known as a Sprung structure. It is much like a gigantic permanent tent. It's wide open and the challenges of sound in such a building created obstacles that no one had tackled before. Shannon helped to overcome these challenges, and, as a result, worship in our new building would end up being amazing. He has an ability to tackle the difficult and make it easy. That is the true talent of a master. I had no idea that I would ever see him again, or that our paths would ever need to cross again, or the impact he would have on my life and my internal scars.

Fast forward twenty years and we meet again. Shannon called me to speak about a book project he was working on to help people find freedom in Christ. It just so happened that I was deeply involved in writing my own material and teaching freedom in my church, so we were on common ground. As we began collaborating together, I began to realize that he had created a program that was far superior to what I had been working on. Once again, I found that I was ignorant to many things that would end up really helping me. For so many issues in life, there are more books, more articles, more information, and more advice than you could ever possibly read—but, many of them have one thing in common. They can tell you a lot about a subject, but nearly all of them fail to tell you how to actually do what they offer—how to effectively apply it to your life. This is where this book exceeds so many that I have read. Shannon actually tells you how to find that freedom. He has a plan that fits anyone, because it is not so much like a plan, as it is a conversation with him about your obstacles—then developing a unique pathway leading you to that freedom.

I found myself immediately putting into practice this plan and finding a final healing of those lifelong scars of being burned, and the rejection and difficulty in life that they brought. I am more free now than before I started. What you don't know really can hurt you. I thank Shannon for this book because, once again, I have been delivered from my own ignorance in the best kind of way. I am excited for all who will read and apply the truths of this book, because the outcome will not only be a finished book, it can also be a delivered life—that's what Jesus said would happen whenever any of his followers lock themselves into the grace and truth he so abundantly provides. May God richly bless you as you journey through these pages, and may you share these truths with the others who may be trapped in the bondage of their thoughts of the past, something they may not even realize. It's time to be delivered—enjoy the journey.

Pastor Kenny Chinn
Northside Church
Wilmington, North Carolina

PREFACE

I wrote this book to challenge an all too often—all too common, wide-spread, and even prevalent Christian perspective and outlook on life, by a little bit, or, maybe, for some of you, by a lot. My extensive research over the last few years in particular, informs me that an increasing number of believers want to actually experience and interact with God, on a much more personal level. That's one reason why America is experiencing such a decline in church attendance today. A lot of Christians, both young & old, no longer want to be told *"about God"* so much—they want to actually discover him, connect with him, and relate *"one-on-one"* with him, for themselves. Jesus wants to let you know that he is up for this - **The challenge is, are you?**

So, in response, we'll take a close look at what I call the ***"God's Eye View of Life,"*** and how that influences the typical day-to-day Christian lifestyle. Here's why—in the God's eye view of life, it is not very meaningful just how successful or unsuccessful your life is, right now—right at this particular moment in time.

Turns out that it's way more valuable to figure out where you are going in your life, rather than where you are at, or, where you have been. Here's what I mean by that—*your current trajectory in life matters substantially more than what your current results may reveal...* That trajectory begs this question: Where are your current habits likely to lead you through this next month, next year, next decade—**what's trending in your life right now**—you're going somewhere, right? The key is, where are you going next—what path are you on and where will it lead you? Something to think about isn't it—I encourage you to consider how much spiritual freedom and fulfillment you've acquired up to this point in your life, and, whether you'd like to acquire more. That just makes good sense, doesn't it?

So, let's talk about some effective, pragmatic, and personal theology that we can put into operation designed to move us toward that freedom, and away from a crisis of some kind—how about distilling all of this down to just 4, essential tactics, in the form of these following sound bites:

- *Find Out What God Likes and Do Those Things.*
- *Find Out What God Does Not Like and Don't Do Those Things.*
- *Find Out What God Wants from You and Give It to Him.*
- *Find Out What Freedom Will Cost You and Pay That Price.*

You won't find a 7-step plan, or 12-step program in this book—only authentic, biblical freedom. Okay, what do you think? You're hearing me today, and considering whether you would like to increase your spiritual freedom, health & well-being, by a little bit, or perhaps, by a lot. So, it really doesn't matter whether your lifestyle just needs a minor course correction, or, whether your life is being hammered hard by some kind of addiction. I know my **Freedom Renewed Program** *(FRP)* in this book, and the Action-Plan on my website, will help you get there and put you on the right path. That's why I developed it in the first place—to provide a God honoring plan to invest your life into - That's what I've been doing with it for years now – It's effective—it simply works, and it works really well.

It's more than a devotional, and way more than a bible study. It's a very comprehensive, **Christian Lifestyle System** that you can plug your life into, patterned off the Gospel, and designed to connect you with Jesus, more consistently, and more effectively, on a daily basis—and, with good reason. Writers like me cannot fix any of the spiritual issues that I document throughout every chapter of this book - **but, Jesus can** – and he promises to do that for everyone who chooses to earnestly seek him out, and then believe and adopt all that he has to say.

ACKNOWLEDGEMENT

This book could not, and would not have been written, apart from the pervasive, and wonderful presence, of my very best friend, confidant, life-coach, Lord, Savior, and the lover of my soul, Jesus Christ. His vast number of interventions throughout my life, directly by his Holy Spirit, and through an abundant number of Christian brothers and sisters, are at the core of this work.

Especially my cherished wife Pamela *(Pammy)*. Her unswerving encouragement, wise counsel, prolific bouts of proof-reading, and her abundant love and support for me, and this work, have been a formidable catalyst—helping me to remain focused over these many years, on getting this book completed. In addition, there have been many dear friends of mine, and several gifted preachers and bible teachers, whom I've known for years in ministry, who's words have found their way into this book. A favorite couple, in particular, whom Pammy and I cherish, is Scott and Daphne Weyer. They live very nearby, and have given so much of their time, resources, and spiritual insight into this work—my gratitude to all is absolutely boundless.

FREEDOM THROUGH GRACE

INTRODUCTION

My Freedom Renewed website – www.shannonericsson.com – begins like this:

> *"There is a Crisis in the Land...... Life comes at us really fast at times, and we all want to avoid a destructive crisis of some kind getting a grip on our life.....***We want FREEDOM** *- but, it can be so elusive and difficult to attain....... even for seasoned Christians.*

More to the point – *"There is a Crisis in the Church."* – Even the most Bible Thinking, God Walking, Upright Christian Believer will experience seasons of life that make them vulnerable and susceptible to the trouble that Jesus spoke about in his Gospels—here's what he said: **"In this world, you will have trouble..."**

Turns out of course, that he was spot-on. Some believers are just becoming aware of this trouble and recognize that it's beginning to influence them and their lifestyle, and they're seeking a *"tune-up,"* at the very least, to strengthen their relationship with Jesus—and for good reason. They're wanting to avoid some kind of crisis developing in their life that could really hammer them. Many have talked to me about a battle they are having with spiritual discipline—especially younger guys—it's about their thought-life, and how they are struggling to take every thought captive to the obedience of Christ, like the bible says. They are realizing that their life has veered off course a little bit, and they are looking for an effective way to get it back on track, moving forward again. They long to ignite, or, to reignite their faith, and their love of God like they know they need to do—like so many of them used to do.

However, many others know they need way more than a tune-up—they need a total spiritual life overhaul. A multitude of believers are looking for fulfillment in all the wrong places resulting in a crisis of substance abuse and even long-term addiction hammering their souls. In addition, our families are having to take on the emotional upheaval and debilitating stress caused by this Covid pandemic winding down on the world stage, and now, ramping up on the world stage, comes war, and rumors of war, just like Jesus said would happen, in the end days of this age. Mom's and dad's grappling with increased levels of anxiety, insecurity and depression in their children that they've never experienced before. They struggle mightily just trying to cope with the reality that life demands of them, in the wake of this menace. For some it's economic, family, or work-related stress. Some Christians have lost their marriage, a loved one, or their career. Others lose their health, or their 401k, or life savings.

All too often, Christians recoil from stress and painful events by yielding to one or more scourges of life such as anger, eating or drinking too much, drug addiction, alcoholism, sexual immorality like porn or adultery—even seemingly innocuous things, especially relevant today, in this culture we live in. *Check this out:*

Who would have thought that Christians would be getting hooked on romance novels, digital gaming, gambling, and social media of all kinds? An insightful book of research on this subject that I have found, comes from one of America's leading psychiatrists and authors, Dr. Anna Lembke, MD. I paraphrase the following from her – ***Dopamine Nation*** – book:[1]

> *"Americans especially, are becoming heavily influenced to **overconsuming** all kinds of things, because of the ease of accessing and acquiring, all kinds of things. We're all running from pain. We take pills—we drink booze—we gorge on chocolate cake—we binge on romance novels. We'll do almost anything to distract ourselves from ourselves—yet all this trying to insulate ourselves from pain seems only to have made it worse. The reason we're all so miserable just might be because we're working so hard to avoid being miserable."*

Though these things can provide some escape and relief, it's only temporary— and then reality shows up again exacerbating the turmoil of life, especially if you're a Christian, because of guilt. It's a soul-crushing cycle that many

---

[1] ***"Dopamine Nation"*** – Publisher: Penguin Random House; New York, 2021

Christians have a deep desire to stop, but they don't know how—and, not because of bible ignorance—turns out that their current plan is just not sufficiently effective. *They need a new one; a better one—an effective one...*

Are you, or someone you know and care about having to live like that? Truth is, no one desires to live like that. We want to determine and control our temperament, attitude, and behavior in a way that produces a deep-rooted contentment and fulfillment from our lifestyle. Isn't that it—doesn't that sound right to you? So, what would you think if I told you that kind of hope, renewed freedom and lifestyle is not only possible, but very attainable and very available, right now...?

There certainly is a crisis of spiritual freedom weaving its way through the church today—however, there is also, and forever has been, a profusion of really good news that comes in the form of our Lord and Savior, Jesus Christ. **He knows everything and he can do anything.**

Trouble is, there's also a multitude of Christians out there in the church today who are blissfully unaware of that—their need-to-know Jesus, way more effectively than they do now—has also become a crisis for them, and it is growing more prevalent in church life today.

An increasing number of Christians experience Jesus more as an acquaintance, or historical icon—akin to George Washington, or Abe Lincoln. They just don't know him well enough to consistently walk in the authentic, biblical freedom that he has provided us. Their spiritual foundation is very weak, making them vulnerable for some kind of train-wreck coming down the line, in their not-to-distant future.

Many are becoming aware of this and are getting inspired to do something about it. Now, that's some really good news. Here's why—the primary motivation for these believers to think about purchasing this book is clearly to either fix, or to avoid, the bad habits and destructive lifestyle issues that I write about—my research distinctly tells me that.

However, there's something else—something bigger. Every believer who chooses to begin adopting my FRP can anticipate something unforeseen and wonderful happening in their life—they'll be drawn much closer to Jesus than they ever were before. Most won't see that coming—but, that's what happens when you hang out with Jesus—they just don't know it yet, but they will... This book will put them on the right path. But, like I said before, life comes at us really fast at times, and the well-worn method of simply reading and memorizing scripture just isn't enough this day and age. You need a plan, or process, to help you focus and consistently apply those biblical principles of truth. This book offers that plan and process—and it's distinctive, in a number of ways.

And, here's one of them—a very key reason for writing this book the way that I have... Turns out that a large number of believers shared that they were not interested in putting a *"Band-Aid"* on the issues of life they were struggling with—they knew that a couple of seminars or a weekend drive-by retreat just would not be sufficient to plug their life into. And further, it didn't matter whether their spiritual need was relatively minor, rekindling a little more discipline, or whether that need was massive, reordering their entire lifestyle. They wanted their spiritual condition fixed—NO MORE BAND AIDS! That's what the FRP in this book is all about—providing a plan that actually works, and works really well, for ordinary Christians, and church leaders alike—even for non-believers who are curious about God and his power. Truth is... that's exactly why I put an action-plan on my website and why I wrote this book—and that's exactly what the program in both of them has been meticulously designed to accomplish within any and every freedom-seeker who will seriously invest themselves in it.

So, what do you think—how does that sound to you? Is it time to experience that fun, joy and fulfillment in your life again—are you interested?

Almighty God, the creator of the heavens and the earth, has a message for you. There is something that he wants you to know, about yourself or someone you care for, that you simply do not know right now. You really need to hear this, for yourself or for them—It truly is a life-changer. That freedom message begins here in the Old Testament book of Jeremiah:

> **Jer. 33:3** *"Call to me and I will answer you, and will tell you great and hidden things that you have not known..." (NRSV)*

There is a clear and compelling logic woven into this message of freedom that I encourage you to consider and think about in the following two points:

1. God knows that if your personal relationship with Jesus was sufficiently effective right now, you wouldn't have need to acquire an increased level of authentic, exhilarating, biblical freedom—*You'd actually be living it.* Isn't that right—what do you think?

2. God deeply desires to reveal those great and hidden things to you. However, He alone understands the motive behind every thought. So, God wants you to know that if you determine to seek him for yourself or to help someone you love, with authentic sincerity in your heart, he will be found by you *(1Chr. 28:9)*. He is waiting for you to take the first step and call out to him.

> *He stands ready, right now, to begin renewing and reinvigorating your hope and your hunger for the deep things of God. Question is, are you ready...? He always rewards those who diligently seek him* **(Heb. 11:6)**.

I can tell you that this message is all about **Authentic Freedom**—not just some old clichés about freedom to live-out a few hopes and dreams or even answers to some prayers that you've likely pondered over and over—but the kind of change in life that can truly set you or them on a path to experience a more fulfilling, and even exhilarating life-style, characterized with much deeper joy and peace. That's what God's message and his reward looks like.

That hidden message that God wants you to know is also revealed here in the New Testament book of Galatians, with a little more perspective:

> **Gal. 5:1** *It is for freedom that Christ has set us free. Stand firm, then, and do not let yourselves be burdened again by a yoke of slavery... (NIV)*

Jesus wants each and every Christian follower of his to experience the kind of freedom and abundant life-style that I have just described, however, the truth is that there are a multitude of us in the church today who are not free to live like that. So, if you or someone you love and care about are in need of that kind of freedom, this book is for you. That's exactly why I wrote it—acquiring, or re-acquiring an abundant lifestyle of authentic, exhilarating, biblical freedom. It's time to have fun and really enjoy life again—*what do you think? Are you ready for that?*

Jesus himself said, from John 16:33, *"I have told you these things, so that in me you may have peace. In this world you will have trouble. But take heart! I have overcome the world."* Jesus is making a strategic point here by inference. He is counseling us to actually anticipate the arrival of trouble in this life and to prepare ourselves for it—and not to run from it, but, like him, to overcome it. There is a way—he always makes a way for those who seek him with all their heart.

This experience of freedom, documented in Galatians 5:1, is wrapped up in the person of Jesus Christ, and the unsearchable riches of your knowledge of him—of just how well you know him. And that unique kind of formidable and powerful knowledge my friend, is the great and hidden thing that Almighty God wants you to know, and know so well, so effectively, that your life will be wonderfully changed forever more.

That freedom you are seeking—that you might even be desperate to acquire, is inextricably linked, both now and forever, to your working knowledge and relationship with Jesus. **Following here, is a very easy and effective sound-bite to memorize that will lock this unassailable truth into your brain:**

- *Insufficient Knowledge of Jesus*—Always Results in Insufficient Freedom, Insufficient Joy and Insufficient Peace in Your Life.

Therefore, at the very least, I have authored this book for that very reason—that your personal relationship with Jesus will have been made significantly stronger and more effective as a result of reading, studying, and applying what I've written.

And further, that many of you will actually acquire that *Freedom through Grace* that I write about—and begin living it out with a new found joy and exhilaration. That's what Jesus wants for you - But, there's that trouble he talks about... We need to deal with it.

Let's begin examining some of that trouble...

Life struggles, temptations, and our response to them, affects all people, from all walks of life—including Christians—including Christian church leaders. We are all vulnerable. We are all at risk. We all battle with this, in some way, throughout almost every day of our life. And, God has already documented the response he expects us to make, here, from the book of Hebrews:

> **Heb. 12:1** *let us throw off everything that hinders and the sin that so easily entangles, and let us run with perseverance the race marked out for us. (NIV)*

Begs a question – Can you fulfill this scripture right now?

Are you able to consistently and faithfully fulfill what God is instructing every Christian to do here? Can you do this all of the time—Some of the time—A little of the time—Every once in a while—or, like so very many Christians, would you have to say—Hardly ever, or even, not at all - *I just keep striking out*. Your answer will reveal a lot about how well you know Jesus right now. God knows just how easy it is for any of us to become entangled in some kind of sinful behavior, and also, what it takes to throw it off and stay clear of it. However, it turns out this is way easier said than done. In fact, many Christians possess sufficient intellectual knowledge of what they need to do. Knowledge of the biblical truth designed to set them free is not their main issue.

They have discovered, much to their dismay, that the discipline, willpower, habits, and overall life strategy they have adopted for themselves is not as effective as it needs to be. Try as they might, their numerous attempts to overcome destructive habits and lifestyles still fall short of success. And, it is certainly not because of any lack of desire. Every Christian I am aware of strongly desires to do what God is instructing them to do, not only here in Hebrews 12, but throughout the entire bible.

What an enigma. They may know what to do, but they are just not able to develop a method, or a plan for themselves that really works; Like Jesus said: *"The spirit is willing, but the flesh is weak."* For example, here's the issue documented in Romans by the Apostle Paul:

> **Rom. 7:18-19** *I know that nothing good lives in me, that is, in my sinful nature. For I have the desire to do what is good, but I cannot carry it out. For what I do is not the good I want to do; no, the evil I do not want to do—this I keep on doing.* (NIV)

This passage of scripture accurately describes the conflict and bewilderment that results when Christians consistently yield themselves to sin. They may clearly recognize, understand, and desire to conform their lifestyle in a way that fulfills the teaching of Christ, but have not been able, or are not currently able, to consistently make that happen.

So many have just given up. They're Out-of-Gas or, their spiritual gas tank is almost empty – *Running on Fumes*. They have yet to find what it takes to get themselves free.

The problem looks just like this: *"No Jesus – No Gas!"*

The solution looks just like this: *"Know Jesus well – Lots of Gas!"*

Jesus clearly doesn't want you to live like that. He wants you to be free so you can determine and control your temperament, attitude, and behavior in a way that produces that deep-rooted contentment and fulfillment throughout all the days of your life, like I stated earlier. This is true whether you believe in God or not. However, there is a certain type of person I am convicted to emphasize and reach out to with this program:

Let me describe that person – **it just might be you:**

*"**Outwardly**, you may be a normal functioning man or woman trying your best to succeed with your life.... Your family, close friends and associates may have no idea that you are having any significant problems. But **Inwardly**, where no one but you and God can see, you are really struggling to get free."*

Does that describe you? ***Definitely...? Maybe...? Sometimes...?***
You'd almost certainly be surprised at just how many wonderful men and women of God are having to deal with this, and, they absolutely hate it.

They're having to struggle outwardly, conforming to what they know looks like a God honoring lifestyle, but inwardly, they have not yet been able to find an effective way to throw off the stuff in their life that causes trouble and distress. This can be a very miserable way to live.

THE PROBLEM
Here's the rub—I write a lot about it throughout my FRP—it's all about *"the cry of every human heart to be loved, to be accepted and to be respected."* Turns out that God deliberately created this longing within every one of us, and, it also turns out that God is the only one who can effectively fulfill it, through Jesus.

However, we all like sheep have gone astray, and are prone to wander, just as the bible states—so, because that is true, our minds can easily be deceived into thinking that we can satisfy that very powerful yearning for love, acceptance & respect by indulging in all kinds of destructive behavior. As a result, many of us end up getting heavily influenced by it, or, even addicted to it. *That's the crisis*—and, it's getting worse in the church—not better.

Many Christians like those I've just described have become trapped in a destructive behavior cycle. This cycle starts by yielding to a temptation of some kind—then comes remorse and sorrow and many times even some intense anger at one-self.

That's followed by conviction and confession to God—then a short-lived state of repentance providing a temporary respite of freedom and peace - Only then to repeat the cycle by yielding to temptation again and again resulting in more defeat and misery. The cycle goes on and on, sometimes for years and yes, even decades for some Christians. This process describes the actions of a Yo-Yo, and can become a very merciless cycle of misery for those held fast by the grasp of it. A Yo-Yo travels up and down, **but never forward—it doesn't "go" anywhere.** Some believers have been living like this for years, living in denial with some kind of binding affliction, and having to become extremely stealthy to keep from exposing their lifestyle addiction or destructive behavior to others.

However, there is a way to either effectively inoculate one-self from being driven like this in the first place, or to get yourself free, and keep yourself free, from the tenacious grip of one of these afflictions. That's what the program and this book is all about—Intended to benefit any Christian seeking consistent personal freedom from destructive habits and lifestyles. Over time, it is designed to develop within you the knowledge, wisdom, fortitude, tenacity, grit and perseverance that will help you live your life in a more consistent state of freedom. That's why I developed this program and wrote this book—providing ordinary believers, and even non-believers, with a freedom plan that actually works, and works really well.

This book is not just another Christian self-help encyclopedia to wander through and try to digest. I didn't want to write yet another self-help tome for the Christian DIY book market, of which there are many. Let me explain – A real perplexity that begs an answer to a number of questions, beginning with these – Why are so many Christians, in this generation, becoming so afflicted with destructive lifestyles? What is causing this and why are they so deeply rooted, entrenched and difficult to get rid of? When I began developing this program and researching the effectiveness of existing books about the subject matter, I discovered something very compelling. A significant amount of the information needed to accurately and authentically define both questions of what was causing these debilitating lifestyles, and what can be done about it, was either not very clear at all, or, was missing entirely.

However, please don't get me wrong here… Many great and inspirational Christian books have been authored over the years, and many of them have brought me notable insight, enjoyment, and benefit. In my research, I could easily find support from bible study companion guides and other clinical resources from Christian and even secular behavior therapists, scientists and related professionals in the marketplace. There are numerous books and resources providing lots of good advice, lots of beneficial guidance. But I found nothing to substantially, or adequately, answer these questions of mine—after a lot of research, it become apparent to me that a new and unique development method could be employed that would be far more effective.

THE SOLUTION

I began developing this program in 1986. It occurred to me that if simply reading and memorizing scripture could produce the desired freedom from a destructive lifestyle, then a book like this would not be needed. Christians have been using scripture for eons. That is not the issue.

Statistical facts verify that this kind of program definitely is needed for so many of the reasons I have already documented within these last few pages.

So, what makes this FRP unique? Actually, a number of factors.

First, the program embedded within the pages of this book has been produced using a meticulous process of searching out and compiling, over many years, specific axioms of biblical truth, complimented with other freedom oriented, authoritative, and beneficial sources—however, and please take particular note here, that these other sources are never used in place of sacred, holy scripture, or, altering in any way, the authentic canon of scripture, found only, and exclusively, in the authorized versions of the Christian bible.

These other sources include the development and implementation of very efficient life management skills, the clinical workings of the mind from experts within pertinent fields of behavior sciences, advanced training methods of high-performance athletes and business professionals, accelerated and advanced learning techniques, and other applicable resources. Then **integrating all of this into an actual working plan** that is always pragmatic, productive, exceedingly effective and very rewarding.

This program of mine focuses exclusively on a plan of effective tactics designed to apply, authentic, biblical truth in ones' life. Further, I have also developed my process, in this way, to seriously avoid wasting your time and spinning your wheels. I have purposely researched only those specific and highly relevant principles and precepts from scripture, and also from these other particular sources, **that really matter.**

However, I can't tell you that this program is super easy and requires little effort to get through it. *(If I did, you would have some difficulty trusting me and believing that this program is worth very much)*. In fact, the study can be challenging, and even daunting at times.

Nonetheless, I have worked painstakingly hard to make both, the study process, and the retaining of knowledge, to be as easy for the reader as I can possibly make it. Here's another time-saver—at specific milestones of introducing essential precepts of biblical freedom, I document a Key-Principle to really help the reader "Lock-In" the crucial truth being presented.

For example, here's one of these essential key-principles:

> **Key #3** – *Jesus Christ is more intent on helping you and teaching you how to obtain a vibrant, functional, and stronghold busting lifestyle than He is about exposing your weaknesses and failures to public humiliation.*

So, this program is definitely not designed to be a quick drive-by presentation of information like you might receive from reading a few self-help books, or attending a couple of weekend seminars or workshops.

But, it doesn't stop there. The program goes on to identify, develop and help you maintain what is needed to avoid these freedom sucking bandits for the rest of your life. This FRP of mine will help provide that needed structure to plug your life into and develop some long-term stability—a functional and formidable spiritual foundation that you can reliably build your life upon.

This book meticulously and systematically reveals the *What, Why and How* all of this destructive behavior is happening to well-intentioned Christians navigating life right now, today. And, most importantly, this book illuminates an exceedingly effective method of actually helping to acquire that life-changing freedom sought after by so many. So, I reiterate; this program simply works – *IT REALLY WORKS!*

WHY WRITE THIS BOOK - SOME OF MY PERSONAL MOTIVATION
Considerable research has convinced me over the years that a significant percentage of Christians are experiencing cycles and seasons of misery in their lifestyles.

It is not like being in a state of inward denial, for they know their affliction very well. It is because this insidious and hidden state is real, and afflicts a multitude of wonderful people in the Church, that I have developed so much passion and dogged-determination to design this program and write this book. So, how have I become aware of these spiritual issues, you may ask?

Good question; let me offer some background.
My career, as a professional ministry consultant, has put me in almost daily contact and relation with literally hundreds of pastors, administrators, ministers of music and worship, gifted bible teachers, and other leadership within the Christian Church Community across our nation. In this capacity, I have personally experienced many of the denominational structures that identify Baptists, Pentecostals, Methodists, Presbyterians, and the other many expressions of faith within the Christian Church, taken as a whole.

So, I have learned to develop a very keen insight, knowledge and expertise of both evangelical and liturgical expressions of ministry, and, have also not been confined to construct this book from a single denominational viewpoint. This has been invaluable to me and I've been able to design this program for a very wide appeal within the Christian Church, at large.

You see, in order to perform my work really well, it is essential that I *"get to know"* these ministers and their ministry performance goals and mandates with considerable accuracy, effectiveness, and depth. Most of these Church projects of mine, over the last 25+ years, have taken from several months to sometimes several years to complete. This has provided me a more than sufficient time frame to establish very strong and trusting relationships with many. Through this network of endearing relationships, there have been extensive discussions and sometimes deep concerns being revealed. And, even great sorrow expressed at times, with many intercessory prayer sessions conducted when well-intentioned men and women of God, with great skills and service to offer, seemingly lose so much when life *"breaks down"* for them.

Therefore, I have developed a sincere sense and conviction that I am writing this book not so much to a group of readers that I do not know, but rather, to very dear friends whom I have a very real connection with, and care a great deal about. I also have a lot of empathy with Christians who struggle with addictive behavior. I was saved myself while in my 20's from a lifestyle of being a functional alcoholic. I know the struggle very well, and have had to be vigilant and diligent in my pursuit to know and relate to Jesus effectively enough to maintain my own spiritual freedom. *I get it.... I really do get it...!*

And so, now you have explored the introduction, probably scanned the table of contents and have been evaluating what this program is all about. The syntax of the program within this book has purposely been developed to ensure a very high return on the investment of time, research and study that each of you will choose to employ.

I know very well that you will need to develop a formidable Strategy and Life Action Plan to establish a rewarding lifestyle of freedom for yourself. I strongly believe that this book will help you do that very effectively.

I have also endeavored to design some flexibility in how you study and take-in this program. Some of you may only be looking for a very solid reference to just help you get back on the path of a more rewarding lifestyle. You may simply want to eliminate some errors in judgment before they lead to the formation of bad habits. If that lines up with your thinking, then I can encourage you to read and study the introductory sections, chapters 1 & 2, and then read and study the Key Principles, located throughout the book. This will save time and give you a quick overview of the overall freedom program.

On the other hand, if you know that just a refresher course will not be sufficient for you, and that you realize your desire or your need for a very comprehensive plan – A plan designed to completely re-order your thinking about life stuff and your behavior(s), then I recommend a different approach.

Here's what that could look like:

Read through the entire book without taking any extensive notes, but definitely documenting for yourself sections of the book that you realize will need further study. I strongly recommend that you do this without any regard for how much time this may take you to complete. Take all the time that you need. Then go back through the book as often as needed, but each time focus a lot more attention and detailed study on those sections that require more concentration. That's also when you should take extensive notes. I especially encourage you to start a written journal—it will become invaluable to you, as the Holy Spirit of God uses it to renew your mind more quickly, and more effectively.

This book has been deliberately designed to be very challenging at times, for many effective and beneficial reasons. However, I know you will also find it extremely compelling and rewarding. And now...... I thank you for your initial interest and consideration to read through this book Introduction. I sincerely hope that you enjoyed it and that these words of mine have given you a number of life changing things to think about...... Wishing you the very best as you begin now to plan and develop your own Freedom Strategy, studying your way through the pages of this book...... ***GODSPEED!***

PART 1
CHALLENGING THE STATUS QUO

God knows that if your personal relationship with Jesus was sufficiently effective right now, you wouldn't have need to acquire an increased level of authentic, exhilarating, biblical freedom—*You'd actually be living it.* Isn't that right?

Therefore, part 1 of this book will challenge you to believe, adopt and understand this fact—that somewhere along the line, the relative strength of your spiritual foundation has failed you at some point, or, it is not where you and God would like it to be, isn't that it? The first part of this book is designed to help you thoroughly assess the path of life that you are currently on, and, whether you need to, or would benefit by, making some changes in your lifestyle.

These next couple of chapters will begin making you aware of just where you are at right now, and what your particular path to freedom will look like, as you navigate the Christian lifestyle.

CHAPTER 1
CHALLENGE

The first part of this chapter will likely be a challenge to you. A challenge to focus your thinking, and then to believe something different...
- about yourself
- about God
- about how life works, compared to what you have been believing

Here's the reason why—the bible boldly declares what a Christian's normal lifestyle should look like, from **God's unique perspective**, according to his biblical standard. I write of this standard, documented here in Hebrews 12:1, often throughout my book, and the Action-Plan series on my website. Here it is again for your reference:

> **Heb. 12:1** - *let us throw off everything that hinders and the sin that so easily entangles, and let us run with perseverance the race marked out for us. (NIV)*

God is clearly speaking to Christians here in this passage of scripture. I restate the question, regarding this scripture, from my Intro again FYR... can you do this all of the time...some of the time, when you feel like it, or, like so many believers, I can hardly ever do this at all—I just keep striking out...! God is using this scripture passage here as an example to declare that every believer should be able to consistently live their lives, not in perfect compliance—but in earnest compliance, with this particular scripture, here in the book of Hebrews, and others like it, documented throughout the bible.

This is God's perspective of a normal Christian lifestyle.

Therefore, you are challenged to believe, adopt and understand this fact—that somewhere along the line, the relative strength of your spiritual foundation has failed you at some point, or, it is not where you and God would like it to be, isn't that it?

God is informing you here in Hebrews 12, that you need to fix it—you need to find out what went wrong, or, what's going wrong, and call out to Jesus for help—it's time to get it corrected. What do you think? Sound right to you?

That's your first Challenge—opening your mind up, and making a sincere commitment to thoroughly assess your existing belief system, your core values and habits, and how they influence, determine or outright control your behavior. Your life has veered off course a little, or a lot, and you need to get it back on track.

The question is, are you ready for that? The first step of this challenge is very simple, but also very profound—and, it is absolutely essential to your spiritual freedom. Here it is in one word **– DETERMINATION –** You've become very aware that your spiritual foundation is just not strong enough to continue building your life upon it the way that you want, and the way that you know God wants. You know that you need to change it—you need to fix it. Isn't that right?

Okay...we'll open this up. You've read through my introduction to this book—you've developed, at the very least, a sufficient amount of curiosity to take the next step and invest yourself into this program. Let's build on that—you see, your success in acquiring that authentic, biblical freedom is absolutely contingent upon just how determined you become—how much intensity you are able to develop as you make your way through this program. So, what does that look like—take a look at this key principle from my Freedom Renewed Program:

*Find out what Spiritual Freedom will cost you, and **pay that price.***

Truth is, that price you need to pay is always determined by God himself, as he looks on your heart, measures your faith and evaluates just how much **GRIT** you have. He sets that price based upon his good and perfect will and plan for you, but also, upon those results—that particular price is unique to you, and each one of us, who have determined to follow Jesus. Here's a relevant example:

Consider what the 56 signers of the Declaration of Independence committed themselves to pay, getting free from the tyranny they were under, way back in the 16th century. Take a look:

- Five signers were captured by the British as traitors and tortured before they died.
- Twelve had their homes ransacked and burned.
- Two lost their sons serving in the Revolutionary Army, another had two sons captured.
- Nine of the 56 fought and died from wounds or hardships of the Revolutionary War.
- They signed and they pledged their lives, their fortunes, and their sacred honor to each other and to our new nation. They all signed the Declaration of Independence knowing full well that the penalty would be death if they were captured.

I reference this epic account of our Founding Fathers and what they paid getting free from tyranny, for a really good and strategic reason—it is directly in context with getting oneself free from the tyranny of alcoholism, drug addiction, porn & sexual immorality, excessive anger, gluttony, etc.

You get the picture...

I encourage you here to stop and think about what I have just written—especially about your own determination. Your circumstances and status in life is certainly different than the founding fathers of our nation, however, there is one glaring exception that you definitely share with them.

They fully realized that the freedom from tyranny they were seeking would cost them something—it was not free, and, it would not just be given to them; they would have to fight for it. Just like you and me, they all had to struggle and wrestle with their own willingness to pay that cost, as the Lord began to reveal it to them. The cost of freedom that God reveals to you and me will be different than what they had to pay, but, the principle in force is exactly the same. Here it is...*When you determine to get yourself free from some form of spiritual tyranny in this life,* **you will be opposed.** Your adversary the devil wants to put his boot on your neck and keep it there throughout your entire life—that's just a fact. Therefore, ask yourself a couple of strategic questions and ponder what comes to your mind as an answer:

1. How determined are you to acquire that authentic, biblical freedom experience that I am writing about—**just how important is it to you**, and how bad do you want, or even crave, that kind of freedom?
2. It's going to cost you something—so, how willing are you to actually pay the price that God asks of you, once he reveals what that cost is? Think about that throughout your study on every page of this program.

AUTHENTIC FREEDOM REQUIRES STRUGGLE

God knows very well what a struggle this process of acquiring and maintaining spiritual freedom is to every one of us. He purposely created each of us with that struggle in mind. You might ask why did God do this? The answer to that question is manifold and just one of the tenets that may challenge you in this study. However, it must be learned really well if you are to acquire a lifestyle of freedom for yourself.

A good example of that *"life-struggle"* is found by observing a brood of chicks being hatched from their eggs. A normal, healthy mother chicken hen will not help or aid her chicks as they begin the process of hatching out of their eggs, even if a chick is really struggling to peck its way out of the shell. The reason is that the hen knows instinctively that if the chick is given an easy way out of the egg shell, that chick will end up being very weak and will likely not survive very long.

And so it is with all living things, including you and me. God has intentionally designed struggle within life into his creation as a necessary component of growth, health, strength and vitality. He did this **on-purpose.** The point here is that Jesus Christ is the designer and creator of life. He is the one who has created all the heavens and the earth, including you, me and every other living thing.

And, he has designed life for human beings in such a way that almost all things we value require effort, and sometimes very hard work on our part to achieve and/or acquire. Here's another example of this life struggle—to gain physical strength and enhanced vitality, a person must exercise, sometimes with a rigorous training regimen involving lifting weights, calisthenics, etc. Muscles require resistance to grow and become stronger.

Gaining physical strength requires personal effort working and struggling against resistance to be successful. Same thing is true for mental strength and critical thinking ability. A person must apply effort and exercise their minds by studying, gaining knowledge and learning new techniques about all kinds of things to increase the acuity, adeptness and mental functions to gain new cerebral strength, vitality and health.

The opposite is also true. If you tie a person's arm to their side, preventing the physical use of that limb, it will atrophy, and over time, become practically useless. Same thing happens with brain cells. Should a person neglect the exercise and health of their brains, mental decline will set in and accelerate over time with age. That's just how life works. And, so it is also with the health and well-being of your spirit and soul—*a defined struggle.*

FREEDOM – TIME TO LAUNCH
WEAPONS AND TACTICS – The Bible has a lot to say about getting yourself free of bad habits, addiction(s) and a destructive lifestyle. It also characterizes this conflict as being a definite, and deadly warfare—a real struggle. Not at all like a contest, a skirmish or a simple scrimmage game of some sort—it is deadly serious. Your adversary, the devil, is not playing around—he's not seeking you out to just slap you on the wrist - he fully intends to steal every good thing that God has given you, and then to kill you, that is... IF YOU LET HIM.

That being the case, I encourage you to focus your attention on the following scripture passages that reveal some very strategic tools, weapons, and tactics that God has made available to every believer in waging this warfare, both offensively and defensively:

> ***2 Cor. 10:3-5*** *For though we live in the world, we do not wage war as the world does. The weapons we fight with are not the weapons of the world. On the contrary, they have divine power to demolish strongholds. We demolish arguments and every pretension that sets itself up against the knowledge of God, and we take captive every thought to make it obedient to Christ. (NIV)*

> ***Eph. 6:11-12*** *Put on all of God's armor so that you will be able to stand firm against all strategies and tricks of the Devil. For we are not fighting against people made of flesh and blood, but against the evil rulers and authorities of the unseen world, against those mighty powers of darkness who rule this world, and against wicked spirits in the heavenly realms. (NLT)*

I also encourage you to read and study these scriptures, with a focus on what jumps out at you—*what kind of action* you think the Lord is coaching you to take. This spiritual warfare is not about bullets and bombs. It is supernatural, and you will be engaging the enemy of your soul with your mind and your spirit—as Jesus, *The Lion of Judah*, prepares you, and then leads you into combat.

Therefore, your mind will become one of your most formidable weapons of spiritual warfare—but, for that to happen effectively, it must be transformed from being corrupted by repetitive sin and destructive behavior, to being sufficiently renewed, by and through Gods word—and that is a work of the Holy Spirit who has already begun his good work in you, which he promises to finish.

That last statement may surprise many of you, grappling with some expression of spiritual discipline. I've had quite a number of believers' question that, wondering how God could be working in their life when they are experiencing so much chaos, trouble and discontent—it looks very much like an enigma, or paradox to them. Truth is however, whenever we get ourselves into trouble, God goes to work making us aware of that trouble, and where it will lead if we fail to correct it. He warns us, either by his word, or by his Holy Spirit, or both. He knows that trouble will come our way from time to time, and he wants us to know exactly what to do about it, and how to handle it, when it does.

THE SILVER BULLET – Problem is, when some kind of trouble is first revealed in a typical Christians life, they almost always try to fix it by putting a **Band-Aid** on it. They want to resolve it and get rid of it quickly, and that band-aid represents the easiest, and the most immediate response to fix whatever the trouble might be. That method works well with minor frustrations that happen in your life once in a while, but not so much with trouble that just keeps on showing up—the kind of trouble that you cannot fix with a band-aid any more – What about that?

It can be really hard to wrap your brain around this. You realize that you need to step it up and elevate your game plan to a higher level, but change can be really hard—especially trying to fit this extra time, energy and hard work into your existing schedule, when you're likely pinned down enough already. Isn't that right?

Every one of us would love to have a Silver Bullet solution to resolve that kind of trouble. Isn't that also right? Truth is however, we actually do have that proverbial Silver-Bullet available. *The bullet has a name...***JESUS.**

The Apostle Paul said it like this in the book of Romans:
> ***Rom. 7:24-25*** *I've tried everything and nothing helps. I'm at the end of my rope. Is there no one who can do anything for me? Isn't that the real question?*
>
> *The answer, thank God, is that Jesus Christ can and does. He acted to set things right in this life of contradictions where I want to serve God with all my heart and mind, but am pulled by the influence of sin to do something totally different. (MESSAGE)*

The key tactic here is simply getting to know Jesus better than you do now, and learning to trust him to do all the heavy lifting in your life¬—simple, but not easy. You want real change in your life to acquire authentic freedom?

You will be opposed—there will be hindrances, obstacles and outright war coming against you, so, get yourself ready. You and Jesus working together are substantially more formidable than you think. *He will make you more than a conqueror...*

PREPARE YOUR MIND – All expressions of sin, and many, if not most, afflictions of mental health and well-being, **begin within the mind**, of every one of us—Christians and non-Christians alike. Specifically, the sub-conscious part of our mind. Established research from clinical behavior scientists and therapists have cited that 95% of what we think, and then, how we act and behave, all emanate from our sub-conscious mind. Does that surprise you? It did me...

Begs a question... why is that important to you? *It is within the sub-conscious mind that you begin to increase the intensity of your determination*—you begin to ramp-up your desire to find out what authentic, biblical freedom is going to cost you. You take on a new understanding of *"hard-work"* to mean, ***"hard and deeper thinking."*** You earnestly begin that arduous mental work of deliberately meditating about how much you really do want this, and how much it's going to cost—you prepare your mind to take this new work on—you get yourself ready—you anticipate the change in your lifestyle. This is where acquiring that freedom actually begins.

You understand that from now on, *hard work = hard thinking*. For Noah, that meant taking on the building of his ARK—for you, it means finding out what authentic freedom will cost you, and then committing yourself to pay that price—very much a mental and spiritual discipline issue.

> **1 Pet. 1:13** *Therefore prepare your minds for action; discipline yourselves; set all your hope on the grace that Jesus Christ will bring you when he is revealed. (NRSV)*

The Bible records these timeless words that actually form the foundation of authentic, biblical freedom: **"For as he thinks within himself, so he is"** *(Prov. 23:7)*. The next question for you to resolve after ramping up the intensity of your determination, reads like this: How willing are you to take this on? The answer to that question will come in the form of you simply making a sincere **COMMITMENT** to yourself and to God, from deep within your mind, that you are going to get this done—it then becomes - just a matter of time...

INFORM YOUR MIND - So, you need to begin the process of letting your mind know that you want to, and that you fully intend to, make some changes. However, you'll want to inform your mind of this in a way that works well to promote an *authentic, long-term change in your life*. You'll be replacing some bad habits with some new habits. Change is coming—let your mind know that. These transactions will actually take place within the sub-conscious part of your mind, and, you'll need to use a language method that your sub-conscious mind will effectively respond to. For example, it will not be very effective at all for you to just read off a list of do's & don'ts that you'd like your sub-conscious mind to respond to and make happen in your life—your brain and your mind do not work that way. They are extremely complex and definitely not intuitive or easy to understand and predict.

A multitude of books, scientific journals and very advanced research studies have proven that to be true—so, for our limited purposes right here and now, it's only important to focus our attention on a proven method, to communicate effectively, with the sub-conscious part of your mind.

There are a few characteristics of how that part of your mind functions, that you do need to know something about—that is, if you are to experience some degree of success without having to *spin-your-wheels* and waste your time. Your sub-conscious mind is an active, integral part of your authentic identity—of who you really are. Your sub-conscious mind knows all about you—everything, down to the last detail, and, here's why that fact is so essential to your success:

One of the most strategic characteristics of your sub-conscious mind is that it always knows exactly what is most precious and valuable to you—what you hold dear, and what your desires really are, at any and every moment of time throughout your entire life. That's exactly how God created it to function, and, it doesn't matter one whit to your sub-conscious mind whether those values and desires of yours are right, wrong, good, or bad.

It only matters and focuses on getting you whatever you actually value and desire—what it is that you want, irrespective of whether it is good, beneficial or healthy for you. Your sub-conscious mind will also know how much you really care about someone or something in your life—it will accurately measure the intensity and magnitude of exactly how determined you are to stay on your present course without change, or, whether you really are serious about making a change in your life that you actually believe in.

It doesn't respond to what is true or false, unless, and until, you actually determine, and commit yourself, to sincerely increase your love of God with all of your heart, all of your mind, all of your soul, and all of your strength—and, to do that effectively, it is really essential, and not optional, to completely renew that mind of yours.

Therefore, wishing, hoping and a whole host of good intentions that you may develop to change the way you think, act and behave simply does not, and will not work. Effective, real and beneficial change to your sub-conscious mind is not a trivial pursuit, and almost always requires a sincere, serious and very strong commitment to pay the price and do the work required—I say almost because God can rescue, deliver and change you in an instant, by his grace and miraculous power anytime he chooses.

He's done that for me and for a vast multitude of believers down through the ages, and, he'll continue doing that as he sees fit every moment of every day, till he returns—but, he is especially delighted when one of us determines to resist evil and fight for that freedom. So, for now, I encourage you to inform your sub-conscious mind that you are directing a new change to come into your life.

You'll be expecting some new desires, values and habits to be developed to put your life on a new course. But, to be effective, you need to learn, practice and use the language of your sub-conscious mind—something like this... Deliberately imagine, and then meditate, on how wonderful you will feel when you actually overcome and prevail against every hindrance and obstacle working against your spiritual freedom. Your sub-conscious mind will respond to that kind of action—*especially if you do it consistently.*

Visualize yourself, in your mind's eye, actually experiencing that, and how it will make you feel, over and over again, as often as you can do it. This takes time and effort, mental and spiritual discipline, but, if you sincerely believe this, your sub-conscious mind will begin to change and you will truly begin to experience that authentic, biblical freedom you've been hoping for.

Hope will give way to faith—followed by freedom...

Your job is to convince your mind that this is extremely valuable to you and that you indeed, are going to make this commitment to get it done. The work of the Lord in this endeavor—on your behalf, is first to build and perfect your faith to believe this to be true—that you'll actually be able to do this, and then to equip and enable you, with everything needed to make it actually happen.

What do you think—can you grip this and believe it for yourself?

This first chapter involves a lot of mental work—that's where your spiritual freedom actually begins—developing a new mind-set—a formidable attitude—an attitude like Jesus has, so you can think and act more like him. Isn't that it? However, this is not new to manking—check it out:

> **Josh. 1:8** *This book of the law shall not depart out of your mouth; you shall meditate on it day and night, so that you may be careful to act in accordance with all that is written in it. For then you shall make your way prosperous, and then you shall be successful. (NRSV)*

Are you ready for that—you'll be making some new choices.

FREEDOM – CHOICES

You also read in this book intro that *"It was for freedom that Christ has set us free."* Remember that? Let's unpack that a little—load the following scripture into your brain:

> **1Cor. 6:12** *"All things are lawful for me," but not all things are beneficial. "All things are lawful for me," but I will not be dominated by anything. (NRSV)*

God is documenting here that he has given free-will to all mankind—we are all free to choose how we will live and navigate life—with, or without, his involvement. However, he also qualifies this free-will. He reveals that not all of our choices are to be considered as being beneficial to us. He infers that some choices are beneficial for us, but, some are not—and, **that's the rub, isn't it?**

God does not, and will not, make this choice for us. He will not make us think like Jesus—we must make that choice ourselves. He expects each one of us to exercise responsibility and choose wisely. So, the next time that you are tempted to take that drink, or that joint, or that porn image, or whatever thing that you know is definitely not beneficial to you, take on the following challenge.

STOP AND THINK—challenge yourself to reason and consider this choice from a different perspective than you usually do. Gods' perspective and encouragement to you is to take on, and have the same attitude as Jesus, so you can then think more like him, and act more like him. That's clearly what he wants for you—question is, **do you believe that?** Especially, if you've been yielding yourself to temptation(s) for a while, you know it's not that easy—it can be a challenge, a really tough slog. Consider the following case history I recently reviewed:

A very famous celebrity, who is a well-known actor, had an incredible experience with the presence and the still-small-voice of Almighty God. He had been going through a particularly rough patch of life and he found himself face down on the floor—he was exhausted and he was exasperated because of it. This experience was exceedingly rare for him in that he was not given to be so emotional. He was very distraught and he declared the following words, out loud:

"this is difficult...why is this so damned difficult."

Immediately following this declaration, he heard the following remarkable words spoken to him from within his own mind - it was the voice of God - this is what God spoke to him:

"it's supposed to be difficult."

Almighty God showed up in the form of his Holy Spirit and spoke those words to him. That's the first time anything like that ever happened to him and it totally changed the rest of his life. Up until that time, he believed that God existed and that he created all the heavens and the Earth—but, although he considered himself to be a Christian, he really did not know Jesus, hardly at all—he was more like an acquaintance, or historical icon that he was familiar with. However, after hearing God speak to him in such a personal way, he knew right then that he, and all the rest of us, were not alone, and would never be alone. God, indeed was with us, would never leave us, and loved us completely. His life would never be the same.

So, don't let yourself get discouraged here. It may feel like you are drinking water from a fire hose, and, that all of this is just too overwhelming. But, it's not—you can do this like a multitude of believers, just like you, have already done. Just let these words of mine begin to slowly sink into your brain. Just let your mind adjust and become aware that you will be making some wonderful changes.

You are reading this right now, and that should encourage you to realize that God is already at work renewing your mind to help you navigate these new choices. It's not a coincidence...He put you here and now, deliberately on-purpose, for that very reason. This truth of his, is clearly at work in you, and will ultimately set you free. That's just a fact—that's how it works.

Now, check this out:

> **Rom. 12:1-2** *Do not be conformed to this world, but be transformed by the renewing of your minds, so that you may discern what is the will of God—what is good and acceptable and perfect. (NRSV)*

Here's another one:

> **1Pet. 5:8** *Be self-controlled and alert. Your enemy the devil prowls around like a roaring lion looking for someone to devour. (NRSV)*

Someone like YOU....!

FREEDOM – OBSTACLES

Okay, if you're really serious about this, you're realizing here that you need to get a grip on the issue—you'll be confronting one or more bad habits that have either led you into experiencing a destructive lifestyle, or have you heading that way. However, you're not alone—take a look at some more facts:

I speak with a lot of believers and study a lot of case-histories conducting research for my freedom renewed program and my writing. They all tell me that the following issues are prevalent and have been instrumental in causing them to suffer such a loss of spiritual discipline. Therefore, I encourage you to study this list well and see if you identify in some way.

> 1. **Immediate Gratification** - We are all sinners, by birth and by choice. In addition, we are all born into this world with selfishness being a dominant trait of our human nature—we all tend to want things right away, and, we do not want to wait very long to acquire those things that we desire. Believers who are experiencing a loss of spiritual discipline in their life almost always suffer with inadequate **impulse control**. They lack sufficient self-control over their thoughts and their behavior.

Many are no longer willing, or even capable of taking every *thought captive to the obedience of Christ*, like the bible instructs us all to do, in 2 Cor. 10:5. God speaks to this issue in the bible:

> *1 Th. 4:4 that each one of you know how to control your own body*
> ** in holiness and honor, (NRSV)*
> ** **Paraphrased to read:** "That each of you should learn, and know how, to control the members of your own body and mind, in a way that is holy and honorable to God."*

Behavior scientists and therapists cite a clinical lack of impulse control as being a very dominant cause of addictive behavior—for Christians suffering some kind of addiction, it shows up as a great difficulty to control or resist, strong urges and temptations leading them to various expressions of sin they are confronted with.

So, how are we to respond to that? How about this challenge:

Remember what I stated earlier, that an effective response begins with a new mind-set, an attitude just like God is instructing us to do in *1 Pet. 1:13*—it begins in the mind with a fervent determination and commitment to do whatever it takes to get completely rid of this propensity and susceptibility, of yielding yourself so easily to sinful behavior—do this: Acquire an attitude - **Resist it; push back hard** - Just like Jesus. Not so easy to do at first, but really necessary.

Next comes adopting an effective freedom strategy, and action-plan, and putting them both into reliable and consistent operation. That's where this program of mine comes into play—it's formidable and effective to help you prevail over those temptations that have been kicking your butt.

This new mind set will involve you learning how to **weaponize** the *spiritual virtues of humility and patience* that will then lead you to increasing the unsearchable riches of the knowledge of Jesus in your life. However, don't go thinking that you will - *jump right into this* - Truth is, achieving an effective, spiritual change is not a trivial pursuit and it often takes a lot of time and effort—but, it can also result in the greatest fulfillment that you'll ever experience—you will look back and absolutely cherish your decision to do this; to make this commitment.

2. **Contentment** – This second challenge also involves *the current level of contentment* you have in your life. One of the best and most pragmatic examples of this comes from the Apostle Paul, in the book of Philippians:

> **Phil. 4:12** *I know what it is to be in need, and I know what it is to have plenty.* **I have learned the secret of being content in any and every situation,** *whether well fed or hungry, whether living in plenty or in want. (NIV)*

For many believers I have discussed this issue with, the predominant cause of becoming discontented and unhappy with their life comes from an abundance of failure being experienced. Especially failing to prevail and overcome some kind of sinful behavior. They all agree— this really sucks and wars against their souls and contentment in life. Every one of them want to take their life back and experience that sheer enjoyment of life again. *So, that begs another question:*

What's the best and most effective way to look at this life sucking bandit of yours—plundering you of all that joy you should be experiencing? You need to figure this out—you want to be effective and you need a very formidable plan. So, how do you prepare your mind to evaluate this—to get and effecive grip on it?

First of all, you know the difference of whether this sucker is right or wrong for you—yes, isn't that correct? That perspective is obvious to every Christian, but, what if you looked at it from a different perspective—a way to evaluate just how and why it is hammering you so easily, effectively and so often. What would that look like?

Turns out that the most effective approach is to evaluate each choice as to whether you think it will be either **beneficial or harmful** to you, rather than thinking whether it is *right or wrong*—here's why:

Our human nature will always have a predisposition to be at odds with God, throughout our entire lifetime—even as committed followers of Christ.

Therefore, as a result, Christian psychologists inform us that whenever we are confronted with obeying God, *because of a clear choice of right and wrong,* our human nature will make it much easier to consider rebelling against God—because we are simply so prone to doing that.

However, if we consider the same choice as being either beneficial or hurtful to our life in some way, that same human nature will lead us to favor the more beneficial choice, and will resist the harmful one. I really think that is why God inspired the Apostle Paul to use the phrase, *"all things are beneficial"* rather than using what is *"right or wrong"* when he wrote that scripture in 1 Cor. 6:12—God loves us and does not want us to get hurt. He also knows exactly how are minds work and just how easily enticed we can be, so, use this following tactic whenever you are tempted to sin. *Deliberately think about how harmful and hurtful that sin will be to you—and, how crappy you will feel if you yield yourself to it.* Take up this challenge—you'll be really glad that you did.

3. **Comfort Zone** – One aspect of our human nature is that we all acquire a comfort-zone for ourselves. Every human being has one. I'm sure you've all heard of that before. Ideally, the comfort-zone is actually a lifestyle, or a mind-set, where there exist very few surprises in your life. A place where you are in control of circumstances and events as much as possible. You know pretty much what is going on and what to expect on a day-to-day basis.

Your comfort-zone is similar to an *"auto-pilot"* in an airplane, and *"cruise-control"* in a car. However, in contrast, your comfort-zone is powered-up and turned-on all the time. It is literally a series of habits that you perform over and over almost every day. It defines and activates how you behave—how you typically respond to certain situations, circumstances and events in your life. It makes up and defines a huge part of your identity—**knowing who you are, by experiencing and observing, what you do.**

Jesus defined it like this: You will know them by their fruits, that is, how they act and by what they do. *(Matt. 7:16)*. I reiterate this again from the book of Proverbs: *"For as he thinks within himself, so he is."* (Prov. 23:7)

Your comfort-zone is primarily made up of your core-values. Those internal beliefs that you hold in extremely high regard and respect, whether you are able to live them out or not, and, whether they are beneficial or harmful for your lifestyle. Your core-values make up the guiding principles behind all of your habits, some good, some bad and some destructive—those habits that dictate your behavior, and define your lifestyle.

So, prepare your mind to almost certainly be challenged by this chapter intentionally shaping your core-vales, and moving you out of your comfort-zone by a little bit, or by a lot. This program is very focused upon your core-value system that enables your comfort-zone—habit-by-habit, and how it influences your lifestyle.

A THREE-PART CHALLENGE – GET READY
So, do as the scripture in 1 Pet. 1:13 directs you to do: *"Prepare your mind for action."* Get really serious with yourself about this—ramp up your intensity.

Be on the lookout for these three adversaries within your mind to "show up" and try to stop you from forming this essential habit that you desperately need to get all this started. **Don't let them win—vehemently oppose them with** *all of your might!* A huge part of achieving success in overcoming spiritual adversaries is first, becoming aware and vigilant, then learning to detect, recognize and identify those adversaries. You want more faith? *You want more effective faith—leading to freedom?*

You will be opposed. So, the question is...

What will you do about it when it happens?

When the devil detects that you have made this commitment to increase your faith in Jesus—to get to know him more, Satan and his demonic kingdom will actively oppose you, more than he does now. You can expect him to *step-it-up—this is spiritual warfare.* His mission, at first, is simply to make you less effective in your spiritual life. The devil comes only to steal, kill and destroy you, in every way that he can *(John 10:10),* and he knows that if he can start his mission by just distracting you a little bit, getting your life off course a little and making you less effective spiritually, then he might be able to keep his mission against you alive.

Satan also knows that if he does nothing, you will indeed become more effective in God's kingdom, and become a potent threat. So, he will actively come against you. He understands very well that if you succeed in forming this habit to just show up and increase your knowledge and relationship with Jesus, that his mission to keep **his boot on your neck** will fail miserably.

In context with this spiritual warfare, particularly applied to you, comes a famous quote by Edmund Burke, circa 1770 - He famously said these words:

"The only thing necessary for the triumph of evil is for good men to do nothing."

So, as you personally experience this spiritual warfare conflict, perhaps in a new way, remember this word from God to you—Jesus would say something like this to you: *"Refuse to do nothing,"* but instead, *"exercise your faith, display strength and take effective action."* Here's why—always remember these words:

Complacency - is a fierce Enemy!

Renew your mind with this fact—*this particular and very strategic truth*—that if you choose to do nothing, or, you choose a plan of action that is woefully inadequate and ineffective, then that spiritual crisis you're becoming aware of will come on you like a bandit, and, you will absolutely hate it—you will rue that day like a plague, because **you'll have known that you could have avoided it**. That's why the Holy Spirit of God reveals this kind of strategic truth to you. He coaches you, and even warns you to pay heed. He wants to harness your attention on this issue in your life, right now—at this very moment—WHILE YOU STILL HAVE A CHOICE—a choice to actually do something about it.

Here's why - every time a destructive lifestyle of some kind advances and develops into an actual crisis, *that choice will no longer be available to you*—the result of that crisis will actually FORCE you into a result that you will almost certainly not control, not like and will not enjoy.

Therefore, gain some spiritual strength from these two, very formidable messages from the Lord—make them both personal.

> **Luke 14:11** *For all who exalt themselves will be humbled, and those who humble themselves will be exalted." (NRSV)*
>
> **2 Chr. 7:14** *if my people who are called by my name humble themselves, pray, seek my face, and turn from their wicked ways, then I will hear from heaven, and will forgive their sin and heal their land. (NRSV)*

Jesus would also say something like this to you: *"Don't just stand there... DO SOMETHING—do something effective."* Choose to humble yourself willingly, and effectively, otherwise you'll be humbled by a crisis coming your way at some point in your life. That's why God advises and coaches all of us in Isaiah 66:2 to **Fear and tremble at his word**—because his word is always, and empirically, TRUE.

I really encourage you here, and soon, to exercise effective action to believe, adopt and activate this next step in choosing to avoid a crisis coming your way by weaponizing humility in your life—while you still have this choice.

Here it is:

> **Jam. 4:10** *Humble yourselves before the Lord, and he will exalt you. (NRSV)*

Learn to overcome these three attributes that I've listed, of your human nature, whenever you become aware of any of them showing up in your mind. *Take effective action.* Choose to humble yourself and tremble at Gods' word on every occasion as you navigate life. Show up deliberately and make it a habit. You won't regret it. Exercise godly wisdom and choose to humble yourselves voluntarily, so that God will exalt you—trust me here... **God will do it way better than you.**

Okay, let's take a break before we move on. I'm sure that some of you may very well be feeling somewhat overwhelmed by all this. But, like God would say to you—*let not your heart be troubled...*

He knows that you are not currently able, and perhaps not even willing, to make all this happen in your life right now. At times like these, let him comfort you with these words from the bible...

> **Psa. 91:4** - *He will cover you with his feathers, and under his wings you will find refuge; his faithfulness will be your shield and rampart. (NIV)*

Jesus has your back—when your own love, loyalty and faithfulness to him fails—*his faithfulness to you will fail not.* His love for you is so intense, and his Gospel is so powerful, that he will literally **stand-in-the-gap** for you and shepherd you through every struggle of life. Especially in those times when you are just too weak spiritually to carry-on. Jesus is really that good, and his Gospel is really that powerful. His love for you never fails, so, place your trust completely in him and believe what he says about you, and his plan for your life. He will perfect his love for you, in your weakness—that's how he rolls...

> **Jer. 29:11** - *For I know the plans I have for you declares the Lord, "plans to prosper you and not to harm you; plans to give you hope and a future." (NIV)*

Got that down? All right, let's move on a little further on in this key scripture recorded in Hebrews 12:1. God inspired the writer to talk about a race. Let's take a closer look at that race.

THE RACE

This chapter confronts you with putting some wings on this new challenge—you are about to enter a new competition in your life. The bible identifies this competition as *"a race"* that every Christian enters at the time of salvation, as I recorded in Heb. 12:1. The last line of that scripture reveals that we are entering a race—*let us run with perseverance the* **race** *marked out for us*. Remember that? A race means that there is competition so, who are you competing against? You will not be competing with any of your contemporaries in this generation, or, Billy Graham in the last one. No, you will be competing strictly, and very specifically, with yourself, that is—*YOUR OLD SELF.* Reads like this in the bible:

> **Rom. 6:6** *For we know that* **our old self** *was crucified with him so that the body of sin might be done away with, that we should no longer be slaves to sin—(NIV)*

Our old-self was crucified—*or was it?* For many Christians, that old self is very much alive and well—and, is still in control... **How about your old self?**

THE COMPETITION

Is it way more active than you'd like it to be? In addition, the bible declares that our old self should no longer be calling the shots in our life. Further, it is actually, and literally, to be displaced with a new self and a new identity—reads like this:

> **2Cor. 5:17** *Therefore, if anyone is in Christ, he is a new creation; the old has gone, the new has come! (NIV)*

> *Eph. 4:24 and to clothe yourselves with the new self, created according to the likeness of God in true righteousness and holiness. (NRSV)*

The bible mandates every Christian to **"put on Christ"** just like we would put on a new suit of clothes. Looks like this:

> **Rom. 13:14** *But clothe yourself with the Lord Jesus Christ (the Messiah), and make no provision for (indulging) the flesh (put a stop to thinking about the evil cravings of your physical nature) to (gratify its) desires (lusts). (AMP)*

Pragmatically speaking, God gives each of us a brand-new suit—but a number of us often leave that suit hanging in the closet, rather than putting it on. Here's what I mean by that:

When we become *born-again* and God adopts us as sons and daughters into his family, our spirit comes alive—we are given a new spiritual nature and a new identity in Christ. However, our human nature—**our old self,** that we are all born with, is only displaced, and not replaced, and it remains in operation throughout all the days of our life. For many of us, we just run into the closet every once in a while, and take a look at that *new identity in Christ suit* hanging there, but fail to power-up and put it on.

And, that human nature of ours, which is completely selfish, will continue to seek its' own way, every minute of every day, right up to the day that we die. No exceptions—and that's another rub isn't it...

That sets up a definite tension and conflict that every Christian is faced with—that's the competition—that's the race defined in Hebrews 12, and we must learn how to compete effectively, if we are to win that race. Jesus defined this race as a conflict in a number of profound and compelling ways in the bible—he not only defines the conflict, but, reveals exactly what we should do about it, that is, if we are to prevail against it, like he intends for us to do.

Jesus is making a strategic point here by inference. He is coaching us to take a measure of this race, and just how prepared we are to actually run and effectively compete in it. He is revealing that the race we are to run is unique to each one of us. The difficulty of it, and the distance that we are to run is determined by the condition of our hearts and our minds, by God, and God alone. He measures each one of us and then, just like Hebrews 12:1 lays down, he tells us that *"we are to run with perseverance the race marked out for us."* God is the one who marks out this race, and it is unique to each believer.

In addition, he says we are to run with perseverance. He knows that when we enter into this race—when we deliberately choose to follow Jesus—we will have to endure hardships from time-to-time. He is also inferring that this race is almost certain to be more like a marathon (26.2 miles), and a lot less like a short 50-yard sprint. His inference also informs us that we will certainly need to train ourselves, physically, mentally, and spiritually to effectively take on the challenge of this race. That's what my FRP in this book is all about—to help you train, and to get you ready to compete in this race effectively, and then, to go on and win this thing—even if it takes the rest of your life. So, that begs this question again: ***Are you ready for this?***

PERSPECTIVE – LIFESTYLE

I began this chapter by challenging the status-quo of your life. That challenge involves getting your mind prepared for action—something new—a change in the way you've been accustomed to think about life stuff. I intend to build on that now by challenging your perspective and outlook on life a little bit, or, maybe, for some of you, a lot. An outlook to be much more like God's perspective on life. We'll take a close look at what I call the *God's Eye View of Life* in this first chapter and how that influences your day-to-day Christian lifestyle. Here's why—in the God's eye view of your life, it is not very meaningful just how successful or unsuccessful your life is, right now—your status-quo, right at this particular moment in time. I wrote this down in the Introduction to this book, and, I reiterate here again for emphasis...

"Turns out that it's way more valuable to figure out where you are going in your life, rather than where you are at, or, where you have been."

That's how Jesus thinks—that's how you want to think. Here's what I mean by that—*your current trajectory* in life matters substantially more than what your current results may reveal. Begs yet another question:

Where are your current habits likely to lead you through this next month, next year, next decade? And, *what's trending in your life right now*—what are you thinking about—how far out are you looking—where are you going next—what path are you on and where will it lead you? *Start thinking more like that... God thinks long-term—he always takes into account today, tomorrow, and forever.*

PERSPECTIVE – DAILY

So, the Gods' Eye View of Life is also to be adopted and applied on a daily basis. That process is a working part of what is simply known as *Godly Wisdom*. Almost all of us develop some kind of a daily to-do list to plan our way into navigating, and managing how we respond to life stuff. I have a number of specific tactics to optimize that list for greater impact and effectiveness, but, the very first part of developing that list is all in your mind.

That process begins as you consider and plan-out your daily to-do list. However, instead of focusing all of your attention on that first activity, you deliberately focus your attention on how you will feel, at the *end of your work day*, after you have crushed it—nailing everything on your list after giving 110%+ on the effort. You intentionally think about and meditate on the exhilaration, and on the fulfillment, that you will experience, as you look back on all the good work that you completed. Before you put your hand on that first good work, you deliberately visualize, in your mind's eye, how you will feel after completing what you know God has prepared for you to do on that particular day. It's a specific mind-set... an attitude—Christ's attitude. God himself set a daily example of that mind-set that he wants each of us to imitate and follow, way back in the early chapters of Genesis. *Take a look...*

PERSPECTIVE – GOD'S EXAMPLE

God has established exactly how you should feel and what you should be thinking about at the end of every work day.

I call it, the **well-done witness of good work**. It's a deliberate mind-set that you seek after and adopt for yourself at the beginning of every day—to be purposely realized and experienced at the end of every day. God first set this example for each of us to imitate and experience early in the book of Genesis, as he was completing his 6 days of creating all the heavens, the earth, and everything in them. The bible records what he was thinking and experiencing at that moment when he looked back on his work—God said this:

> **Gen. 1:31** And God saw everything that He had made, and behold, it was very good (suitable, pleasant) and He approved it completely. And there was evening and there was morning, a sixth day. (AMP)

So, what is it that the Lord wants us to take away from this and apply to our own lifestyle on a daily basis? Every Christian comes to the understanding that God is purposely shaping each and every one of us to be more like Jesus— the bible says that we are actually made in his image, and challenges every one of us to seek out and adopt his attitude—to think, act and ultimately to navigate our lives by his example.

God himself establishes what that is to look like right here:

> **Eph. 5:1** THEREFORE BE imitators of God (copy Him and follow His example), as well-beloved children (imitate their father). (AMP)

God looked back on his 6 days of creation and the bible records his response— what he thought about his work; he thought it was: **Very Good**—that's what he was thinking. Paraphrased, it reads something like this: Wow, that work I just completed was very good—it was awesome!

Therefore, that is exactly what each of us should be thinking and experiencing as we look back on what we accomplish each and every day. That's a big part of the **reward** that God himself provides every believer who seeks him with diligence—who lives their life intentionally to love, honor and follow Jesus— it's a functional and extremely powerful result of the Gospel of Christ, put into operation:

> **Heb. 11:6** *But without faith it is impossible to please and be satisfactory to Him. For whoever would come near to God must [necessarily] believe that God exists and that He is the rewarder of those who earnestly and diligently seek Him [out]. (AMP)*

*The Gods Eye View of Life—**It's a mind-set***

Hold that thought as I introduce a couple of issues that have a significant influence on acquiring, maintaining and sustaining authentic, biblical freedom for oneself over a long period of time—*over years and decades*. I've researched a multitude of case histories from ordinary Christians, and church leaders alike, who are struggling with the crisis I describe on my website and within the Intro to this book. My research puts me in contact with hundreds of believers from all walks of life, many of them in some capacity of church leadership.

Turns out that almost every believer has experienced seasons of spiritual dysfunction of some kind and had to deal with the results—instead of experiencing that *well-done-witness-of-good-work* at the end of their day, and feeling very good and awesome about it, they experience a load of trouble, and feel really crappy about it. Fact is, navigating the Christian life includes confronting bad habits and sometimes entrenched, hard to get rid of, addictions, whenever they show up—even though the bible tells us in Galatians 5:1 that - *it was, and is for freedom that Christ has set us free.* Knowing that this scripture is absolutely true... It begs another question:

Why is acquiring authentic biblical freedom so difficult?

Actually, there are a number of issues that can adversely influence, or even prevent, this kind of spiritual freedom from being consistently experienced. I'm specifically talking about the kind of hindrances and encumbrances that we are to throw-off—to get rid of—to completely remove from our lifestyles, as documented in Hebrews 12:1.

I listed some examples of those issues earlier in this session, that I encourage you to continue thinking about. In addition to those, the following 3 always come up, and are often prevalent, when I discuss this stuff with other believers. Your experience is likely in this mix of freedom obstacles somewhere, so, check this out and see what you think:

1. **Spiritual Dysfunction** – Almost all bad habits and destructive lifestyles can be traced back to being caused by, or being influenced by, the condition of a person's soul and spirit—especially a weak or ineffective spiritual foundation that Jesus commented on in his Gospels (Matt. 7:24-27). *It's actually impossible to build a strong spiritual lifestyle on a weak spiritual foundation...*

2. **Love of God Lost or impaired** – Jesus laid down his greatest commandment in the Gospel of Mark 12:28-34 – *"Love the Lord your God with all your heart and with all your mind and with all your soul and with all your strength. The second is this: Love your neighbor as yourself."*

   In regards to a believer experiencing the loss or impairment of their spiritual freedom, Jesus has this to say in Rev. 2:4-5.... *"But I have this against you, that you have left your first love. Therefore, remember from where you have fallen, and **repent and do the deeds you did at first;"***

3. **Becoming Double Minded** – This is what happens to any and every Christian who experiences either issue above, to any significant degree. We become double-minded. James 1:8 informs us that a double-minded man (or woman) is unstable in all their ways. James 4:8 goes on to inform us what we should do about it; *"Draw near to God and He will draw near to you. Cleanse your hands, you sinners; and purify your hearts, you double-minded."* However, as many have realized, this is substantially easier said, than it is effectively done.

Okay, I've just documented several reasons that Christians of all kinds end up compromising, impairing or, outright losing their spiritual freedom that can only be acquired through Christ. He had a few things to say about that:

> ***John 14:6*** *Jesus answered, "I am the way and the truth and the life. No one comes to the Father except through me. (NIV)*
>
> ***Matt. 7:13-14*** *(Jesus speaking) "Enter through the narrow gate. For wide is the gate and broad is the road that leads to destruction, and many enter through it. But small is the gate and narrow the road that leads to life, and only a few find it. (NIV)*

Truth is, authentic, biblical freedom can only be discovered, acquired, maintained and sustained over an extended period of time—*like the rest of your life*, through only one source—Jesus the Christ. And, Jesus reveals that there are only two pathways available to all of mankind:

1. **The narrow gate—follow Jesus—leads to life**
2. **The wide gate—follow the ways of the world—leads to destruction**

There is a path leading to each of these gates. A double-minded believer is often jumping from one path to the other, depending upon what life is throwing their way—depending more upon *how they feel about something*, rather than what God and his word has to say. Jesus encourages and coaches all his followers to not do this—to not think and live this way—he says that it's not wise, safe, beneficial or fulfilling.

He tells us that no man can serve two masters, and that each of us must choose which one of these masters we will serve—and further, that the master we choose to serve, very often, will ultimately become the master of our life. You want authentic biblical freedom? **Let Jesus master your life...He'll do it way better than you.**

Therefore, settle this issue in your mind—there really is only one way—one path of life that is truly safe and secure—of incalculable benefit and fulfilling for a Christian to follow. It's Jesus, and Jesus all the time. However, it is also Jesus who said, "*the spirit is willing, but the flesh is weak.*" That amazing statement answers this question, and the previous one, a few pages back:

Why do so many Christians easily choose a path to destruction?

The flesh is weak—Turns out of course, that Jesus was exactly right about that, especially the weakness of our wills and just how easily our minds can be deceived. The fact is, our minds do not, and cannot, function like a compass, that always points to the North—our minds simply do not work that way. Our minds do not always point to the truth—as a result, many of us end up getting heavily influenced by, or even addicted to, the immediate, but only temporary relief, provided by drugs, booze, porn and a whole list of others, just to escape the rigors of life for a while, trying to cope with the demands that life requires of us at times. That's the crisis, and, it's getting worse in the church—not better. *So again... what are we to do—here's what we do:*

TIME NOW TO PLAN – BUT, NOT JUST ANY PLAN
Most believers I talk with consider these issues as individual goals to set for themselves to achieve. However, there is some specific, and very effective research into this subject—especially over the last 5 years in particular. It reveals that using a goal-based system to navigate the Christian life, is just not very productive. There's a better way to do life. How about this— something really valuable for you to think about, and to lock your brain into:

New goals do not deliver optimum results—**NEW LIFESTYLES DO.**

We'll take a good look at this—how your short, mid and long-term goals and core values can be designed into a God-honoring, freedom loving lifestyle—a whole new way of living. A formidable system that you can plug your life into.

In addition, I want to weave into this chapter how the Gospel of Christ actually becomes that system—your new lifestyle. Turns out that it is way more wonderful and powerful, than most Christians realize, or, experience.

God's in there—he lives in there, and, he wants all of us in there with him.

The bible reveals that living the Christian lifestyle, from within the Gospel of Christ, is not an outcome—but more of a dynamic, living process.

The Gospel functions in our life like a *Strong Tower*—a safe and secure place for Christians to run into whenever the worries and stresses of life come their way. That's where you will find the grace of God.

That's the place where you will practice and hone your understanding and application of Gods' grace—especially in those times when your faith falters and you end up yielding yourself to the sin that so easily entices you. You'll run in there and discover the incredible and wonderful truth that even though your sin may abound in your life at times, the inimitable, unfailing grace of God will abound all the more, to rescue you—to restore you—to bring you back to your senses and renew the fun & fulfillment of life again—he gives you a *Spiritual-Mulligan*—a do-over—a new lease on life. But, don't wait until the next issue develops to run in there—get in there now... Do it daily— live in there with Jesus every day. Hang out with him... You'll love it and so will he.

For this reason, all of your energy should go into developing a system of godly habits, that can supercharge your comfort-zone—not making better goals or chasing better results. Here's why:

We all develop some kind of a routine in our life we call our comfort-zone that I talk about a lot in this program. It has been written: **We are what we think** (Prov. 23:7). Remember that one? Here's another one: **We create our habits, and then our habits create us.** Our comfort-zones exist and function through the habits we learn and adopt, like I stated earlier, some good.... some bad.... some destructive.

A lifetime of good and godly habits can be the result for anyone who seeks to increase the unsearchable riches of their knowledge of Christ. Check out these words:

> *"Excellence is an art won by training and habituation. We do not act rightly because we have virtue or excellence, but we rather have those because we have acted rightly. We are what we repeatedly do.* **Excellence, then, is not an act but a habit."** - Aristotle

One thing for certain to think about—the determined commitment you make to God and yourself, that you will tenaciously maintain the pursuit of increasing your knowledge of Jesus, both intellectually and relationally, will absolutely end up being the most rewarding habit that you will ever form and put into operation within your lifetime. I intend to convince you of that, throughout every chapter of this book and my FRP, embedded within it. **However – This is lifetime stuff – We are just getting started here.**

Acquiring this new lifestyle and the attitude of Jesus that you require to master the sin in your life is not an event, but a process and a daily pursuit that you will develop into a very powerful habit. This wonderful and formidable habit will become an essential component of your new lifestyle—your new comfort-zone. Won't happen overnight, so give yourself all the time you need, and set your thinking to coincide with God's schedule and timing, not yours. Learn to trust him.

PERSPECTIVE – GOD'S TIME FRAME

I know of God rescuing and even delivering believers from a crisis of some kind, in an instant of time using his miraculous power—I've also seen other times when he took many months, years and even a decade or two to complete a work like this when he begins one of his rescue operations. The timing key here is that God looks on the heart—he knows the condition of our hearts, every moment of every day throughout our entire life. That's why he says this in the book of Proverbs:

> **Prov. 4:23** *Keep and guard your heart with all vigilance and above all that you guard, for* ***out of it flow the springs of life****. (AMP)*

Therefore, when you detect the springs of life drying up in your life... Take a close look at your own heart—don't let your love of God and people grow cold. **Here's why—you do not want Jesus saying this about you:**

> **Matt. 15:8** *'This people honors me with their lips, but their hearts are far from me; (NRSV)*

That's why you need to guard your heart with all diligence—God's looking at it. He always has, and always will, give you his best, and, he wants your best in return. That's his heart put on display for you—his best. **What does your best look like right now?**

We all can tell when we are functioning at our best throughout the day. That's the time span when your brain is functioning really well at peak performance. Rarely does that time span exceed somewhere between 1 and 3 hours for most of us.

That begs an essential question for you to ask yourself: Who is currently getting that peak-performance time from you right now? The best time from your brain every day—who or what currently gets that? Who or what are you giving it to? **Is it Jesus...? Weed...? A six pack? You get the picture...**

SPIRITUAL FOUNDATION

The actual strength of your spiritual foundation will prove to be the main determinant of just how much authentic, biblical freedom you will be able to acquire, sustain and enjoy, over your entire lifetime. Here's the primary reason why that is—out of your spiritual foundation will flow your behavior; how you act and what you actually do, moment-by-moment. Your spiritual foundation is an accurate measure of where your heart is, and how much abundant, and fulfilling life, flows out of it. That's why God wants you to guard it so much, and so fervently.

Your real priorities, that is, what you truly value, will always be determined by your actions—by how you act, and not according to your hopes, good intentions and feelings.... Only what you actually do—reveals what your priorities and values actually are.

Therefore, changing your belief system, in order to strengthen your spiritual foundation, is not a trifling quest—however, Jesus himself provides more evidence of why you would be strongly motivated to do this, and to do it really well. Here's a load of strategic truth from his words within the book of Matthew:

Check This Out:

> **Matt. 7:24-27** *(Jesus speaking)* *"Therefore, everyone who hears these words of mine and puts them into practice is like a wise man who built his house on the rock.*
>
> *The rain came down, the streams rose, and the winds blew and beat against that house; yet it did not fall, because it had its foundation on the rock.*
>
> *But everyone who hears these words of mine and does not put them into practice is like a foolish man who built his house on sand.*
>
> *The rain came down, the streams rose, and the winds blew and beat against that house, and it fell with a great crash." (NIV)*

This program is designed to teach you that a change in your behavior is not the sole-result of your willpower, but first on *what you believe*, and then on how you act – *putting what you believe into action*. Truth is, your willpower can only take you so far...

That renowned Hollywood theologian, Clint Eastwood, famously said these words in one of his movies: ***"A man has got to know his limitations."*** Remember that one? Turns out that there is a very profound insight to be found in this sentence from Clint Eastwood. Here it is:

> *The resources required to develop and sustain a lifestyle of freedom are definitely not found within any of us. Believe and accept the fact that human willpower, combined with intellect, cleverness, education and desire is not sufficient for a person to free themselves from, or prevent the occurrence of, a destructive lifestyle.*

Eastwood was right—You need to know your own limitations...!

It further turns out that the essential resource required to develop and sustain a lifestyle of freedom for each of us is none other than the Son of the Living God, Jesus Christ.

Many of you know this to be true. Intellectually, you've got that down. Believing this is not your main issue... Navigating your life up to this point has exposed the truth that you have not yet developed an effective strategy and life-action-plan. Isn't that it?

You strongly want to put what you believe into consistent operation. Problem is however, that you run out of spiritual gas almost every time you try. So, the question lingers: My life has been hijacked...

How can I resolve this difficult dilemma and take it back?

So, we start out this first chapter defining and understanding that a multitude of Christians are currently experiencing a debilitating and even a destructive lifestyle, and that they simply lack an effective way to get themselves free of it. Let's focus our attention right there as we continue.

Heb. 12:1 clearly reveals and documents the instruction from God of what He considers to be a normal and typical response for any Christian navigating life. But, God also regards our response perfectly, because He knows our weaknesses. So, I restate the question again:

What to do—how do we get our life back?

God answers that question in the very next scripture that he inspired the writer of Hebrews *(most probably the Apostle Paul)*, to write. Here it is:

Solution-1:

> *Heb. 12:2 Let us fix our eyes on Jesus, the author and perfecter of our faith, who for the joy set before him endured the cross, scorning its shame, and sat down at the right hand of the throne of God. (NIV)*

Fix our eyes on Jesus Indeed... Could it really be that simple? Further, God also confirms and validates the answer to that question in many passages of scripture throughout the pages of the bible. Look at this one...

Solution-2:

> **Rom. 7:24-25** *What a wretched man I am! Who will rescue me from this body of death? Thanks be to God—through Jesus Christ our Lord! (NIV)*

So then, *what to do...?* **Here's what we do** - We look to Jesus, the author and perfecter of our faith. All life, and all freedom, begins with him.

Jesus knows everything and he can do anything, especially providing all things needed, not only for your freedom, but, for the totality of life itself. This chapter begins right there focusing on Jesus, and challenges you to examine your personal knowledge of Him.

Whether that knowledge is sufficient or not. Whether you really need to increase your knowledge of Jesus. This first book of mine, in every chapter, explores and details that knowledge of Christ, in many ways, and on many levels, because that knowledge, and how you apply it, is absolutely essential to acquiring, and then navigating your Christian life in a consistent state of freedom.

He truly is the impregnable cornerstone of your spiritual foundation —apart from him, authentic biblical freedom simply cannot be acquired and sustained for very long. Do you think it is a coincidence that God states the Christian dilemma in Heb. 12:1 and then immediately reveals what to do about it in Heb. 12:2...? I certainly don't.

So, this key phrase from verse 2 can be opened up a little more, let's take a look: *"Let us fix our eyes on Jesus."* Okay, how does that happen? Fix our eyes on Jesus how exactly? By learning how to acquire his *attitude*. Let's go there.

Check This Out:

> **Phil. 2:5** *Your attitude should be the same as that of Christ Jesus: (NIV)*
>
> **Eph. 4:23** *...to be made new in the attitude of your minds; (NIV)*

Acquiring the attitude of Christ is inextricably linked to developing the freedom strategy and life-action-plan you will need to get yourself free—or, to keep yourself from falling prey to one of these destructive scourges. It works like this: As you begin to acquire his attitude, you begin to *think like him*.... Jesus said it himself in the book of John:

> *John 15:5 (Jesus speaking)* *"I am the vine; you are the branches. If a man remains in me and I in him, he will bear much fruit; apart from me you can do nothing. (NIV)*

What Jesus says is always amazing, compelling, and many times even miraculous. What Jesus does not say, but infers, can also be equal in comparison. Here in this John 15:5 passage of scripture, Jesus infers that this pursuit of freedom by you is not to be attempted as a *Lone-Ranger*. He says this: **"Apart from me you can do nothing."** He means that Christians will not be successful navigating life by themselves only, with little reliance on him, especially if they are seeking to break-free from a destructive lifestyle. In fact, acquiring that attitude of Christ, is actually a self-fulfilling prophecy.

It reads like this: To the degree that you are successfully enjoying authentic biblical freedom, will also be evidenced that you have successfully been acquiring and maintaining the attitude of Christ within your mind. That's exactly how it works...In addition, that attitude of Christ, so crucial and essential to acquiring and maintaining your spiritual freedom is one of the precious promises and provisions that God makes to you here in the book of 2nd Peter:

> *2 Pet. 1:3-4* *His divine power has given us everything we need for life and godliness, through our knowledge of him who called us by his own glory and goodness.*
>
> *Through these he has given us his very great and precious promises, so that through them you may participate in the divine nature and escape the corruption in the world caused by evil desires. (NIV)*

God provides you *EVERYTHING NEEDED FOR LIFE*. Including sufficient knowledge of Jesus. Further, this passage of scripture provides you a guarantee. One of my favorite bible commentaries includes a paraphrase of this guarantee. The wording reads like this:

That even **IF** you are not perfectly consistent, but you are sufficiently consistent, to fulfill this scripture, **THEN** you can expect to never stumble or, at the very least, rarely stumble, in your walk with God. Does that appeal to you?

But...GET STARTED! You will be very joyful when the Holy Spirit of God begins to increase your awareness and sensitivities of these attributes in your life, which are all woven into the person of Jesus Christ. You will discover that you are becoming more God conscious and less sin conscious in your day-to-day thinking.

Get started indeed. Calibrate your thinking. Connect the dots in this passage of scripture. I mean, didn't you invest yourself into this action-plan of mine to realize and acquire what one very strategic sentence from God is offering you in this passage: *"to escape the corruption in the world caused by evil desires."* Isn't that it? Isn't that true? Yes! Indeed, it is true and it only happens when we increase what? *Check it out:*

"Increase Our knowledge of Jesus"

It is this specific, precise and highly detailed knowledge of Jesus that really matters to God and to you. Here's a very essential one of the many reasons why:

> **Dan 11:32** .... *the people who know their God will display strength and take action....* (NASB)

Once again, connect the dots. **It is the people who know their God** who display strength and act effectively. Further, that is what so many Christians are lacking; that ability, or spiritual strength, to do just that; to *Display that*

Strength and Take that Action. That's what is missing, and, it is inseparably linked to how well you know Jesus.

Meditate on that—*you need to KNOW JESUS REALLY WELL!* Almost certainly better than you know him now. So, you might ask... just how well do I really need to know him? Okay, good question—let's break that down some more...

SUFFICIENT KNOWLEDGE
Before you can master the sin in your life, you must first begin learning how it works its way into your life. At that point, you'll be ready to acquire a sufficient base of spiritual knowledge thereby enabling you to effectively *resist* the sin that so easily entices you.

The action-plan on my website is designed to get you started immediately, and so is the FRP in this book, especially, to help you follow through, to progress more effectively. Your success in resisting sin is *intrinsically-linked* to your relationship with God, through Jesus. What does that mean? In this context, you must know Jesus really well, to master the sin in your life. So, that process usually looks something like this: Over time, your relationship with Jesus will grow and will be tested through experiences and you, at some point, will arrive at a place whereby you know him sufficiently well. When you arrive, *at that point*, you are able to begin mastering the consistent sin in your life. Pragmatically, that's how it works.

Your ability to successfully resist, and eventually master, the sin in your life will track and follow your relationship with Jesus that gets deeper with experience over time. The deeper you come to know God, the more faith you will have, and the more successful you will be, in resisting sin. The following two scriptures illuminate this:

> **Dan. 11:32** *...but the people who **know** their God will display strength and take action. (NASB)*
>
> **Gen. 4:1** *and Adam **knew** Eve as his wife, and she became pregnant and bore Cain.... (AMP)*

The word used in the original language (Hebrew), for the English word "Know or Knew" found in the above two scriptures is the word—**YADA.**

The context here is that the word used when Adam *"knew"* his wife Eve, is the same word used in the book of Daniel when the people who *"know"* their God displayed strength and acted. Let's connect these dots...

Now, for them to display that kind of strength and take that kind of action, they had to **know** God with the same depth, love and intimacy that Adam possessed, when he **knew** his wife Eve—his knowledge of her leading up to child birth.

The significance of this distinctive form of knowledge actually expresses the dedication, selfless love and intimacy that we develop, form and attach to our spouses. That significant distinction is meant to be identical with how God desires us to know and relate to him through Jesus.

This is God's message to you and he wants you to understand this really well, so, he compares knowing him with how a husband and wife know each other through a marriage relationship that grows stronger and more intimate over time. The process is analogous. We are to fall in love with, and learn to know Jesus, in a related way that we fell in love with and know our husband or wife. So, pragmatically speaking, we find out what Jesus loves... and we do those things.

Conversely, we find out what Jesus hates or dislikes... and we refrain from doing those things. Very similar to falling in love with our husband or wife. Simply put, but very profound and not at all that easy to accomplish...

We have to work at it and actively resist our own selfishness, on a daily basis.

If Jesus is just an acquaintance of yours, or, more like an icon of history in your mind, your relationship with him is woefully inadequate—absolutely insufficient—and that, my friend, puts you at significant risk of a spiritual train-wreck coming your way.

God has designed our spiritual life experience like that on purpose. If it was really that easy, God knows we would not place such a high value on it. He also knows that we will really only struggle and fight for issues in life that we highly value and care about. How about you...

Do you value and care enough for your marriage, and/or your relationship with God enough that you will fight to maintain it? *Further, is that value sufficient enough to confront your own selfishness?*

Think long and hard about this. Your relationship with God, and your relationship with your spouse, are gifts that god has given you. Your adversary, the devil, wants to take them both away from you... The question is, *will you let him do that, or,* **will you fight to hold onto those precious gifts?** Where do you place that value? For many of you, the answer to that question is a personal and spiritual life challenge. That is why I place it here early in this action-plan. Now, consider this:

SUFFICIENT SPIRITUAL STRENGTH
There is an excellent, pragmatic and compelling reason that God has determined our spiritual life to function in this way. He wants it to be exceedingly strong, not weak. He will test the strength of our spiritual life and faith as often as he deems necessary to ensure that strength. How does God do that, you might ask:

Check this out:

> **Heb. 12:28-29** *Therefore, since we are receiving* **a kingdom that cannot be shaken***, let us be thankful, and so worship God acceptably with reverence and awe, for our "God is a consuming fire." (NIV)*

God will often test things by shaking them. He shakes things to reveal weakness. He shakes all kinds of things; He shakes individuals, marriages, families, churches, businesses, organizations, nations, etc.

You get the picture....

However, like the scripture says, God's kingdom cannot be shaken. It is perfectly strong and we are receiving the gift of adoption into this family and kingdom of his through Jesus.

But, how about you... ***Is he shaking you to reveal some weakness?***

Or, does he need to shake you in some way? Is your faith in him sufficiently strong right now, or, does God need to shake it making you aware of any weakness? Think about it.

What do we take away from this? We are able to see and respond to our spouse through our human senses. However, we cannot see Jesus, but must relate and respond to him through faith, not sight; and, that is not so easy at times. Not so easy indeed. Therefore, I encourage you to think and pray the following paragraph with sound reasoning and clear logic...

Connect these dots; That **IF** your current knowledge of Jesus was sufficient, and your relationship with him sufficiently strong, **THEN** you would not be experiencing a destructive lifestyle, or being influenced by a series of bad habits. Isn't that true? What do you think? Do you agree? I really encourage you to **settle this in your mind.** You want to be able to think and respond like Jesus whenever you are confronted with a temptation to sin – especially a besetting sin. Challenge your own thinking here. Take what time you may need and really think and reason about how well you know Jesus at this point in your life.

Make a sincere assessment of not only your thoughts, but how those thoughts lead you to act and behave like you do. Connect those dots to link how your thought-life controls what you actually do on a daily basis. *Got it?*

Ask yourself, is your knowledge of Jesus sufficient? *(probably not)*. Is it lacking, or insufficient? *(almost certainly)*. Is your relationship with him sufficiently strong?

You and God both know that answer...

The first few chapters of this book are specifically focused on helping you to increase the unsearchable riches of your knowledge of Jesus, and precisely why you need to do that. Your working knowledge of the attitude of Christ is absolutely essential in this pursuit of freedom.

So, beginning in this chapter, you are challenged to open your mind up to refining the **what you believe**, and the **why you believe it**, knowledge of Jesus.

In context with these last several paragraphs, let's introduce another key, and essential principle that must be wholeheartedly believed and adopted prior to learning and applying the many other essential principles of freedom in this program.

Reads like this:

> **Key #2** – *You must first acquire, and then apply, sufficient power and force that is **demonstrably stronger** than whatever it is you are trying to overcome or dominate."*
> *(This key principle specifically applies to internal strongholds, habits or behaviors that bind us to a destructive lifestyle).*

JESUS CHRIST - THE PERSONIFICATION OF TRUTH

That sufficient power and force documented in this key principle is only to be found within the person of Jesus Christ. The resources required to develop and sustain a lifestyle of freedom are definitely not found within any of us. In addition to being simple & profound, it is absolutely, and irrefutably true. Jesus Christ himself, on a myriad of differing, but related levels, possesses in himself, the very truth that all freedom is based upon.

> *John 8:32* "*Then you will know the truth, and the truth will set you free.*" *(NIV)*

Paraphrased, it reads like this: **"Then you will know Jesus, and Jesus will set you free."** Once again, you will not find what is required to produce a high-performance and spiritually fulfilling lifestyle within you, as a part of your human nature. *It simply is not there.* And second, this key principle infers that there is only one resource that possesses the power and force that is demonstrably stronger than whatever internal stronghold is binding you, and that resource is Jesus himself. You will not find it in a medical doctor, a psychologist or psychiatrist or counselor, or even a pastor or priest.

These professional people can certainly be of assistance, and can help you in a number of beneficial ways, and God can, and definitely does, use them to the great benefit of many.

However, in and of themselves, they do not possess the power and resources you will require to develop a high-performance lifestyle or get yourself free from debilitating habit(s) and behavior(s) that are wreaking havoc in your life—so, burn this truth into your brain:

> *1 Tim. 2:5 For there is one God and one mediator between God and men, the man Christ Jesus, (NIV)*

Further, most, if not all, of these debilitating habits and destructive lifestyles are the result of a **spiritual deficiency** of some kind, and only a **spiritual solution** from God will truly be effective. So, once you accept the first challenge to open your mind up to some new knowledge and tactics, the next challenge, coming right after it, looks like this: You activate and maintain these two essential principles of truth to gain personal freedom for yourself, understanding that they both require the direct involvement of God, through the person of Jesus Christ.

It is as simple and yet as profound as that!

Therefore, your first course of action is to connect with, and wholeheartedly trust Jesus himself, one-on-one, **before** you consider turning to anyone else for help. He may very well lead you to a trustworthy person or source, that can be incredibly effective, helping you in a time of need. On the other hand, he may not. The next chapter focuses considerable attention on this with a lot of detail—stay tuned.

Ok, all that being said.... Be wise – Be very wise, and incline your heart to always seek God, and his kingdom, **FIRST**—to *Fix your eyes on Jesus, the author and perfecter of your faith.* The yoke of Christ, and that yoke upon you, is at the heart of God's provision for your freedom. That is the challenge that you, me, and all of humanity must grapple with.... The plan of almighty God through the person of Jesus Christ. Either he is who he says he is, as recorded throughout the Old and New Testaments of the bible, or he is a complete fraud. What do you think...?

That means *the person of Jesus Christ*, not just his teaching. Jesus himself, acting through his Holy Spirit, is the only way for Christians to acquire a high-performance lifestyle of freedom. Many people have tried to build a *"structure"* for themselves of learning and adhering to the principles and precepts that Christ has taught, but, without having to form any, or very little, personal relationship and accountability with him.

The concept of adopting Christ's teachings alone academically, without adopting a personal relationship with him really does have some notable benefit, but ultimately will not provide the freedom you are seeking, especially if you have been trapped in a destructive lifestyle.

CHRIST ALONE PROVIDES WHAT'S MISSING – HIS POWER
Christ alone possesses and provides his divine, supernatural, & overcoming power to each one of us who will seek him out and learn how to obliterate these internal strongholds. In addition, reading the bible, or just going to church will not, in and of themselves, cause you to power-up and destroy destructive habits. Jesus himself is that distinctive reason why Christians experience such fulfillment, leading to freedom, in their lifestyles. Always remember moving forward in this study that, *apart from Christ, you can do nothing (John 15:5).*

Our Father in heaven desires very close, personal relationships with each one of us. However, he is not impressed with any of our learned knowledge and intellect, no matter how great we think that may be. Not at all. In fact, he knows that we need him desperately, moment by moment, as we live out our lives. He created us with that relationship in mind, and, he sent Jesus to ensure that we have a way to reconcile our relationship back to him. Consider the early creation story in Genesis 3:8, about God looking for Adam, as he walked in the garden of Eden.

I think God is wanting us to take a very introspective look into the window of this particular scripture, of just how much he enjoyed spending time with Adam and Eve. As you read through this early description of creation, you easily get the sense of just how much God enjoyed his personal relationship with them—he likely walked with them quite often, and, you clearly form the impression that God really cherished this personal time he spent with them. Guess what? **He still does.** Turns out that this is not a coincidence, placed so early here in the bible, but, a very powerful spiritual warfare tactic that Jesus is wanting us to adopt. So, the next time that you find yourself bound up with some worry or anxious thought—***GO FOR A WALK WITH GOD.*** Just you and him. Get immediately away from the anxiety, or the temptation to sin, even the fear, or whatever else might be hammering your soul and your brain. It will absolutely delight Jesus that you have decided to take a walk around the block, or a dedicated hike in the mountains, or a stroll along the beach—just to connect with him—just because you want to spend some personal quality time to get to know him better. HE DELIGHTS IN THAT KIND OF A CHOICE.

Hebrews 12:2 tells us to ***"fix our eyes on Jesus."*** When you decide to fix your eyes on him, you are moving away from whatever else may be bothering, or distracting you from what really matters in life. Taking a walk with him is not only a really good way to do that, it is also a formidable, and powerful tactic of spiritual warfare. You'll discover that the cares and things of this world begin to fall away, every time that you choose to do this.

Many of my Christian friends have discovered this tactic of walking with God - one-on-one - investing a lot of quality time, just getting to know him better. Over time, you'll find out that those formidable attributes of Gods' divine nature just began to rub off on you—the more time you spend with him, the more time you dedicate to know him, the better you will like him. Jesus is so cool, loving and rewarding, you'll soon be going out-of-your-way to spend even more time in his presence. That is really smart. That is really wise. So, remember that this first principle of freedom involves both knowledge **and** a viable, fruitful relationship with God, through Jesus. Remove either one, and you are stuck once again with your own willpower. That is like taking a sea voyage across the Pacific Ocean in a rowboat. You attempt, or continue that, and you will be doomed to failure.

However, the same sea voyage worked out with God's plan in your life made operational through Christ, will dominate the sea and every storm that rises up against you! The will, plan, teaching and mission of Jesus Christ is purposely designed and intended to set people free and keep them free. There exists a wealth of scripture that verifies this loving relationship with God through Jesus; One of my very favorites starts out like this:

> *Matt. 11:29 (Jesus speaking) Take my yoke upon you...*

God has purposely designed our human nature to be dependent upon him in order to function as fully as he has intended we should. We definitely have not been designed to live and navigate life all alone, by ourselves, without any participation by God. We are designed to be *Yoked to Christ*. However, God doesn't force himself, or even the evidence of his existence upon us. Want some proof? Take a good look at this, from a historical icon, who knows this truth really well:

Here's some really good, historical evidence of that fact—the great French mathematical genius Blaise Pascal, who came to know God through Jesus Christ at the age of 31, put it this way:

> *"God is willing to appear openly to those who seek him with all their heart, and to be hidden from those who flee from him with all their heart. God so regulates the knowledge of himself that he has given indications and evidence of himself which are visible to those who seek him and not to those who do not seek him. There is enough light for those to see who only desire to see, and enough obscurity for those who have a contrary disposition." -*
> **Blaise Pascal**

That being the case.... Be wise - Be very wise, incline your heart to seek God, to *Fix your eyes on Jesus, the author & perfecter of your faith.* The yoke of Christ, and that yoke upon you, is at the heart of God's provision for your freedom.

You really do need a viable, healthy and personal relationship with Jesus Christ to effectively obliterate destructive habits and behaviors that war against your freedom and the joy of life. It is **HIS POWER**, not yours... He does the **HEAVY LIFTING**, not you. It is this relational partnership with Jesus, by his Spirit, that enables the overwhelming spiritual power required to develop, establish and maintain a viable and rewarding personal experience of authentic, biblical freedom for oneself. As I said earlier, **you just have to get to know him really well!**

Therefore, I encourage each of you to ask and pray that Jesus, by his Spirit, would develop a new **spiritual-stronghold** within you—a new work within your mind that not only challenges, and competes against any and every ungodly and wicked spiritual stronghold that you have already developed, but, completely overwhelms and eviscerates the power of those existing spiritual strongholds that may very well be holding you captive in some way, right now. As I just wrote, let Jesus do the *Heavy-Lifting* that you cannot possibly accomplish.

And always remember this point; You cannot overcome evil in your life through just an intellectual pursuit of bible study lasting a few years—it's way more rigorous than that. This process of acquiring and maintaining spiritual freedom is not solely academic or educational, but, it is primarily **relational**, through the person of Jesus Christ. That is the challenge that you, me, and all of humanity must grapple with.... The plan of almighty God through the person of Jesus Christ.

As I close out this first chapter, let me leave you with some powerful encouragement, especially if you are experiencing a rough-patch in your life, and you think that you have little to no chance of putting these new tactics into operation. *Here's Jesus again—he wants you to know this:*

> ***Matt. 11:29, 30*** - *(Jesus speaking) "Take my yoke upon you and learn from me, for I am gentle and humble in heart, and you will find rest for your souls. For my yoke is easy and my burden is light." (NIV)*

Jesus, our Lord, absolutely knows each, and all, of our strengths and weaknesses and what each of us is able to bear. He never requires anything from us that we cannot accomplish in and through him.

HIS YOKE IS EASY AND HIS BURDEN IS LIGHT! So, don't ever think the Lord would put something on you that you cannot handle. That is simply not true.

I encourage you now to go back over this chapter to determine a *"starting-point"* to develop your new freedom-strategy and action-plan. Clinical research has established that the hardest part of making a substantial change in your life is simply taking that first step...

SO, GET IT STARTED....

Godspeed My Friend.

CHAPTER 2
PATHWAYS

THE PATH... To summarize up to this point: Christianity alone, through the person of Jesus Christ, by his Spirit, provides the opportunity to experience authentic spiritual freedom. There are a couple of pathways, or methods, documented in the bible that can lead you to it. These pathways of establishing or restoring a lifestyle of freedom are described in the following sections utilizing a very simplistic narrative, by design. The intent is to document the distinctive differences of these pathways causing you to intently *focus your mind* on one method in particular. That is all we need to accomplish at this point. What path to take. Therefore, read, and pray through this chapter to see which one the Lord will lead you to follow.

CHURCH CENTRIC PATHWAY
Should you realize that you, or someone you care about, are ensnared, or are even just being influenced, or trapped by a destructive lifestyle of some kind, you may decide to follow what I call the Church Centric method of restoring that freedom. Here's a brief description of how this method works:

First, *(assuming here that an effective bible believing / teaching church is being attended)*, it is recognized and concluded that the freedom being sought after has not yet been acquired. Next, addressing the reader personally here, you recognize your accountability to God and you confess your sins to him and ask for, and receive, his forgiveness, based upon your faith. You then seek out other Christians to make yourself accountable to. This is quite often done through your local church or through a Christian counselor. There are many accountability, or sometimes called overcomer groups formed at the local level in most evangelical churches. So, you confess your sins first to God, then one to another as the bible teaches:

> ***James 5:16*** *Therefore confess your sins to each other and pray for each other so that you may be healed. The prayer of a righteous man is powerful and effective. (NIV)*

In most Church accountability groups, the process of confessing these besetting sins is not addressed to the entire group, but usually, to only one or two mature Christians who have shown themselves to be trustworthy confidants who then function as a mentor and a coach to help the besieged Christian disciple work toward getting themselves free, as the bible documents:

> ***Phil. 2:12*** ......*continue to work out your salvation with fear and trembling (NIV)*

This Church Centric process can, and usually does, work really well. However, this method does not always work well. There is a risk of unintended consequences that has been known to happen, and you need to be made aware of this potential issue, assess to see if it is relative to you, and what to do about it.

Here's the issue of concern: *You will be entrusting people,* in addition to Jesus, with the knowledge of your moral failure(s). Therefore, these other Christians, whom you will be confiding in, need to be exceedingly honest and trustworthy. You need to be sufficiently convinced of their *"Christian-credentials."*

They need to have established a rock-solid testimony, living out the life of a mature, competent follower of Christ who knows Jesus really well, and who can be trusted completely with your welfare. A person who looks something like this:

> ***Gal. 6:1-2*** *Brethren, even if a man is caught in any trespass,* **you who are spiritual, restore such a one in a spirit of gentleness;** *each one looking to yourself, lest you too be tempted. Bear one another's burdens, and thus fulfill the law of Christ. (NIV)*

The success and effectiveness of this process is directly dependent upon you and God, but also upon these other Christians. Jesus will clearly do his part, perfectly—every time.

However, should even one of these brothers and / or sisters in Christ whom you have trusted fail you in this regard, your testimony can be seriously impugned with potentially very tragic results that you might have to live with for the rest of your life. Therefore, you need to understand very well what you risk when you decide to use this Church Centric method, and choose to rely upon others. Be very wise as you consider this—employ only a very well-reasoned, well thought-out and prayerful approach to this decision.

Many, many Christians know this pathway can be potentially perilous to their reputation and **good name,**[2] and have decided not to pursue this course of action because of that risk—there is sometimes a very large price to pay for some believers who choose this process, especially when it fails to produce the intended results of restorative freedom.

Because this price of unintended consequences represents such risk of testimony and livelihood, many Christians, especially professional and ministry leadership in the church, refuse to put themselves at risk and pay that price. Instead, they maintain a struggle to outwardly conform to what they know looks like a God honoring lifestyle, but inwardly, they have not yet been able to find an effective answer. This can be, at times, a very miserable way to live.

Therefore, the Church Centric process of acquiring personal, spiritual freedom is not without personal, and sometimes professional risk, and this risk is fairly well known within the church community.

The Christian reader, who is currently struggling with besetting sin(s) or some kind of entrenched addiction, will have to weigh taking on this risk, against not making any change at all, thereby continuing in conviction, pain and misery. It has become very clear to me through research over the years, that for every believer who chooses to risk possible loss of testimony, and even livelihood, through this church centric process of restoration, there exists several others who choose not to—they know all too well what has happened to many who have lost so much when that process fails for them.

---

[2] God desires your reputation and your name to be of great value. Scripture records this: Prov. 22:1 - *A good name* is more desirable than great riches; to be esteemed is better than silver or gold. (NIV)

This dilemma begs a question: How many of you have experienced what you thought was a friend, or even a trusted confidant, turn against you at some point in time, and expose the very confidence you placed in them?

Unexpected and unforeseen consequences—that's the rub. Therefore, be aware, be very aware. Consider, think, reason, ponder and pray a lot about this before committing yourself. This life will teach you that a true friend, who can honor your confidence and be found trustworthy, is sometimes very rare indeed.

Check this out—It is truly spoken:

> "Your best friends usually know the greatest things about you,
> but often think the worst of you,
> **while Jesus...**
> Knows all the absolute worst things about you
> but always thinks the Best of You."

God does not want to see you fail! Jesus wants you to succeed wildly in your life, on every level that honors him and his will for you. He wants each of us to live life abundantly *(John 10:10)* and to enjoy each and every moment of it. God knows very well how the JOY in your life will absolutely EXPLODE within you at the time you successfully develop your freedom strategy, put it into operation, and then begin to experience those exhilarating results.

He wants you to personally experience that explosion of joy for yourself, and he will oppose anything that diminishes that powerful episode and milestone in your life. Gods' matchless and priceless gift to you is his son Jesus Christ and the freedom that can only come from and through him.

So, even though you, or someone you deeply care about, may have been corrupted and developed a destructive lifestyle, Jesus will provide everything needed to overcome all of that. He'll put you on the right path—that's why I wrote this book. He will hold you accountable. He will also expect you to exercise personal responsibility.

He looks at your faith and the condition of your heart, and will help you on every level that you decide to humble yourself and seek him on. Consider these scriptural truths:

> **Nah. 1:7** *"The LORD is good, a refuge in times of trouble. He cares for those who trust in him" (NIV)*
>
> **Psa. 46:1** *"GOD is our Refuge and Strength (mighty and impenetrable to temptation), a very present and well-proved help in trouble." (AMP)*
>
> **Is. 49:25** *"For I will contend with the one who contends with you." (NASB)*

Therefore, know for certain, that the value of your reputation, your good name, is very significant in God's eyes. He desires every good thing for you and your life. He works quite often *"behind the scenes,"* without our direct awareness or knowledge, to establish love, respect and dignity with others for each of us whom he loves. So, consider, once again, the following scriptural truth:

> **Pro. 22:1** - ***A good name*** *is more desirable than great riches; to be esteemed is better than silver or gold. (NIV)*

In that context, I restate this attribute of God's nature that I have truly come to love, that makes the following key principle of freedom literally come alive.

> ***Key #3*** *- Jesus Christ is more intent on helping you and teaching you how to obtain a vibrant, functional, and stronghold busting lifestyle than He is about exposing your weaknesses and failures to public humiliation.*

Never, ever forget that about him. It's a part of his nature. It's who he is and how he responds to us—much more according to his loving kindness, and not nearly as often, according to our iniquity—according to what we actually deserve for breaking Gods' laws so often. He loves you that much, his Gospel is that powerful, his grace will always abound more than your sin abounds, and, God really is that good! He knows our deepest desire wanting to secure any needed restoration and personal freedom without the embarrassment and humiliation of public exposure.

My research for this book and relevant observations of life inform me that public humiliation used for correction is certainly not God's preference, and is quite often only experienced when other people are involved, and at fault in some way.

But—God also knows so very well how to deal with a stubborn heart and an unruly attitude within every one of us whenever he needs to. In context with that, the bible teaches us that God's desire and his plan for securing restoration and a good name necessitates voluntary repentance on our part—that's what we are to do. He will always lead us to do exactly that—to immediately repent of any sin we may commit. His enduring patience with our selfishness and disobedience is truly legend and defies all human understanding, as he leads us back to that precious relationship and fellowship with him, that he values so highly. His ways are higher than our ways and his thoughts are higher than our thoughts. Exponentially higher!

The bible further teaches us that it is actually his kindness that leads us to repentance in the first place. Check it out:

> **Rom. 2:4** *Or do you show contempt for the riches of his kindness, tolerance and patience, not realizing that God's kindness leads you toward repentance? (NIV)*

So, when weighing the attributes of this Church Centric strategy vs the following God Centric strategy for yourself or a loved one, carefully evaluate the Christians within your inner circle of friends. Those whom you may consider to call upon for help and counsel. You may not really know what you can expect from them—**refuse to be naïve about this.**

On the other hand, Jesus, working through his Holy Spirit, may in fact lead you to trust and confide in one or two brothers or sisters in Christ, as the case may be, and use them as vessels of honor to counsel and coach you onto that pathway to freedom that God wants you to be on. The key for you here is to take your time—think, reason and pray this decision through.

Tenaciously resist any temptation from your human nature to act impulsively, making a snap decision, as you seek relief from a destructive lifestyle you so desperately desire and need to acquire.

JESUS, OUR HIGH PRIEST – WHO NEVER CHANGES
In addition, tenaciously resist the temptation from your human nature to turn your personal responsibility to master this besetting sin over to others—in addition to Jesus. Consider again, the following scripture:

> *1Tim. 2:5 For there is one God and one mediator between God and men, the man Christ Jesus, (NIV)*

Jesus is the only one who really knows your heart, and he is also the only one who has the power you require to obliterate every obstacle and stronghold within you that is keeping you captive. He can also lead, guide and / or direct you into a relationship with a brother or sister in Christ and / or into participating in a Church Centric *"Overcomers"* group of some kind to at least begin developing your freedom strategy. The key here is to not be impulsive and to not rush into this. Instead, think, pray and plan your way into this decision. It will have short-term, mid-term, long-term and even eternal impact upon the effectiveness, the joy, and the very quality of your life experience.

All that being said, the last several paragraphs document what you can expect from Jesus, whether you choose the Church Centric or God Centric pathway to personal freedom. He will always lead you to his good, acceptable and perfect will and plan for your life, including which of these paths to choose—however, he puts that choice into your hands to decide. Therefore, after you effectively think, pray and plan about these two pathways to freedom, should you decide the Church Centric strategy might just be too risky, and therefore may not work out for you in your particular situation, do not worry or be anxious about it. Not at all—not even to stress about it.

God has provided a way through the wilderness for anyone who determines that they just cannot confidently resolve the potential risk associated with the Church Centric method of restoration. God has not, and will never, leave you to fend for yourself, to pursue your personal, spiritual freedom; especially fitting if you find that you are just not sure about the Church Centric method—that you simply have not been able to develop the faith, confidence and peace that this method will work out and will effectively produce the results you so strongly desire and need in your life, and that Jesus clearly wants you to have. Okay, so what's next? *Let's check it out.*

GOD CENTRIC PATHWAY
Considerable research and study of the scriptures, woven throughout both the Old and New Testaments, has led a multitude of God's people to find and follow this approach to establish and maintain a lifestyle of authentic, biblical freedom. This God Centric pathway has been in place, and has been used by God down through the passage of time to draw his people closer to himself, and, in the process, to teach them how to acquire and maintain a very effective, constructive and abundant lifestyle.

The success and effectiveness of this process is not principally dependent upon other Christians, but almost exclusively upon God and you. God will clearly do his part perfectly, every time, just as he does with the Church Centric method. So, the risk of any failure is primarily upon you. This fact of exercising self-control should really encourage you.

However, in saying that, please don't think that this method leaves you alone to function like the Lone-Ranger, as mentioned previously. Not at all. God's plan for your life clearly intends you to be a functional part of his church, to take your unique place within the body of Christ exercising the ministry of the gifts that he has equipped you with. Those gifts are unique to you because you are unique yourself. God intentionally made you that way. Further, the example of Jesus himself, and others in the bible, will encourage you to seek out perhaps from one to three very close and trusted friends to navigate the Christian life with. There is great joy in this fellowship that God intends for you to thoroughly enjoy, that simply cannot be experienced by trying to navigate the journey by yourself.

GODS ABOUNDING PROVISION
In addition to Christian friends and the church, the bible documents a truly incredible array of provisions that God has made available to equip you with, both for ministry and to acquire and sustain your own freedom from bad habits, from besetting sin(s), and from a destructive lifestyle.

> ***Key #4 –*** *God has provided each of us with **EVERYTHING** needed for life. Including **A SPECIFIC PLAN** to discover and put into operation, and, each good work that his plan equips you to accomplish.*

This starts with a couple of strategic scriptures I documented in the last chapter, but, providing a different perspective from the Amplified Bible shown here:

> ***2Pet. 1:3*** *For His divine power has bestowed upon us all things that [are requisite and suited] to life and godliness, through the (full, personal) knowledge of Him Who called us by and to His own glory and excellence (virtue). (AMP)*
>
> ***Phil. 4:19*** *And my God will liberally supply (fill to the full) your every need according to his riches in glory in Christ Jesus. (AMP)*

The bible abounds with God's provision for those who have decided to get really serious about seeking him with steadfast diligence. There is even a wonderful assurance in scripture that this God Centric approach works through a process of acquiring, and then applying, the gift of faith that God has given you. ***Your faith—this is where it starts.*** So, let's go over the following passages of scripture, restating a few points that build upon what you read in the last chapter. I often repeat this assurance from scripture, on many levels, and show you exactly how and why it is steadfast, and most importantly, how to achieve it for yourself, in direct relationship with Jesus, by his Spirit. There is a strategic sequence of core values documented here, beginning with faith. Focus your attention on the sequence of these core values documented here in 2 Peter, and, **believe that they are all attainable by you:**

> **2 Pet. 1:5-7** *For this very reason, make every effort to add to your faith goodness; and to goodness, knowledge; and to knowledge, self-control; and to self-control, perseverance; and to perseverance, godliness and to godliness, brotherly kindness; and to brotherly kindness, love. (NIV)*
>
> **2 Pet. 1:8** *For if you possess these qualities in increasing measure, they will keep you from being ineffective and unproductive in your knowledge of our Lord Jesus Christ. (NIV)*

As practicing disciples of Christ, we are all positioned somewhere within this framework of core values regarding our spiritual faith, growth and effectiveness. Verse 8 states that if we possess these qualities, **read**: *we possess all of these qualities in increasing measure,* then we have the certainty that we will not be ineffective and unproductive in our knowledge of Jesus. We'll be increasing the unsearchable richness of knowing him more deeply and completely. Always remember and meditate often on that linkage; *your freedom is inextricably influenced by, and linked to,* **how well you know Jesus.**

Another bible commentary I refer to very often states a valid conclusion to be formed after studying this passage of scripture. This is what it states—***you will never stumble.*** These qualities show a progression from Christian infancy to the full and fruitful attainment of spiritual maturity and freedom throughout a person's life. Further, the phrase, *"in increasing measure"* literally means that spiritual growth is in process. It's dynamic, it's alive in you and actually happening.

However, there are so many Christians who experience significant difficulty learning how to get themselves plugged-into this process, learning how to achieve this result for themselves. Many, all to often, find themselves functioning in their spiritual lives like the Yo-Yo described in previous sections of this program. They travel up and down but rarely forward—very little growth and development of a viable and effective spiritual foundation for themselves to build their life upon. Their comfort-zone of debilitating habits keeps getting in the way, holding them in this vicious lifecycle.

Does that describe you in some way?

Therefore, throughout this book, I will unpack, parse and detail what this particular scripture *(2 Pet. 1:5-8)* means, and exactly how we can achieve these results that are guaranteed to increase our knowledge of Jesus. This God Centric approach really begins the formation of your life's spiritual foundation, and defines the starting point of anyone seeking to be free. All of the core values that you acquire in your life, beginning with your faith, are first to be deeply-rooted in this foundation of biblical truth. Let's go there and see what truth has to do with it.

BIBLICAL TRUTH—THE FOUNDATION OF FREEDOM
In fact, the formation of every destructive habit in your life can be traced back to a weak foundation of biblical truth. A very profound statement, but absolutely true. Conversely, this statement reveals another essential component of biblical truth—the assurance of this guarantee, paraphrased here from 2 Peter 1:8 that we have been focused upon. Here it is:

> *It is virtually impossible for a destructive habit to be formed within any person who effectively operates on a God-Centric foundation of biblical truth.*

This does not mean that you will never sin again. On the contrary, we are all sinners by birth and by choice, saved by grace, and will remain so throughout our entire lifetime.

However, we can and must learn how to control ourselves in a way that is holy and honorable to God, as it is written from the Amplified Bible:

> ***1 Thess. 4:4*** *That each one of you should know how to possess (control, manage) his own body in consecration (purity, separated from things profane) and honor, (AMP)*
>
> ***Rom. 6:14*** *For sin shall not (any longer) exert dominion over you, since now you are not under Law (as slaves), but under grace (as subjects of God's favor and mercy). (AMP)*

As we learn to master the sin that can so easily entice and entangle us, we will be controlling ourselves in such a way that we no longer are ruled and mastered by the power of sin.

We will stop sinning consistently.

We will overcome bad habits and besetting sin. We will win more spiritual warfare battles over sin than we lose. When that process begins to start working in our lives, we will be well on our way to experiencing the development of our unique freedom strategy and life-action-plan. You see, to acquire a new strategy based upon biblical truth, and then to practice living your life with consistent freedom, requires that you learn to view life much more from God's longer-term perspective—rather than from your own, short-sighted, human nature.

But, you and I are not born with the ability to do that. It must be deliberately learned. Remember studying that in the last chapter? Developing, refining or changing your spiritual life foundation, including your core values that make up your comfort-zone, to be in conformance with God's perspective, requires a very diligent pursuit of learning the truth. This pursuit cannot be a haphazard or an intermittent process; it will never work that way. I really encourage you again, right now, to prepare and focus your mind like you did in the last chapter. There's some new stuff coming your way that just might challenge you some more—you up for that?

Check out these next paragraphs revealing what I like to call God's Classroom—a new concept for you to think about and to dwell on. It bears some similarity to our K through 12 plus college educational system, but is much more rigorous and thorough. This next section is intentionally written to describe what a diligent and deliberate learning experience looks like from God's perspective. It is not so much about the what you're going to learn, but much more about the how you are going to learn it. Therefore, the bible instructs us often to gird our minds for action—to be on the alert—to be vigilant and diligent... *(1 Pet. 1:13 & 5:8,9)*. Now would be a good time for you to do just that. **Biblical truth**—*the foundation of your new spiritual lifestyle.*

GODS' CLASSROOM – THE CRUCIBLE OF LEARNING

Consider this: The Lord begins revealing the attributes of his divine nature in the pages of the Old Testament. He tells his people how to learn about him, his precepts and commandments. He describes, in a very pragmatic and practical way, exactly what the process of learning should look like— that is, the process of learning to navigate life more from his perspective. Moses, writing in the book of Deuteronomy, records these instructions from God regarding the process of learning his commandments, precepts and principles:

> ***Deut. 6:6-9*** *"These commandments that I give you today are to be upon your hearts. Impress them on your children. Talk about them when you sit at home and when you walk along the road, when you lie down and when you get up. Tie them as symbols on your hands and bind them on your foreheads. Write them on the doorframes of your houses and on your gates." (NIV)*

Further on, in Deuteronomy 11, Moses adds a distinction of learning that is unique to how God is instructing his people, including all of us in the Christian church, down through the annals of time to this present day:

> ***Deut. 11:18*** *"Fix these words of mine in your hearts and minds" (NIV)*

The meaning being that a Christian man or woman needs to develop and establish a lifestyle that promotes and sustains a consistent and lifelong learning routine of biblical precepts and commandments from God's Word, and fellowship with Jesus through the Holy Spirit of God. Notice in particular how different the learning and teaching methodology is comparing Deut. 6:6-9 with our school system here in America, or any other nation for that matter. The school system provides a structured format of learning for 6+ hours a day, 5 days a week, from the age of 5 for kindergarten through the early 20's completing college. Some go on to post graduate and doctoral studies.

However, **God's Classroom** learning program starts when you get up and continues throughout the day until you go to bed at the end of the day—ALL DAY—EVERY DAY—UNTIL YOU DIE..!

Quite a comparison. However, please don't get lost on the context. We can learn to function in society and develop a vocation through the school system, without expending the full extent of our lives, on a daily basis. Practicing Christians have been doing that for millennia.

God also wants us to realize that we will never complete our knowledge, comprehension or understanding of him, even in this lifetime. He is simply that great, that awesome and complex. His ways and thoughts are exponentially higher than our ways and our thoughts. But, we can, and we should, evaluate how we think about him and how we perceive him to be within our own mind. In addition, we can and we should make ourselves much more aware that God is with us and dwells within each of us 24/7, regardless of whether we feel like he does or not. **HE DOES—he really does, every day.** Consider this scripture:

> *1 Th. 5:16-18 Rejoice always, pray without ceasing, give thanks in all circumstances; for this is the will of God in Christ Jesus for you. (NRSV)*

God's classroom does not end every morning after you finish spending some time reading a few bible verses and investing a few moments in a daily devotional. Not at all. The bible instructs and encourages us to develop and to practice being knowingly aware of God dwelling within us by his Holy Spirit throughout the day, EVERY DAY. Jesus wants our mental and spiritual awareness of him to be sustained throughout the entire day, never letting up; but, not to "dog us" about his presence. Not at all. Only to teach, train, bless, protect and provide for us and keep us out of harm's way. His unchanging nature, and his great love for us, can do nothing less.

However, he also knows so very well that we all like sheep have gone astray— he clearly understands just how easily any of us can be deceived. Check out this next key:

> **Key #5** - *Do not think that becoming **Easily Deceived** could not happen to you. Refuse to think that way. Instead, realize that we are easily susceptible to being deceived and deluded about God's will in our lives at any point in time. That is why we need a Shepherd in the first place, and that is why our need for Jesus, his grace and his truth is often DESPERATE.* **Always Remember** *- Apart from him, we can do nothing... (John 15:5)*

The bible tells us that Jesus wants to provide Abundant-Life *(John 10:10)* to us, imparted by his Holy Spirit, through every day circumstances of living. So, when you experience one or more wonderful events during the day, like answered prayer, you should rejoice and thank God, in that moment; don't wait until tomorrow morning prayer time. In contrast, when you experience a circumstance that adds some stress to your life, you should pray and ask God to help you, right then. That's what *"pray without ceasing"* means. It is very much an on-going process.

God's classroom in the bible is instructing us to maintain and sustain our awareness that God is with us at all times of the day and night, whether we can sense his presence or not. We are to live by faith, not by sight—it is a lifestyle, framed by the Gospel of Christ, and certainly not to be experienced only by our physical senses—what we see and how we feel. God initiates our new relationship with him at the very moment we are born again, and, his desire is to experience a very close bond of personal fellowship with each of us without respect to any timeframe. It's Jesus—everyday—all the time— continuously.

We will in fact, be spending eternity with him in a never-ending learning process focused upon those attributes of his divine nature, but never completely comprehending them. He is that far above our ability to understand him and his ways, which the bible says are unsearchable.

However, he clearly intends and instructs each of us to be growing and increasing in those unsearchable riches of our knowledge of Jesus Christ. So, he encourages us to develop the godly discipline of a proactive mind set and attitude throughout our entire lives, focused upon learning, understanding and comprehending all that we can about him and his kingdom. In addition to the passages in Deuteronomy documented here, Old and New Testament scripture is replete with numerous descriptions of God's learning process:

> ***Josh. 1:8*** *Do not let this Book of the Law depart from your mouth; meditate on it day and night, so that you may be careful to do everything written in it. Then you will be prosperous and successful. (NIV)*
>
> ***Psa. 119:15*** *I meditate on your precepts and consider your ways. (NIV)*
>
> ***Psa. 119:97*** *Oh, how I love your law! I meditate on it all day long. (NIV)*

There is a very good reason that God's classroom is much different than what the world's system provides. God knows our human nature, and just how easy it is for us to stray from his commands. So, he teaches and even admonishes us to virtually saturate our minds with his word from the bible. Not just from an educational, intellectual standpoint, but, his word is also the bread-of-life that nourishes our spirit. Therefore, to the degree that we increase our knowledge of Jesus, we maintain, and sustain, the health and well-being of our spirits. And, what do we receive in return from him?

He provides us abundant life – **What a deal.**

Truly a Win-Win transaction. He is definitely a rewarder to all those who seek him with diligence. Check this out:

> **John 10:10** *The thief does not come except to steal, and to kill, and to destroy. I have come that they may have life, and that they may have it more abundantly. (NKJV)*

God's Classroom—very different from just learning how to read and write, or learning, and even mastering, a vocation or career. The thought here is to dissuade any of you from thinking that just going through the school and college or seminary system will provide all you need to develop and secure a strong spiritual foundation to build your life upon that will lead you to a higher-performance lifestyle of personal freedom. It will not. However, the bible is not teaching or admonishing us to take upon ourselves anything that is so arduous and difficult that we could not possibly accomplish it.

Or, that only a very select few, with extremely disciplined minds can accomplish what it takes to acquire a lifestyle of spiritual freedom. No, no, not at all. The bible is replete revealing God's amazing grace and lovingkindness, in many ways and on many levels. *Check these scriptures out:*

> **Matt. 11:29, 30** *(Jesus speaking)* "*Take my yoke upon you and learn from me, for I am gentle and humble in heart, and you will find rest for your souls. For my yoke is easy and my burden is light.*" *(NIV)*
>
> **Acts 15:10** *Now then, why do you try to test God by putting on the necks of the disciples a yoke that neither we nor our fathers have been able to bear? (NIV)*
>
> **1 Cor. 10:13** *No testing has overtaken you that is not common to everyone. God is faithful, and he will not let you be tested beyond your strength, but with the testing he will also provide the way out so that you may be able to endure it. (NRSV)*
>
> **Joel 2:13** *"Rend your heart and not your garments. Return to the LORD your God, for he is gracious and compassionate, slow to anger and abounding in love, and he relents from sending calamity." (NIV)*

The bible is teaching and admonishing us to abide in Christ, with his word richly abiding in us, and then learn to walk in and by the spirit, in such a way that we will not carry out the evil desires that can well up from within our own hearts and minds.

Further, that we will learn to control our bodies, including our minds, in a way that is holy and honorable to the Lord. Remember, it is our adversary the devil—and it is sin—not God, who is the evil taskmaster in our lives, seeking to put all of us, and keep all of us, in deep and terrible bondage.

Jesus, our Lord, absolutely knows each of our strengths and weaknesses and what each of us is able to bear. He never requires anything from us that we cannot accomplish in and through him.

HIS YOKE IS EASY AND HIS BURDEN IS LIGHT. So, don't ever think the Lord would put something on you that you cannot handle. That is simply not true. You read that in the last chapter, for a very good reason - It's absolutely, unequivocally, TRUE. **Got that down? Did you Nail-It—Do you believe It?** Good. Now you should continue to plan on ordering, or re-ordering, your life to discover, learn, and conform your thoughts, choices, and actions to this God Centric way of doing life.

ACCOUNTABILITY—YES INDEED, DIRECTLY TO GOD
Dealing with your sin, you make yourself directly accountable to God. You confess your sins first to God, then you repent and make any necessary restitutions, but with a new, single-minded determination to overcome whatever is causing the repetition of sinful thoughts and behavior in your life. One clarification to this. The bible documents what we are to do if we sin directly against another person, or they sin against us:

> **Matt. 18:15** *"If your brother sins against you, go and show him his fault, just between the two of you. If he listens to you, you have won your brother over... (NIV)*

> ***Matt. 5:23-24*** *"Therefore, if you are offering your gift at the altar and there remember that your brother has something against you, leave your gift there in front of the altar. First go and be reconciled to your brother; then come and offer your gift. (NIV)*

Want more evidence to confirm and validate your part of this new freedom strategy? Consider the following—the very first use of the word "sin" in the bible is found in Gen. 4:7. God himself is speaking to Cain in this passage.

God knows that Cain is contemplating the murder of his brother Abel, and God directly challenges Cain to exercise his personal responsibility and resist the temptation. Here is God himself, speaking directly to Cain:

> ***Gen. 4:7*** *"If you do what is right, will you not be accepted? But if you do not do what is right, sin is crouching at your door; it desires to have you,* ***but you must master it.****" (NIV)*

In this case, God is putting the responsibility for mastering sin personally upon Cain, and also, upon each of us who follow. God does not leave us alone to accomplish this, but, he wants us to learn how to overcome evil and get free from this debilitating, habitual practice of sin.

So, understand that the type of sin God is talking about here is the consistent, or, besetting sin that we regularly yield ourselves to, thereby entrapping us to a destructive lifestyle—and not so much about sin in our lives that is more innocuous and of lessor consequence.

God was talking to Cain about the besetting sin of anger in this case. God knew that this tremendous anger from Cain, was hardening his heart and corrupting his mind, to the degree that Cain was contemplating the murder of his brother Abel, and, in fact, that is exactly what the consequence of this besetting sin of anger produced.

Cain murdered his brother Abel. As a result, Cain lost his freedom for the rest of his life. This result was not God's desired will for Cain or for any of us.

However, God holds each of us accountable and makes each of us personally responsible to seek, find and acquire the knowledge needed to develop our own unique freedom strategy. But, he won't do this for us. It is ours to make happen. God created us to, and fully expects us to, take dominion and exercise control over our human faculties.

He clearly has established this responsibility for each of us to adhere to. He has also provided everything we need to perform that responsibility. His perfect nature can do nothing less. However, he also expects each one of us to learn everything we need to know, and also expects us to learn how to acquire everything we need from him, in order to perform this responsibility.

Cain failed to do that—*God offered—Cain rejected—**Abel was murdered.*** Connect the dots... God promises to hold nothing back from a person who will diligently seek him. In fact, it is that person who receives God's reward and blessing:

> ***Heb. 11:6*** *But without faith it is impossible to please and be satisfactory to Him. For whoever would come near to God must (necessarily) believe that God exists and that He is the* **rewarder** *of those who earnestly and diligently seek Him. (AMP)*

GOD'S NORMAL LIFESTYLE – AUTHENTIC FREEDOM
Therefore, God has established that the control of a consistent pattern of debilitating sin can and must be mastered by any and every Christian seeking a lifestyle of freedom. We cannot eliminate sin from influencing our lives, but we can learn to absolutely prevent it from ruling over our lives in a consistent manner.

We are to master, and completely rid ourselves of all bad habits that contribute, or lead us to a destructive lifestyle. That is clearly God's desire, plan and will for each of us. This mastery over destructive, sinful habits is an exacting process that must be learned, working in partnership and very close context with God's Holy Spirit, because we are not born with that ability.

However, a lifestyle of freedom is what awaits every Christian who will seek God with diligence. That truly is his default-lifestyle.

In summary of this God Centric method of acquiring personal, spiritual freedom, you accept full responsibility to assess, determine and correct the spiritual weakness, and to make any restitution your sin(s) may have caused, as you submit to God's leadership in your life. You accept this responsibility with the understanding and acknowledgment that you cannot earn it, and that God himself will be providing everything needed to equip you as you fulfill this, according to his riches, glory and grace through Christ Jesus *(Phil. 4:19)*.

Therefore, as you acknowledge your accountability to God in this way, you also commit to exercising your personal responsibility as you diligently seek his will and plan for your life. This will require you to make an honest and truthful assessment of your faith and spiritual growth, often, but especially when you are first seeking to make a change your life. Like I stated before, that assessment is not a trivial matter. A truly honest assessment will challenge you with the fact that something must be definitely wrong with your core values and comfort-zone, or you would not be behaving in a consistently sinful manner. The bible admonishes each one of us about this:

> ***Rom. 12:3*** *"For by the grace given me I say to every one of you: Do not think of yourself more highly than you ought, but rather **think of yourself with sober judgment,** in accordance with the measure of faith God has given you." (NIV)*

This is the distinctive difference between the Church Centric, and God Centric, approach to restorative freedom. Authentic biblical freedom requires you to be personally accountable and responsible for your actions. You can choose to be directly accountable to God alone through the God Centric approach, or to also make yourself answerable to other Christians through the Church Centric approach. The bible teaches and supports both. Further, society has provided a number of organizations like Alcoholics Anonymous, Narcotics Anonymous, Celebrate Recovery, and others that can also be of benefit to a Christian struggling with addictive issues—however, God holds each of us directly and personally accountable and charges each of us with personal responsibility to him and his word.

In addition, other Christians can, and should be involved in this God Centric approach also—the difference is that you choose not to make yourself directly answerable to them for your behavior. To be sure, God has not designed your life to be conducted like the Lone-Ranger, but, will lead you to many godly people throughout your life to be nurtured, discipled, admonished and blessed by. He always encourages us to love one another and to fellowship with one another.

So, this leads to a sixth key principle of God's truth thereby making yourself personally responsible for your actions and behavior. However, God has made that responsibility a choice that you must consider, determine, and put into operation.

> **Key #6** – *You must accept the fact that **You Alone** are absolutely, and personally responsible for the integrity of your character, your core values and unique comfort-zone system of habits you choose to believe, adopt and live by.*

That has always been the case, even before you were born again. Always remember that God himself spoke to Cain about sin and said, **YOU MUST MASTER IT.** However, now that you are born again, you are no longer alone in this struggle, and God has committed to providing you everything needed for that freedom you acquire, or renew, **Like an Eagle** *(Is 40:31) (Ps. 103:5)*.

Well, there they are. Two viable, but different approaches from the bible that can lead you to freedom. What do you think? Do you agree?

Okay, let's see what the bible, life and the next chapter tells us about **FAITH......**

PART 2
BELIEVE GOD BEFORE YOU CAN OBEY GOD

That's not just a novel sound bite to chew on.... It is absolutely essential to successfully, and effectively, navigate the Christian lifestyle. Here's a few points the chapters in part 2 will focus your attention on:

- **Faith** is to your spirit what blood is to your body—IT IS LIFE!
- **Faith** is always essential to navigate life—NEVER OPTIONAL!
- With effective **faith**—PETER WALKED ON WATER TO JESUS!
- Without effective **faith**—IT IS IMPOSSIBLE TO PLEASE GOD!

CHAPTER 3
FAITH

*Before you can **OBEY** God, you have to **BELIEVE** God...*

FAITH - GOD'S PERSPECTIVE
The last chapter introduced you to what I call the God Centric method of acquiring and maintaining, authentic biblical freedom. A key strategy for me was, and is, to illuminate that particular path to freedom and help you get on it, and stay on it. I presented a number of attributes of spiritual freedom documented throughout the bible, but with a Gods' eye view of life, more from his perspective—gleaned from the bible, rather than what is common to us. We'll begin this chapter exploring his perspective on biblical faith, and how faith factors into acquiring and sustaining that spiritual freedom.

The bible establishes that faith is to our spirit what blood is to our body. *It is LIFE—Spiritual LIFE—A very big deal.* The bible also details that God's eyes literally search the world, to and fro, for individuals with faith, and, when he finds it, he always responds. Jesus said this in Luke 7:9: *"I tell you; I have not found such great faith even in Israel."* God is actively looking for it, 24/7. So, consider what he will find when he measures yours. Let's make it greater...!

FAITH and FREEDOM - The bible also establishes two, definitive and distinctive methods for anyone seeking to acquire true, authentic, spiritual freedom for their lifestyles, both of which require sufficient faith:

1. The Freedom acquired through the Grace of God.
2. The Freedom acquired through Obedience to the Lord's commands.

The first experience of freedom that Jesus provides to every one of his Christian believers is provided by his Gospel, through grace, by grace, and grace alone. This freedom experience begins at the initial time of salvation, and then every day afterward whenever a Christian effectively applies the

Gospel and receives forgiveness of sin. Galatians 5:1 boldly declares this truth, *"It was for freedom that Christ has set us Free."*

This method of acquiring spiritual freedom is focused completely upon learning how to consistently believe, and then act upon, the Gospel of Jesus Christ—It is the core of Christianity. There is also a second, and separate expression of freedom that God mandates to every believer; that is the *"Freedom that comes through Obedience."* We will explore and detail that particular method of acquiring freedom in book two of this program.

However, first you acquire and experience the spiritual power of the Gospel put into consistent operation within your life. That initial expression and experience of freedom acquired through grace prepares you to then acquire and experience the freedom that comes through obedience. That's just how life works. So, in this chapter, we explore the freedom acquired by, and through, the grace of God. That's where spiritual freedom actually begins. *Let's take a look......*

FAITH COMES FIRST - Faith is dynamic and has an *"ebb and flow"* to it. In addition, your spiritual faith is not like your mind, which can be easily deceived. In fact, your faith in Christ will need to become unshakable as you acquire that freedom so essential to a thriving, abundant lifestyle. Always remember this: FAITH COMES BEFORE FREEDOM. You will not acquire authentic, biblical freedom without it—believe what God says in the bible first, then he will enable you to obey his commands.

That's why your faith is so precious to God—it accurately reveals the condition of your heart to him. And, that's why Jesus always looks on the condition of your heart—he knows that it accurately reveals just how much you love him. And that, in turn, actually defines why the quantity, and the quality, of your faith in God, is such a big deal to Jesus—because it is such an accurate measure of your love for him. We are mandated to love God, so he will then enable us, to love people. That's where faith fits in—that's how it works... Study the following chart which displays how your faith is out in front, leading you into acquiring that treasured freedom:

FREEDOM STRATEGY PROGRAM
Attributes of Faith & Freedom Chart

The following profile plots a series of Spiritual Warfare Attributes, similar to the Divine Attributes listed in the above scripture reference from 2Peter. However, these spiritual warfare attributes have been selected from a context of a Christian seeking to focus on, and acquire, a lifestyle of Spiritual Freedom. Take particular notice here that it is the attribute of FAITH that effectively LEADS all of the other attributes needed to acquire authentic spiritual freedom. With faith in what you see in this chart, you will, in time, experience the results of your Freedom Strategy...Without faith, you can't even please God.... Study *Mark 5:34 & Matt. 8:10 & 13* in context regarding how faith works from God's unique perspective.

Faith is absolutely required and always leads these other attributes regardless of whether you acquire spiritual freedom exclusively thru the grace of God, or thru grace & obedience.

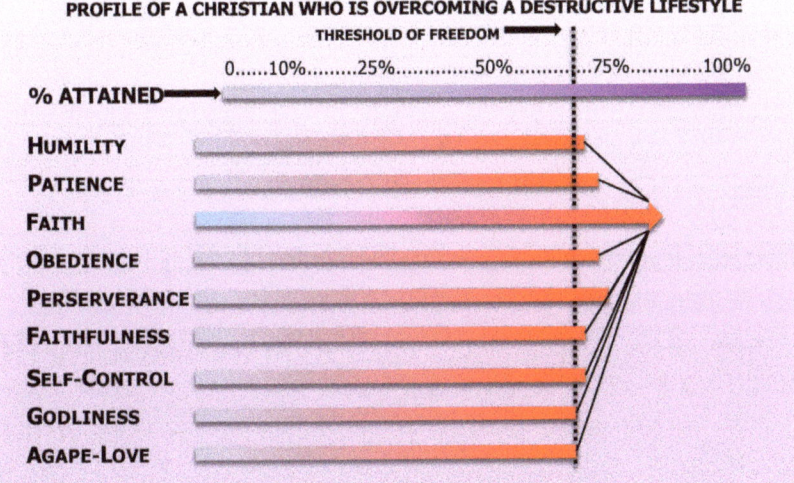

Okay, what should you take away from this? First-things-first, these attributes define your new identity in Christ. However, they are not intrinsic to your human nature, like they are to Gods' divine nature. You are not born with them—but, God mandates every Christian to acquire them, as evidence of our new identity in Christ. As these attributes begin showing up in our lifestyle over time, they become the actual proof that we are becoming more like Jesus. The bible defines this process in 2 Peter 1:5-8, documented very clearly in the last chapter, however, I want you to see with even more clarity, how these individual attributes relate to each other, and, how faith is at the forefront of making up this new identity of yours, in Christ.

These individual attributes listed in this chart accurately represent the *"bricks and mortar"* that God provides you, to form your new spiritual foundation, throughout your lifetime. However, you cannot see them like you can see a bag of cement—they are spiritual, and must be discerned by faith, not by sight. Without faith leading the way - without you actually believing that Jesus has begun this new work in you, and that he will certainly complete it, just like he said he would do - the bible says that you labor in vain. *Check it out:*

> **Psa. 127:1** *Unless the LORD builds the house, those who build it labor in vain..... (NRSV)*
>
> **Phil. 1:6** *being confident of this, that he who began a good work in you will carry it on to completion until the day of Christ Jesus. (NIV)*

And specifically, that's why God informs us throughout the bible to place such a high value on our faith—to guard it with vigilance because it is linked so completely to the condition of our hearts. He tells us to **look out for, and to be on the alert**, to identify and avoid anything that could lead us to less faith, dull or ineffective faith, bad habits, even to the extreme point of addiction. Determine to not let your mind go there. Instead, consider and respond to the choice that the Gospel of Christ makes available to every Christian at the beginning of every day. By choosing to activate your faith every day, you will then be enabled to choose life, just like God inspired Moses to declare, way back when:

> **Deut. 30:15** *"See, I have set before you today life and prosperity, and death and adversity; (NRSV)*
>
> **Deut. 30:19** *... Choose life so that you and your descendants may live, (NRSV)*

Always remember, as Christians, we are to walk and live by faith, not by sight—as it is written:

> **2 Cor. 5:7** *for we walk by faith, not by sight. (NRSV)*

FAITH, ACTION AND VALUES – A key thought for you to load into your mind here at the beginning of this chapter on faith stems from the transaction that God makes with you at the time of your salvation. He offers you the free gift of "Saving-Faith." Spiritual life begins here, when you become born-again. That gift enables you to initially believe that Jesus is who the bible says he is, and that the Gospel of Christ is absolutely true. It is God who enables you to actually believe that in the first place.... It is his gift to you, because of his love for you. Your part of this transaction is simply to accept God's free gift and exercise your belief that it is indeed, true. *When you do that – God sees your faith and responds to it* – He writes your name into his Lamb's Book of Life; he adopts you into his family and kingdom, and grants eternal life to you. DONE DEAL.

God is transactional and we live in a cause & effect world. God makes covenants with mankind, and he also makes deals with us, throughout our lifetimes. For example, in the bible you will often read something to the effect of this following statement:

If you, then I – meaning: *"If you do this, then I will do that."*

Here's a great example of that from the Old Testament book of Exodus:

> **Ex. 23:22** *If you listen carefully to what he says and do all that I say, I will be an enemy to your enemies and will oppose those who oppose you. (NIV)*

Now that's a really good deal, wouldn't you agree?

On another level, that salvation experience of yours is an event, and it happens in a micro-second of time. However, from that point forward, the growth, maintenance, strength, vitality and effectiveness of your faith is not an event, but a process conditioned by many factors, all of them influenced by your personal relationship with Jesus.

When you take effective action to exercise your faith, on what you believe to be true about it, then it will grow and you will exhibit increased levels of spiritual vitality, health, strength and well-being. Conversely, if and when you neglect the health and well-being of your faith, it will atrophy and become weaker. That's just how it works—*cause and effect.*

I write a lot about the core-values that make up your comfort-zone throughout this program of mine. Some of those core values, are more treasurable than others. I encourage you therefore, to put your faith in Jesus and his Gospel at the very top of your treasured values list.

Those highest treasured core values of yours, are the ones that you will fight for, to protect from loss or damage.

In that context, I am purposely intending right here to plant a thought, like a seed, in your mind, from the words I write in this particular chapter on faith. I encourage you to methodically think through these words—especially those key words that you know pertain to you, and your particular lifestyle right now, and take all the time you need. Read and study through this program. Take notes and go back over those notes. Be sure about this. Prepare, study and inform your mind that you intend to do this.

That time may start out very small at first, but Jesus will cause it to grow, as he measures your sincerity—he knows just how serious this issue is to you. Then, when you are ready, pull the trigger and take the action—begin showing up consistently to spend quality time just getting to know him better than you do now— that's where you start—that's your next step of spiritual growth. That's the action Jesus is wanting you, and leading you, to make happen in your life.

Think this through—of all the core-values that you treasure, highly value, and hold dear in your life, make this time of showing up for prayer and devotion to Christ one of the highest. Then follow through to guard and protect your heart, your faith and your mind especially above all others. Fight tenaciously to establish and maintain this new life-giving habit, so essential for your spiritual health and well-being. I think the Amplified Bible version of the following scripture captures the context of this principle really well:

> ***Prov. 4:23** Keep and guard your heart with all vigilance and above all that you guard, for **out of it flow the springs of life**. (AMP)*

LIFE IN THE FAST LANE – Sometimes life comes at you really fast. Other times, not so much. The key principle here is that life is always moving, primarily because your mind is always moving. It's in motion all the time, even when you sleep, and, this issue of trusting God with your time schedule every day can really challenge you.

You've likely heard of the tyranny of the urgent? Your adversary, the devil, wants to keep you in a state of chaos, while Jesus, is always working in your mind to bring order.

Your mind is very *"malleable"* and incredibly capable of either remaining in a fixed state in certain circumstances, or, actively changing perspective in others. God designed it that way on purpose—so he can shape it.

The God's-Eye-View of your life is in motion, almost all of the time. It's like a pendulum you can visualize in your mind's eye, capable of extreme swings in both directions. One extreme can move you towards evil behavior, and the other towards godly, Christ-like behavior. However, your spiritual faith operates very differently. That faith of yours, is the substance that the entire spiritual foundation of your very life is made of. Jesus builds it, and then perfects it within you, truth upon truth, principle upon principle, throughout your entire life—*he's the only one who can....(Heb. 12:2).*

So, what to do... First, **choose life...** Then exercise your faith to meet with Jesus every day that you can, praying to acquire his attitude and taking his yoke of life upon you. Next, put that Christ-Like attitude of yours into action to resolutely guard your heart, faith and mind. You'll need to effectively prevent that pendulum swinging in the wrong direction.

Be aware of your mind always moving—*Your thoughts are always determining your actions and behavior—throughout all of your life.*

Kind of like a Pendulum—Check this out:

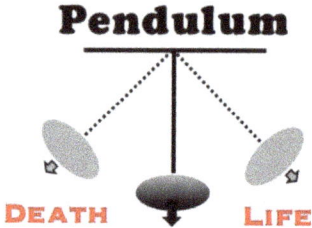

Therefore, shape and control those thoughts to move your life where you and Jesus want it to go. Actively, and clearly think about this. Don't let your life go where you don't want it to go. Resist it like the plague. First, BELIEVE that you can do this—then put that faith into action:

> **1Pet. 1:13** *Therefore, prepare your minds for action;* ***be self-controlled****; set your hope fully on the grace to be given you when Jesus Christ is revealed. (NIV)*
>
> **James 4:7** *Submit yourselves therefore to God, resist the devil, and he will flee from you. (NIV)*

FAITH, FREEDOM and UNBELIEF – One way or another, God always responds to faith - or, the lack of it. That being stated, the bible is replete with many examples of how faith influences your life, especially any besetting sin in your life, one way or another. Let's examine a few of those to see Jesus at work, authoring and perfecting faith, just like he said he would do in Heb. 12:2.

Jesus used *parables* quite often to teach the principles and precepts of grace and truth that his Gospel operates on, and our faith is established by. He did this intentionally and deliberately because he knew that these parables would illustrate a story-line, or put a word-picture within the mind. He also knew that forming a word-picture in the mind's-eye of someone was perhaps the most effective, and the most efficient way to initiate, build and perfect a person's spiritual faith. He simply, but profoundly, designed the human mind to work that way. Here's an example from scripture:

The law of sin and death can be either present and in operation within the mind, or completely absent, **depending upon the condition of a Christian's faith.**

> *Rom. 8:2 ......because through Christ Jesus the law of the Spirit of life set me free from the law of sin and death. (NIV)*

Here is the predictable outcome from scripture clearly revealing the powerful result of what can happen to a Christian who exercises their faith to believe in the sheer, irrefutable, spiritual power of the Gospel of Christ:

> *Rom. 6:14 For sin will have no dominion over you, since you are not under law but under grace. (NRSV)*

This word in Romans 6 that God inspired the Apostle Paul to write is absolutely true—but, do you really believe that it is? How strong is your faith in this particular scripture? God is looking and he wants you to know, and abide in, this specific truth—and, for good reason. Here's why—there is a condition of faith that God has hated and judged, with epic results. That is the condition of no faith, known as the sin of unbelief, leading to unfaithfulness.

There are numerous examples of this throughout both the Old and New Testaments of the bible. Perhaps the most relevant example begins with the following scriptures from the book of Numbers. This egregious example of the sin of unbelief occurred just prior to the Israelites taking possession of the *"promise-land"* that God was giving them. The issue began to surface with the Israelites grumbling against how they thought Moses and Aaron was leading them:

> *Num. 14:2 All the Israelites grumbled against Moses and Aaron... (NIV)*

God did not take this grumbling lightly....

Check out what God said to Moses:

> **Num. 14:11** *The LORD said to Moses, "How long will these people treat me with contempt? How long will they refuse to believe in me, in spite of all the miraculous signs I have performed among them? (NIV)*

"They refuse to believe in me"... The sin of unbelief is the antithesis of faith, and, without faith, it is virtually impossible to please God. Check out what God did to the Israelites because of their unbelief and unfaithfulness on this occasion:

> **Num. 14:33** *Your children will be shepherds here for forty years, suffering for your unfaithfulness, until the last of your bodies lies in the desert. (NIV)*
>
> **Heb. 3:19** *So we see that they were not able to enter, because of their unbelief. (NIV)*

God would not allow that entire generation of Jews to enter the promise land, judging their complete lack of faith, exiling them in the desert for forty years. I'm not hinting, or intimating with this example that it pertains to any of you seeking to acquire a lifestyle of freedom. However, a very accurate intent of all scripture like this example, may very well be to virtually, **"Scare the Hell right out of you."** My intent with this example is really just to inform or confirm to you emphatically how much God hates the specific sin of unbelief—so, consider yourself to be informed and to be made aware...

God hates all sin for sure, but, this one in particular. And, Jesus wants you to know that about your Father in Heaven. So, remember this about God's divine nature, and his hatred of sin. It vigorously reveals another attribute of just... **Who he is.**

Conversely, there are numerous examples of what God does when he is confronted with faith, and the condition of it—especially faith measured in different degrees of effectiveness. *Check out this well-known bible story:*

You all know the famous biblical story of David and Goliath. I encourage you to read through 1 Sam. chapter 17 for this account of it. The key here, that I'd like you to think about, is that David really did kill Goliath—the almost 9ft tall Philistine giant, because he simply, but very profoundly, **BELIEVED THAT HE COULD.** So, how did that happen? David had sufficient faith that he could kill Goliath, because Jesus told him that he could—within his "mind's-eye."

Jesus revealed the thought to David, that he could really do this, and, like Abraham before him, he chose to believe God—so, he acted. *Because of his faith, he displayed strength and he acted...(Dan. 11:32).* And, because he put that faith of his into action, he did in fact, kill Goliath. He believed God first, then, he acted—*that's how it works—that's how Jesus does it...*

Next, read through this amazing and miraculous example of how Jesus develops, perfects, and then responds to Peter's faith on the sea of Galilee:

> *Matt. 14:25-31 During the fourth watch of the night Jesus went out to them, walking on the lake. When the disciples saw him walking on the lake, they were terrified. "It's a ghost," they said, and cried out in fear. But Jesus immediately said to them: "Take courage! It is I. Don't be afraid."*
>
> *"Lord, if it's you," Peter replied, "tell me to come to you on the water." "Come," he said. Then Peter got down out of the boat, **walked on the water** and came toward Jesus. But when he saw the wind, he was afraid and, beginning to sink, cried out, "Lord, save me!" Immediately Jesus reached out his hand and caught him.* ***"You of little faith,"*** *he said,* ***"why did you doubt?"*** *(NIV)*

Okay, what do we understand about faith from this example? First, faith can be an exceedingly powerful catalyst. When Peter requested that Jesus command him to come to him on the water, his faith informed him that Jesus could miraculously make that happen. Peter began this example with sufficient faith because he had seen and experienced Jesus performing miraculous signs and wonders several times.

Pete's faith was based upon EVIDENCE, not conjecture, or presumption. He knew that Jesus could do anything. He possessed strong evidence of his faith in Jesus. So, he obeyed the command of Christ to come. Peter realized, that his faith, at that particular moment, would enable him to obey the command of Christ to actually walk on the water, just as Jesus was walking on the water.

Peter had to believe that he could walk on that water, or, he would have never even gotten out of the boat. But he did get out of the boat because he activated his faith in what Jesus told him he could do. **He took action.** He knew and understood the risk of failing miserably, in the sight of Jesus and the other disciples. He took that risk and exercised his faith. The result—God rewarded Peter's faith in an exceedingly powerful way. This example of faith in action provides us a veritable classic instruction and understanding of what can influence faith when it is put into motion, especially how dynamic it can be.

We do not know how far he walked and how long his faith prevailed. We do know, however, that it was **the condition of Peter's faith** that resulted in the suspension of the law of gravity, that enabled him to walk on the water. Clearly a miracle of Christ, arguably made possible through the faith of Peter. Faith is clearly at work as a catalyst in many miracles performed by Christ throughout the New Testament.

Faith can be variable and is always contingent upon, or can be influenced by, how we are relating to Jesus at any point in time. Here's what I mean by that: Peter's journey of walking on the water was indeed a miracle and was initiated by the condition of his faith. His faith was sufficient to begin walking on the water, but, at some point, "when he saw the wind," his faith weakened, he became fearful, and he began to sink. **Fear is the antithesis of faith.** Accordingly, in a short period of time, Peter's faith went from being sufficient and strong, to becoming very insufficient and weak. Pragmatically speaking, this is what I think happened—Peter's faith was made sufficient for him to experience this walking on the water miracle because he was obedient to the commands of Christ in general, but specifically to the following scripture in Hebrews:

> Heb. 12:2 Let us fix our eyes on Jesus, the author and perfecter of our faith.... (NIV)

As long as his eyes *(read: his heart, mind and will)* were fixed on Jesus, his faith was strong enough to prevail over the law of gravity and he did not sink. However, he became distracted "when he saw the wind" *(read: storm)*, causing him to take his eyes off Jesus, and when he did that, his faith immediately was weakened and he began to sink. That's it...

To summarize this particular section of the chapter, I've documented a few "extreme" examples demonstrating how God responds to faith, both when it is sufficient and strong, and also when it is weak and even non-existent.

I strongly believe that God wants you and me to understand what faith is capable of doing when applied properly, and a few things that can, and do, affect the condition of it. Faith leads to faithfulness when consistently put into action like that. And, faith can also lead to obedience to the commands of Christ, in the same way—when it is effectively exercised.

So, remember that God has given this incredible gift of faith to you, and he expects you and me to exercise personal responsibility to maintain it, and to maintain it at a high enough level of effectiveness, to sustain your freedom. Remember also that your behavior will never be changed exclusively, by an act of your will, but only by what you believe... The working condition of your faith.

> **Key #7** - *Your behavior is not, and will not, be changed by the actions of your will exclusively, but only by what you believe... That is, by and because of, the* **CONDITION OF YOUR FAITH** *at any point in time. The development of your spiritual foundation and your freedom strategy are always linked to the effectiveness of your faith.*

INITIATE ACTION – POWER

This first chapter on faith is designed to set what has been presented so far, into motion. So, where does your knowledge fit in with all of this? Sir Francis Bacon popularized the phrase, *"Knowledge is Power"* – However, according to the bible, he is only half-right.

Check these scriptures out:

> **James 2:14** What good is it, my brothers, if a man claims to have faith but has no deeds?... (NIV)
>
> **James 2:26** As the body without the spirit is dead, so faith without deeds is dead. (NIV)

Therefore, spiritually speaking, that well used phrase can be restated like this: Knowledge - **put into action** - is Power. That's the essence of the Gospel.

So, load the following items from this chapter on faith to focus your mind on, to acquire, and to put into action, as these items come your way:

1. **Situational Awareness** – Do you remember these famous words spoken by Jesus from the cross of Calvary? Do you know what they mean?

   "Forgive them Father, for they know not what they do"

   Indeed, they know not what they do; If they did know, they likely would not do it—like Eve when tempted in the Garden of Eden and like those Jesus spoke to from the cross. If they knew what their sin would cost them, they probably would not have yielded themselves to it. What do you think? Do you agree with that?

   However, **they were not aware.** They could have been, but, they were not. Awareness almost always comes in two stages; First comes intellectual knowledge to our mind, then, at some point later in time, comes heart knowledge. Turns out though, that only heart knowledge is *"Actionable."* Intellectual knowledge needs to be turned into faith.

When that happens, it can be owned and subsequently acted upon because faith reveals what is true, and truth reveals what will happen to you if and when you yield yourself to the sin you are being tempted with. A very significant conviction of mine, in writing the pages of this book, is exactly that purpose happening in your mind...

To Make You Aware....... Exceedingly Aware!

2. **Knowledge of Jesus** – Increase that knowledge; get to know him better than you do now. A 2-part challenge; Increase your intellectual knowledge of Jesus from bible study, and, increase your relational knowledge of Jesus by spending time with him in daily prayer, devotion, and navigating everyday, ordinary, life. *Just Show-Up...*

3. **Attitude of Jesus** – Learn from him. Specifically, learn how to weaponize your humility, patience, contentment, perseverance and your faithfulness, resulting in you becoming less selfish than you are now.

4. **Revise and Upgrade your Comfort-Zone** – Challenge yourself and evaluate the habits you have developed, both good and bad. Commit to refining the knowledge and the core-values that you have based each of these habits on.

5. **Renew your Mind** – Commit to increasing your knowledge and application of Spiritual-Warfare-Tactics. Specifically, to develop and increase your ability to **capture every thought to the obedience of Christ** - *(2 Cor. 10:5)*

The human mind can easily be deceived—consistently winning spiritual warfare battles requires the mind to be hardened as a target. Don't give the devil any opportunity. Eliminate the *Low-Hanging-Fruit* in your thought life that make you an easy target. Our hearts - *that is, our soul and will* - need to be softened, not hardened; Especially when we hear his voice. Here's the key to that:

> *Therefore, harden your mind, not your heart,*
> *and soften your heart, but never your mind.*

This chapter is intended to challenge you by introducing action into the program. Within the Introduction of this book, I documented that this syllabus would not be confined to just an academic experience, but, in fact, be very pragmatic—integrating knowledge, understanding, and action.

It simply would not be very beneficial for you to simply gain some academic knowledge about developing this strategy, without actually experiencing the result—navigating through this process of learning how to actually put it into operation. To own it for yourself, and realize that exhilarating reward that God bestows upon you...!

COMMITMENT - JUST SHOW UP - By now, I'm sure you all have realized that everything concerning the development and sustainment of this freedom strategy is centered on the person, authority and the sheer, unassailable power of Jesus Christ, and getting to know him in a very personal way.

> *Key #8* - *Apart from a very close, effective, personal and intimate relationship with the person of Jesus Christ, none of us can possibly acquire and sustain a life of personal, spiritual freedom.*

The next installment of that process begins right here. There simply is no substitute other than spending time in his presence, if you are to get to know him and learn to trust him more than you ever have before. That's why I tag this chapter with: **JUST SHOW UP...**

That's where we go next. It is very simple, but very profound. It has a lot of similarities with developing a friendship with somebody. You just show up, begin experiencing their nature, personality and temperaments. You spend time with them so you can **get to know them.**

You find out what they like, and, what they don't like. If you are pursuing this person to be more than just a friend, perhaps like a future spouse, then, you will spend even more time with them. You will find out everything you can about them. You will treasure that relationship and set it apart from others. But what about God—about Jesus? He has a personality, a certain temperament and divine nature—He has likes and he has dislikes. So, fix your eyes on Jesus—like it says in Heb. 12:2.

Consider this—the beginning of this new level of spiritual discipline, to Just Show Up, can start with a simple but very sincere prayer request to God. Use the following prayer, or devise one of your own, to initiate the action that will validate your first action step of faith as a new commitment to God:

Pray this often...

Heavenly father, I really want and need to do this. I want to make this commitment of dedication, time and sincere effort to take the yoke of Christ upon myself and to learn of him and from him, more than I ever have before. Please apply the grace and power of your Holy Spirit, in Jesus name, to my life and circumstances, making a way for me to effectively initiate and sustain this new level and discipline of spiritual life. Thank you, Lord, for hearing me as I bring this prayer to you, with thanksgiving, in Jesus name.

Now, keep declaring this prayer and others like it both out loud, and in your mind, to the Lord as often as you can. Be persistent, but trust the Lord and be sensitive to changes in your spiritual awareness, how you feel, and what you think about this, as he begins to work in your heart and your mind.

And, most of all, be authentic. God is very likely to test the sincerity of your heart and your mind for a while. He will measure your faith and your desire for change. How bad do you want this?

Jesus will know the answer to that question. In addition, he has provided us a spiritual weapon for this new discipline—you'll hear it often in this program:

> **Phil. 2:5** Have this attitude in yourselves which was also in Christ Jesus. *(NASB)*

FAITH – WEAPONIZED TACTICS

There are two attributes of Christ's attitude, in particular that you will need to acquire, or re-acquire. The first one is HUMILITY, and the second one is PATIENCE. You and I will never develop these two attributes on a level even close to Jesus, however, we can learn to weaponize each of them, making them significantly more effective in your life than they are now. There is a wonderful scripture written for those who are waiting, or learning to wait, on the Lord as they employ these two weapons of spiritual warfare:

> **Is. 40:31** Yet those who wait for the LORD will gain new strength; They will mount up with wings like eagles, they will run and not get tired, they will walk and not become weary. *(NASB)*

Many of you may already be waiting, praying and devoting time with God at some level of diligence and consistency, but - just how effective are you? - In my research, many Christians commented to me that they know the quality of time spent with Jesus is not very productive, authentic and sincere. Does that describe you? Are you mostly *"spinning your wheels"* out of habit, ritual, or duty, but not growing spiritually like you know you should be?

An old axiom declares that 5 minutes devoted to God with diligence, focus, and zeal is way more effective than 1 hour spent with him - just going through the motions. Therefore, from this point forward, tenaciously determine to achieve a closer relationship with Jesus, and refuse to spin your wheels and waste time any longer. Really anticipate God doing a new work in you. Every meaningful change in life has a starting point...

Make this one yours.

Start right here as you study this program. Refuse *"taking God for granted"* any longer as we are all prone to do. Instead, challenge yourself to know and relate to Jesus with increased reverence, according to the truth of scripture, for good reason: Let the Holy Spirit of God speak to you through his word, and by his *"still, small voice."*

> **Is. 66:2** *"This is the one I esteem: he who is humble and contrite in spirit, and trembles at my word. (NIV)*
>
> **Psa. 15:1-2** *O LORD, who may abide in your tent? Who may dwell on your holy hill? Those who walk blamelessly, and do what is right, and speak the truth from their heart; (NRSV)*

BE DETERMINED – BE AUTHENTIC – As you ponder what these words are meaning to you, and especially, what new action you are thinking might be effective for you, take a look at the following few paragraphs. Think and query yourself about this new commitment to just show up and invest quality time in his presence. Why would you want to do that? Your answer can have a very significant effect on your faith.

God wants you to respond to his love and his gifts, by you giving him the unconditional best of your capabilities.

It has been clearly documented by many who research productivity, effectiveness and efficiency from our lives that most human beings are at their strongest, at their brightest, at their very best at the beginning of the day, early in the morning. That's what God wants from you… the very best of yourself given to him. That includes the best of your time, resources and energy first thing in the morning, then, throughout the rest of your day and throughout the rest of your life, every day that you possibly can. If the best of your day happens to be later in the day or evening, then start there, but determine here to give God that time when you are at your very best.

Your Heavenly Father has already given you his best… JESUS the Christ…!

His most valuable treasure, in the form of his only begotten Son, so that you could be redeemed and reconciled to your Heavenly Father for eternity. Therefore, **determine to reciprocate and give God the very best of your life,** starting with the valuable time that you set aside for him. Instead of only praying on-the-way-to-work, or, on-the-fly, commit yourself to dedicating the most productive and valuable time of your day to meet with God in devotion to him, to get your day started right. The more you know Jesus, the more meaningful and fulfilled your life will be. Give him your very best. He certainly deserves it. You may not make this schedule every day, and sometimes you will simply rebel and throw off the yoke of Christ, as I detail many times throughout this FRP. We all do that from time to time.

That's just a realistic part of our human nature, which is, and always will be, at odds with God's will for our lives. But, **BE DETERMINED** in this new habit-forming commitment.

Be determined to show-up, but, **let Jesus do the heavy-lifting** in your life.

He is not wanting to put you under any severe discipline, or some kind of labor-intensive process at all. His desire for you is not arduous to adopt and put into operation within your life. No, not at all. Consider the words of Jesus again in the following scripture passage which is absolutely faithful and true:

> **Matt. 11:29-30** *"Take my yoke upon you and learn from me, for I am gentle and humble in heart, and you will find rest for your souls. For my yoke is easy and my burden is light." (NIV)*

Jesus will never be the *"Hard-Taskmaster"* in your life, like sin can be. Knowing and serving Christ is exponentially way easier and more rewarding than serving sin.

So, just be authentic.

Let him know how and what you are feeling. Pray and ask him to help you in your unbelief, in your weakness and fatigue, and even in your stubbornness and rebelliousness. In addition, pray and ask him to provide you the faith you need to authentically desire to be in his presence more consistently. And, recognize that you really do have a clinical NEED to experience and enjoy his presence, as much as you possibly can. The more the better, all throughout your day, every day. In his presence, there is liberty, fullness of life, and joy *(Ps. 11:16 - 2Cor. 3:17)*. I mean, you'd really like more of that wouldn't you? The presence of Jesus is always exhilarating, and sometimes even intoxicating *(Eph. 5:18)*—highly desirable and rewarding, and, many times, beyond measure.

MID-CHAPTER SUMMARY – By now, I trust that you have received at least an entry-level amount of incentive to begin making some changes in your life. You have likely been thinking about, or have been significantly reminded of, riding the Yo-Yo and how much that really sucks. You also realize and understand by now that a quick-fix band-aid is not what you need to acquire a powerful and constructive lifestyle.

However, you are also likely thinking about **the challenge you may face** to activate your strong desire to get this new process started. It may be likely that you have not yet initiated or developed an essential habit and discipline of daily prayer, devotion to Christ and immersing your heart and mind effectively in God's Word.

In addition, you also know that you need to discover, experience and relate a much deeper and closer relationship with Jesus than you ever have before. So, I encourage you to pause here and scan through the beginning of this chapter to *"lock-in"* the key parts that stand out to you, or that you know definitely pertain to you, before you move on.

MAKE A "DEAL" WITH GOD

I encourage you to memorize and to hide this following key scripture in your heart and mind from the New International Version (NIV) of the bible:

> ***Matt. 6:33*** *But **seek first** his kingdom and his righteousness, and all these things will be given to you as well. (NIV)*

I encourage you also to think through and add the pragmatic detail from this same scripture to your understanding, but, from the Amplified Bible Version (AMP) of the bible:

> **Matt. 6:33** But **seek** *(aim at and strive after)* **first** *of all his kingdom and his righteousness (his way of doing and being right), and then all these things taken together will be given you besides. (AMP)*

The very first part of just showing up, is simply deciding to seek God, with a new attitude. Then, acting on that commitment to sincerely pursue and acquire that new attitude from Jesus himself, just like he encourages you to do.

So, I urge you to mark down this Matt. 6:33 scripture reference on your calendar as the catalyst to remind yourself of the day you commenced your initial, or renewed, determination of acquiring a sustained lifestyle of personal spiritual freedom. Regard this scripture as a principled axiom of your particular freedom strategy, reasoning through the cause and effect of what God is speaking to you—to put him first, more than I do now...

That **IF YOU** decide and follow through with the consistent action of *seeking first* His Kingdom and His righteousness—**THEN HE** will give you all these things taken together. To paraphrase: He will give you rescue, hope and increased faith leading to deliverance, and eventually, that very elusive, but strongly desired, *Authentic Biblical Freedom*. That's a really good deal for you to consider making with God—don't you think?

I also encourage you to mark this reference down in a very prominent place, or even several places, that you can be reminded by, every time you see it. I can literally guarantee you of what a giant help and comfort this reference will be to you throughout this program. Why do I say that, you might ask?

Here's why: You will lose some spiritual battles all along the way of seeking your freedom, and when you do, you can look back on your calendar and think about this reference. You can recall your motivation when you marked this scripture down. What your attitude was like—how tenacious you were at that moment—even the confidence you experienced from your feelings—from your emotions—making you very glad that you decided to do this. You can remember how committed you were to succeed, even when you may have failed miserably so many times before—*you will recall and know that this definitely was not a coincidence in your life*...When you recall this milestone, you will be comforted and strengthened many times by the Holy Spirit of God.

THE OBSTACLES WITHIN OUR HUMAN NATURE
Human beings are incredibly capable of reasoning their way out of all kinds of beneficial events, circumstances, habits and responsibilities.

We can really become adept and expert at procrastination techniques to put off and delay very important and even critical things, especially from God, that are designed to provide or add spiritual growth, faith, and blessings in our life. It's so easy for us to do that. The tendency of our human nature is to avoid and even to oppose God in our lives. That tendency is also to seek out and acquire that which makes us feel good, and satisfies some level of selfish appetite, that may or may not be good for us. That is our normal and natural way of responding to life, most of the time.

Further on in this book, I write about **the cry of every human heart is to be loved, to be respected and to be accepted.** And, in our attempt to fulfill that longing, our minds can be easily deceived into thinking that we can satisfy that very powerful pursuit for love, respect and acceptance by indulging in all kinds of destructive behavior. As a result, many of us end up getting addicted to it.

God has purposely designed our minds to function that way—he has done this on purpose. Once we have developed a series of habits that in-turn produce a comfort-zone that we put into action, our minds become very difficult to change. So, if your comfort-zone causes you to effectively maintain an abundant lifestyle of freedom, you are indeed very blessed. If it does not, you have work to do.

That is why I have often stated - *you have to really want to do this.*

Further, think about the linkage between your human nature and your spiritual nature. When your spiritual nature is weak and not very effective in governing and directing your life, those selfish and destructive attributes of your human nature will occupy the dominant role of managing your life, thereby causing adverse influence upon the growth, health, strength and well-being of your spirit.

Conversely, when your spiritual nature is strong, healthy and thriving, those destructive attributes of your human nature diminish, lose strength and dominance over your life, while the good and beneficial attributes from your human nature do not suffer at all, in fact, they actually thrive along with your spiritual nature.

That's a much better way to live, isn't it? God means for you to thrive in your enjoyment of life. That abundant life, that thriving lifestyle Jesus offers and imparts to you, as you continue practicing and perfecting the new godly habit of - JUST SHOWING UP - What do you think? Does that make good sense to you?

Therefore, as you cooperate more effectively with Jesus, he will help you and lead you, to effectively transcend the inclination of your human nature to oppose God. He will develop a totally new level of commitment within you that will eventually lead you to be stronger in your spiritual nature than you are in your human nature—that is, if you persevere and refuse to give up. When that condition begins to operate within you, your spirit will dominate the weak and destructive attributes of your human nature. And, you will experience the lifestyle of authentic spiritual freedom through Christ, more often.

OLD THINGS PASS AWAY - ALL THINGS BECOME NEW
Next, some very helpful insight into overcoming and restructuring your comfort zone. There is a key function of your sub-conscious mind that is very instrumental in re-shaping and maintaining your comfort zone.

And that function is known as **Selective-Awareness**. Your brain, especially the sub-conscious part of your brain, is wired and programmed to get you comfortable and keep you comfortable with all kinds of things that you encounter in life. One of those things is known as, *"old patterns of thought."* Your sub-conscious mind works in the background and is always on the alert to things that come your way that interest you—especially things that will fulfill and / or strengthen a habit that you have. It doesn't matter whether that habit is good for you, or whether it is totally destructive and terrible for you. It simply doesn't matter to your sub-conscious mind whether the habit is good or bad. Your sub-conscious mind is amoral. It simply responds to whether you have a habit that needs to be fed, or reinforced, or strengthened. And, the more you feed that habit, again whether it is good or bad, the stronger and more entrenched within you it becomes, thereby reinforcing, and strengthening, that particular appetite. Here's why:

The core-values that make up your comfort-zone, determine where your sub-conscious mind will lead you.

Over time, your sub-conscious mind will develop patterns of thought that are designed to make it somewhat easier for you to act upon fulfilling a habit that you are very used to, and comfortable with. Old patterns of thought more easily stimulate and activate your imagination, because you have experienced the habit so much in your life. Your imagination then takes over and reveals how you will feel when you act upon that thought pattern and then experience in reality what you just imagined happening in your mind.

Quite often, an old pattern of thought is actually what the bible calls a *"temptation"* intended to compel you to commit a sin. This cognitive process happens exceptionally fast within your brain, and, you need to be very vigilant, sober minded and on the alert, just like the following scripture directs you to be, whenever it occurs—whenever you are tempted. You will first need to detect it.

This is where you learn to deploy this new cognitive weapon called, **Selective-Awareness.** Here's how it works, and how you use it:

You inform and direct your mind to alert you anytime and every time one of these old patterns of thoughts occur, tempting you to sin. Once you detect it and become aware of it, then you process it and take the applicable action needed to stop it from deceiving you with another ride on the Yo-Yo - that selective-awareness tactic documented here in 1 Peter:

> **1Pet. 5:8** Be well balanced (temperate, sober of mind), **be vigilant and cautious at all times;** for that enemy of yours, the devil, roams around like a lion roaring (in fierce hunger), seeking someone to seize upon and devour. (AMP)

Someone Like YOU......!! (Remember this one?)

Pragmatically speaking, here's the specific action you put into immediate operation: *Take this thought captive to the obedience of Christ (2 Cor. 10:5).* Cast it out of your mind—don't let it get attached to you. Refuse to dwell upon it, like you are used to doing. Instead, inform your mind that you intend to replace this old pattern of thought with a new one—a good one—a beneficial one that is healthy and safe for you.

However, when you first start initiating a change like this into your life, especially a change intended to move you deeper into your relationship with Jesus, then your sub-conscious mind has little to no old patterns of thought to draw upon from an existing habit—*because, you haven't made it a habit yet*—got it? Do you see how that works in your mind? Think clearly and deeply about this particular process happening within your mind **until you get-it - until you own-it.** That process can really be essential to your faith.

Until you have a working habit formed within your mind, it makes it much more difficult for your mind to deal with. Takes more mental and emotional energy and work for you to make this happen. At first, there is no habit. It doesn't exist yet. It is in the early stages of development. You are just beginning the process of informing and directing your sub-conscious mind that you indeed want to form this new habit. **You are just beginning to show up** in order to experience a deeper and more effective relationship with Jesus.

At this early formative stage, a new habit can be very fragile and vulnerable to failure. Your sub-conscious mind is literally evaluating just how sincere and serious you are about forming this new habit.

So, be cautious and careful that you do not give up and quit too soon. Here's one huge pragmatic reason why you want to give your brain sufficient time to process this—*follow me closely here...* In 2009, A well-known professional health psychology researcher, named Phillippa Lally, at University College in London, examined the habits of 96 people over a 12-week time frame. Her research study results revealed how long it can take to develop and maintain a new habit. The study showed that it can vary considerably depending upon the behavior, the individual, and the circumstances. The new habit time frame took as little as 18 days for some individuals, and others out to 254 days to form a new habit, depending upon how complicated it was.

The results of her research in this study calculated an average of 66 days for this group to form a new habit. Interestingly, that roughly coincides with how long it takes the sub-conscious mind to develop an initial memory-mapping of a new pattern of thought, needed to form a new habit like this. However, you should also notice that God, and his super-natural influence, is not, and probably cannot, be factored into this kind of study. My intention in documenting this research is to provide you a valid perspective, based on actual, scientific study, regarding any new habits that you will be challenged to develop in this program. Further, take a look at this previous investigation:

Another well-known, **but inaccurate**, research study from Dr. Maxwell Maltz, stipulated that it only takes about 21 days to form a new habit. So, if you have been thinking that a new habit like this will likely only take you an average of 21 days to form, like most people think, you'd likely be making an error. There's more to it. It's more complicated. The key thing here that I'd like you to focus on is not so much the time frame that it takes to form a new habit. Whether it takes you 18 days, 180 days, or a number of years doesn't really matter because if you are to achieve success, you simply have to put in the work, either way, regardless of the time it takes you.

So, let this inspire you, and, let it not frustrate you......

Don't let yourself get bummed out because you initially thought this process would be easier, or would only take a couple of weeks. *It's supposed to take longer.*

God designed your mind to function that way, on purpose. It's normal. Once you successfully reshape your comfort-zone to maintain your lifestyle of freedom, you'll be exceedingly glad that Jesus crafted your mind the way he did. Like I stated before, **You Have to Really Want to Do This**— It takes time and it takes effort **(read: WORK)**. But, you are not alone in this process—the Holy Spirit of God will provide you with what your human nature lacks:

> **2Cor. 5:17** *Therefore if any man be in Christ, he is a new creature: old things are passed away; behold, all things are become new. (KJV)*

> *Those old patterns of thought will pass away—***count on it...**

They won't be eliminated, but they will not be dominant in your mind either, and will not be in control of you, like they used to be. Then this will happen: *all things become new,* **including you,** even if you have been born again for 50 years. This is a new beginning, a new work God is beginning, or renewing in you. Because you have Christ in you, by his indwelling Holy Spirit, if you pray and ask Jesus to help you capture and crucify those old patterns of thought, he will, over time, give you what you lack without him:

The **POWER** to actually do this!!

> **Acts 1:8** *But **you will receive power** when the Holy Spirit comes on you; (NIV)*

> **2 Cor. 10:3-5** *For though we live in the world, we do not wage war as the world does. The weapons we fight with are not the weapons of the world. On the contrary, they have divine power to demolish strongholds.*

> We demolish arguments and every pretension that sets itself up against the knowledge of God, and we take captive every thought to make it obedient to Christ. (NIV)

So now, YOU COMMIT TO NEVER, NEVER, EVER GIVE UP! Keep at it. This effort of putting godly habits into place is not easy. It can be a tough slog, so *keep on preparing your mind for **ACTION***. Read, study and memorize these scriptures from the Lord intended to provide you an advanced level of faith and confidence. Keep on resisting, keep on fighting and struggling until this happens: **YOU WIN...!** *He is training you to become More than a Conqueror.*

The bible says so right here:

> **Gal. 6:9** *Let us not become weary in doing good, for at the proper time we will reap a harvest if we do not give up. (NIV)*

Now check this out:

> **Rom. 8:37** *No, in all these things we are more than conquerors through him who loved us. (NIV)*

THE HARDEST PART

There exists an abundance of books and references that have been produced about all aspects of achieving an increase in your ability to manage your life on a daily basis. There is also very clear and compelling evidence that the hardest part of putting this into practice and operation is simply TAKING THE FIRST STEP.

Remember, this first action step required in resisting and mastering sin is that you **make that decision** to diligently seek God, because, if you want to learn how to resist sin, *you will require the personal involvement of Jesus Christ*, on many levels. So, all that starts with a strong incentive to change oneself from yielding to sin, to being enabled and empowered by Gods' Holy Spirit, to resist sin.

The second action step starts by *just showing up* to meet with God every day that you possibly can. Schedule and/or take the time and look very forward to improving your relationship and fellowship with him. Show up—be there! But, also consider this: You really do not need to decide anything right now. No pressure—none. Receive this word from God documented in the bible:

> **Is. 1:18** *"Come now, **let us reason together**," says the LORD. "Though your sins are like scarlet, they shall be as white as snow; though they are red as crimson, they shall be like wool. (NIV)*

Wow...Think through the implication of what this scripture is saying—the God who spoke the entire universe into existence—who is possessed with absolute power and absolute authority over everything in existence—THAT GOD... is revealing his unconditional love for you and me by humbling himself to the degree of actually, and tenderly, inviting us to reason with him about our struggles in life...AMAZING isn't it? And further, it doesn't matter one whit whether our struggle is just trying to gain a little more spiritual discipline, because we need a course correction in our life, or, whether we are held fast in the bondage to some form of sinful addiction.

He is an ever-present help in the time of trouble. (Ps. 46:1), and, he will never, ever quench a sincere expression of faith (Matt. 12:20)—in fact, he will fan it into flames!

Jesus will never "force" his will upon your life at all, ever—he definitely is not the arduous taskmaster that even some believers think he is at times in their life—perish the thought. In fact, he says that if you will just try—to make a sincere effort in seeking him, that he will be found by you, and he will indeed help you *(Eph. 5:10 - Jer. 29:13)*.

Jesus is tenaciously committed to you succeeding in the attainment of true spiritual freedom through the abundant life that he offers you. He wants you to be effective in the mission and ministry of your life that he gives to you. He will spend the rest of your life, if that's what it takes, enabling and empowering you to achieve this.

That is why he encourages you to sincerely, and effectively, use your brain and think about this stuff—*reason with God.* Talk to him in prayer. Tell him your concerns and why you think you can't do this, if that's the case—but, at the very least, commit to sincerely reading through all of this program. It is not a coincidence that you have started. Let this stuff, all of it, the whole Freedom Renewed Program just wash over your brain—take it all in—take your time. Think about the cost to you in time, effort and energy, but, and measure this well, think about the return you will receive once you invest yourself.

Sometimes your feelings and desires coincide with God's will for your life, many times they do not, but, you will never know unless and until you begin meeting with God, through Jesus, in earnest. So, commit to changing and upgrading how you prioritize the things of God in your life from now on. Commit, or re-commit, to giving God something of yourself that he can work with. Give him the best of your time. Give him your focused and undivided attention during that time. Be focused, be deliberate, be intentional, be very sincere, be very honest.

Start slow if you need to—but hear this: *everybody can give God at least 5 minutes at the beginning of the day*, with sincerity and a focused authenticity of being effective and diligent. The Holy Spirit will lead you to dedicate sufficient time in prayer and devotion that will accomplish his plan for your life, but, it has to start some place. Give him at least 5 minutes every day to start and then build upon that as he leads you. Make it happen—you'll never regret it.

The attribute that God first wants you to acquire is just simple faithfulness. You cannot acquire faithfulness if you do not put out the effort and sincerity to just show up. Produce the evidence of faithfulness to God over time, no matter how small the start, and God will provide you with a return on your investment of time, energy and zeal that will absolutely astound you. You will be really glad you did this. Showing up is all about Jesus teaching us and training us to become faithful to God.

Learning to be more like him. He is always faithful to himself, to his Word, and to his unfailing love for each of us, who have decided to commit or recommit our lives to follow Jesus. It is an unchanging attribute of his nature.

JESUS – STANDING IN THE GAP

This chapter is all about faith, so, I encourage you to think about and receive the following amazing and comforting truth about Jesus, his faith, and **his faithfulness.** There will be many, many times when you will absolutely fail in your life to be faithful and obedient to Christ, even after you set apart a new commitment to just show-up from this study, just like the Apostles failed him as recorded in the Gospel accounts. As Jesus himself told his disciples at that time, *The Spirit is willing but the Flesh is weak* - *(Matt. 26:40)*

It is in those particular times of failing when you find yourself absolutely unable and/or unwilling to be faithful to Christ, that he just shows up and proves his unfailing love for you by revealing his faithfulness to you and to his word. When you will not, or even cannot, deliver your faithfulness to him, in any situation, he, that is, JESUS... becomes your faithfulness.

He shows up for you—**he stands in the gap,** and applies whatever is needed on your behalf to get you through the situation. Truly a part of his amazing grace. *Where your sin abounds, his grace does much more abound* - *(Rom. 5:20)*

Remember, his love for you is unconditional. It is not conditioned on your response or behavior at all. The Greek word for this kind of love is called **'Agape,'** and in this context is defined as that attribute of God's divine nature, unique to him, that enables him to love us without any condition on our part to warrant or deserve that loving response from him. In its' simplest definitive form, the bible documents it like this:

> *1 John 4:16 And so we know and rely on the love God has for us.* **God is love.** *Whoever lives in love lives in God, and God in him. (NIV)*

His faithfulness, like his righteousness, becomes yours. It is imputed to you through your faith in Christ.

Now, understand completely and absolutely that Jesus wants you working hard to learn how to reliably and consistently increase your faithfulness to him in every situation as you navigate life. But he also wants you to know and to absolutely count on this fact—that *his faithfulness will be your shield and rampart* anytime and every time that it is needed by you and directed by him, especially in those times when your own faith and faithfulness are failing.

> *Psa. 91:4 he will cover you with his feathers, and under his wings you will find refuge; his faithfulness will be your shield and rampart. (NIV)*

Check out this next Key Principle illuminating his unfailing grace:

> *Key #9* - *When your own Faith and Faithfulness fail you, his will fail you not. He will always Show-Up, Stand-In-The-Gap for you, and deliver you from adversity because **his grace is always sufficient and his love never fails.***

And now, just a word to close out this chapter on faith. Forget about how long it might take before you notice tangible, real results in your life from this study. Let that go. Leave the time frame exclusively to God. Just sincerely commit to do this, then definitely anticipate and expect God to change you accordingly, but, in his time, not yours.

WWII wasn't won in a day, a week or several months. It took over 4 years and was truly epic in scope. The spiritual warfare that you and I are facing and fighting is almost always related to that.

It probably took a lot of time for you to become embroiled in a destructive habit or lifestyle of some kind. So, be patient with this process of getting yourself free. Trust God with how long it may take him to change your heart and renew your mind. Leave that completely to him. The bible teaches us something about God's timing concerning many things. It is often said in scripture: ***In the fullness of time... then God.***

So, let God take his time with you. God, not you, happens to be the only one who knows what is required and how long it will take – **to rebuild you** – to renew your mind and transform your heart.

Truth is, that you will win spiritual warfare battles and you will also lose spiritual warfare battles during this process of attaining spiritual freedom.

However, In the fullness of time, at some point in the process, if you continue just showing up, and applying yourself with thankfulness, sincerity, and diligence, God will begin to give you more wins than losses. You can count on the time coming where you will win more spiritual warfare battles than you lose. Okay, that being said, here's what I'd like you to get out of this first chapter on faith. Don't immediately plan on beginning a new, or renewed, time frame of meeting with God every morning for prayer and devotion.

At this point, if you do that, you might just be setting yourself up for failure. It's too early for that level of commitment. Instead, I strongly recommend that **you begin by simply praying in earnest to God,** whether you set aside time for that or not. Just start praying. You can pray and chew gum at the same time, right?

Pray and ask God to begin revealing his plan for your life, *that would include the new Freedom Strategy and Life Action Plan* that he already has developed for you—his plan for your life *(Jer. 29:11)*, including every good work he has prepared for you *(Eph. 2:10)*, has been residing within the mind of Christ before you were even born.

However, because of his great love for you, and his amazing provision of grace to you, he will almost certainly not be revealing his plan and good works to you, until he has made you ready to sincerely and effectively, make that commitment. He will never set you up for failure. Instead, Jesus will set you up for success and victory over the power of sin in your life, and sufficient faith to believe all that.

Therefore, my strong recommendation to you right here is to read through and study every word of this book completely, taking it all in, before making any serious commitments to display strength and take action. (Dan. 11:32) Then, when you have done that, do this:

> **Eph. 6:13** ...*having done everything, to stand firm. (NRSV)*
>
> **Eph. 6:13** *Therefore put-on God's complete armor, that you may be able to resist and* **stand your ground** *on the evil day (of danger), and,* **having done all** *(the crisis demands),* **to stand** *(firmly in your place). (AMP) - (emphasis mine)*

Now, Display Strength – Take Action and **GODSPEED......!**

CHAPTER 4
FIRM FAITH

FIRM FAITH – ESSENTIAL TO FREEDOM

Without faith being activated and put into operation.... There is no salvation... There is no ability to even please God in any way. Further, without faith being activated and put into operation, there is absolutely no way one can acquire a working and functional lifestyle of spiritual freedom.

Consequently, *Firm-Faith*, comes to each Christian, as we begin showing-up and over time, learn how to relate, cooperate with, and finally, to obey God's Holy Spirit. I introduced this sanctification development in the last chapter—the continuous process of Jesus perfecting our faith in him throughout our entire span of life *(Heb. 12:2)*. It literally means that we are being *set-apart for service to God*. The initial saving-faith that God gifts to each Christian establishes an authentic desire to know God and his kingdom of righteousness. Spiritual life begins in earnest, and, so does our sanctification.

The unsearchable riches of our knowledge of Jesus, and our love of God increases, thereby *transforming our saving-faith into firm-faith*. This is very much a gradual process, and when it begins to happen, a Christian will experience a transition of first, wanting to know-God more, followed by, wanting to serve-God. That's what this chapter is all about. God wants to put you in control, or, back in control, of every part of your life. He will order, or re-order, your very thoughts, including the intent of your heart and will. That means for some believers, this can take the rest of their life here on Earth.

Really...why so long? He's getting us ready. God's plan for every believer is to shape, train and equip each and every one of us to serve effectively in his kingdom—in his Church. That's why he begins his work to sanctify our hearts and our minds immediately at the time of salvation. It takes time... In addition, the time it takes God to do that in each of our lives is predicated on the actual condition of our faith, our hearts and our minds. By his grace, God receives us just-as-we-are, as they say, *"warts and all."* If our faith is weak and our hearts are hard, and we are not very willing to cooperate with the Holy Spirit of God, this can take a significant chunk of time out of our lives.

The primary reason for that can be found within the race we are called to run from Hebrews 12:1; remember that? We are competing against our NEMESIS—*our old-self.* Check out the following description of that race from one of my favorite authors...Here's the quote:

> *In every Christian's heart there is a cross and a throne, and the Christian is on the throne till he puts himself on the cross; if he refuses the cross, he remains on the throne. Perhaps this is at the bottom of the backsliding and worldliness among gospel believers today.* **We want to be saved, but we insist that Christ do all the dying.** *No cross for us, no dethronement, no dying. We remain king within the little kingdom of Man's soul and wear our tinsel crown with all the pride of a Caesar; but we doom ourselves to shadows and weakness and spiritual sterility.* - **A.W. Tozer**

These eloquent words reveal what's at stake for each of us in this race—the upward calling of Christ in our lives. Jesus is calling you...so, run your race to win! Just like the Apostle Paul recorded in his first letter to the Corinthians:

> *1 Cor. 9:24 Do you not know that in a race the runners all compete, but only one receives the prize?* **Run in such a way that you may win it.** *(NRSV)*

Every day that you line up in this race to acquire, or reacquire, a lifestyle of spiritual freedom, you will be opposed. Your own human nature will get in the way. Isn't that right? Of course, it is—I've listed several of these life-sucking obstacles to spiritual freedom already in this book. That's the rub isn't it? You want freedom—there is a price to pay; it's going to cost you something. I documented that cost to challenge you, way back in chapter one. Take another look:

Find out what Spiritual Freedom will cost you, and - **pay that price.**

So, now it's time to introduce what that cost begins to look like, from a very personal point-of-view. I encourage you to load this next scripture reference into your brain, and just begin thinking about it, for now. I will be detailing how significant and essential this word from God is to you throughout the rest of this book. Here it is:

> **Luke 9:23** *(Jesus speaking) Then he said to them all: "If anyone would come after me,* **he must deny himself** *and take up his cross daily and follow me. (NIV)*

Okay, it may not sound like it, but, *this is really good news.* God is revealing here, a mighty weapon of spiritual warfare—at first glance, you can't see it. Truth is...nobody wants to deny themselves anything, including believers, following after Christ. That is how our selfish, human nature initially processes this very candid word from Jesus. My research is replete, with the earliest impressions that most believers experience, when first confronted with this scripture - **they utterly recoil at it** - They equate *'denying oneself'* with some kind of suffering and pain, and they definitely do not want to go there. That begs a question for you... ***What's your response to this word from Jesus? Have you thought about it? I really encourage you to do so...***

Truth is, Jesus had a very good, beneficial, and absolutely essential reason that he spoke these words to each of us, who follow him. From the last chapter, I wrote: *"God is transactional and we live in a cause & effect world."* He makes deals with us, and he always rewards our obedience to his commands. So, if you deny yourself like this scripture declares, when temptation comes your way, what does God do in return? Indeed...***what will God do?***

Here's what God does—he puts that ball in your court. He makes that deal a choice. Remember from chapter one I also documented the following scripture that reveals this choice:

> **1 Cor. 6:12** *"All things are lawful for me," but not all things are beneficial. "All things are lawful for me," but I will not be dominated by anything. (NRSV)*

So, I reiterate what I wrote about this choice—load it into your brain again:

> *"God is documenting here that he has given free-will to all mankind—we are all free to choose how we will live and navigate life, with, or without, his involvement."*

Let's unpack what this choice really comes down to—what it looks like, and what the consequences of this choice could lead you to experience. That's what you want to carefully consider and think about, BEFORE making that choice—**it's about those consequences.** Very candidly, when the temptation to sin hits you squarely in the face, you'll either deny yourself, or you won't. It's really that simple and that stark - Isn't that right? Once you make that choice...well, you will almost certainly have to live with the results, apart from God's grace. So, let's focus on what you stand to gain, if you follow through and deny yourself, when tempted to sin, as Jesus commands. First, just focus your brain on what you will avoid—and then, on what you will really get jazzed about—this is Jesus showing you how to win..!

A DEBILITATING CRISIS – THE FIRST REASON

The introduction of this book, and my website, begins with these words: *"There is a Crisis in the Land"* - However, and more to the point, ***"There is a Crisis in the Church."*** The bible is replete, in both the Old and New Testaments, describing what this crisis looks like, in great detail. The kind of crisis I'm talking about here doesn't just happen to a believer as they navigate an ordinary Christian lifestyle—God would never let that materialize. The kind of crisis I'm writing about here always comes on a Christian through choice—they always 'choose' their way into it. Jesus clearly lays this choice out for every one of us as we motor down life's spiritual highway. Here's what he said:

> **Matt. 7:13-14** *(Jesus speaking)* "Enter through the narrow gate. For wide is the gate and broad is the road that leads to destruction, and many enter through it. But small is the gate and narrow the road that leads to life, and only a few find it. (NIV)

> ***Luke 13:24*** *"Make every effort to enter through the narrow door, because many, I tell you, will try to enter and will not be able to." (NIV)*

Okay, what should we conclude from this? Jesus answers that question very clearly, and very candidly. He speaks to all of mankind through these two scriptures, informing every one of us, that life often presents us with these two, unambiguous options that we must choose from—he describes these choices as two roads, each of them leading to a gate that we must open and go through. And further, he reveals that experience to be at complete, extreme, and polar opposites from each other.

One road will put you on a path that can absolutely lead you to experience a debilitating crisis at some point in your life—a spiritual train wreck that you will hate, and will regret; especially knowing that you could have, and should have, avoided it by repenting of it. This road, or pathway in life, is almost always chosen using a **subjective pattern of thought**—how the choice makes you feel; does it look good; will it taste good; what will you get out of the transaction; it will appeal to the selfishness of your human nature. That appeal can be insidiously strong and compelling—especially if you have corrupted your mind and hardened your heart to such an extent that you have become addicted. *But wait... there's more... I have good news:*

The good news of the Gospel is that, though you may currently be on that road toward a crisis coming in your life, **you don't have to stay on that road.** You can be 16, 60, or, older—doesn't matter your age or how long you've been treading down this road. Doesn't matter how much you've screwed up your life—whether you're just off course a little, or, whether you've broken your brain and are now strongly addicted to one of these scourges I'm writing about. Remember, God really did put this ball in your court. You can change lanes anytime you truly want to. Question is, ***do you want to***—are you ready yet? Jesus has made a way for you to escape the corruption in this world caused by those evil desires that you have yielded yourself to for so long.

He said so right here—check it out:

> ***2 Pet. 1:3-4*** *His divine power has given us everything we need for life and godliness through **our knowledge of him** who called us by his own glory and goodness. Through these he has given us his very great and precious promises, so that through them you may participate in the divine nature and **escape the corruption in the world caused by evil desires**. (NIV)*

Therefore, if you really want to actually acquire that authentic, spiritual freedom you've thought so much about, and hoped to experience for so long—well, God has made a very great and precious promise to you. He has promised to show you how to overcome and escape the following two conditions that are so prevalent among believers today. Take a look:

1. **You are unwilling**, at this point in your life, to deny yourself and pick up your cross daily and follow after Jesus like he commands us to do in Luke 9:23.
2. **You are spiritually powerless** in your life right now because you have become addicted to one of these scourges that I'm writing about.

Truth is, that God has unequivocally provided exactly what you need to overcome and prevail over both of these conditions. This explicit word of God declares that it is his divine power that is required to overcome and prevail over these two conditions—trouble is... **he has it and you don't.**

However, he has embedded all of that divine power exclusively within Jesus, and he has made that divine power available to every one of us who chooses to earnestly seek out, and significantly increase, **our knowledge of him.**

Therefore, if you sincerely choose to know Jesus better than you do now, God has promised to make you willing, or, to deliver you from your addiction, thereby enabling and empowering you to escape that corruption that is hammering your soul. That's the deal. God has declared it. Here it is again:

If you do this...Then he'll do that.

You want more proof? You want more assurance that God himself will begin a new work in you and make this actually happen? He says he will, right here:

> **Phil. 1:6** *For I am confident of this very thing, that He who began a good work in you will perfect it until the day of Christ Jesus. (NASB)*

He doesn't mince words—he is absolutely relentless. God said it and that's that..! *There's no quit in him.* Therefore, consider now, and think deeply about this deal—about this transaction God is calling you to make with him. Jesus knows very well that when you have thought and prayed this through, then committed to begin denying yourself, in order to increase your knowledge of him, that you will have to endure some suffering. That's the price you will pay. So, what happens then? Here's what happens—you begin paying that price, and Almighty God does this:

> **1 Pet. 5:10** *And after you have suffered for a little while, the God of all grace, who has called you to his eternal glory in Christ,* **will himself restore, support, strengthen, and establish you.** *(NRSV)*

Having stated all this, what are we to take away—what is God wanting each of us to know? First of all, he knows that when we decide to follow Jesus, that we will be called upon to suffer at times, all throughout our life, here on Earth—we will be opposed. We are directly, and especially, opposed to follow Jesus even by our own human nature—*our old-self,* rising up within us, more often than we like, against God's perfect will being done in our life. And also, the devil and his minions coming against us for the same reason. However, *God is not the cause of this suffering*—he uses it, but he never causes it. Our suffering is explicitly caused by sin at work in our hearts and our minds.

Therefore, God uses suffering, in amazing and sometimes miraculous ways, as he shows us how to overcome and prevail against every obstacle and the sin that so easily entangles us at times, as we follow Jesus. He knows all about suffering—Jesus is the gold-standard example of suffering for all mankind— he put it on display in the garden of Gethsemane and then on the Cross of

Calvary. I encourage you to study what God has to say about his suffering in Matthew 26, Mark 14 and Isaiah 51, especially.

> **1 Pet. 2:21** *For you have been called for this purpose, since Christ also suffered for you, leaving you an example for you to follow in His steps. (NRSV)*

God has many formidable, and spiritually powerful reasons to use suffering in our lives every time that he deems it beneficial or necessary—his tactics making us more like Jesus.

As our faith firms up, he begins to reveal some hidden qualities that he has embedded within this spiritual tool of suffering—here's a couple of tactics that are put into spiritual operation every time you choose to sincerely deny yourself, and suffer the loss of some sinful experience that you and God both know would be harmful to you, and would dishonor him.

- **A mighty tactic of spiritual warfare** – Using suffering as an offensive weapon of spiritual warfare will first require you to humble yourself. God says that he will exalt you every time you choose to humble yourself for his sake. So, when the next temptation to sin comes your way, instead of yielding yourself to it, choose to exercise humility and deny yourself that temptation, then pick up your cross, and follow the lead of Jesus. God will exalt you in some way, every time.
- **A potent instrument to firm up your faith** – God uses and balances suffering in your life to test and build up your most holy faith and to share in his glory—it has great purpose and significance in his kingdom.

So, think about suffering accurately in light of God's word, and adopt its rewarding and formidable use into your spiritual armory, to increase your knowledge of Jesus. Think of it as a powerful evidence of your love of God.

Here's a really good reason why:

> ***Rom. 8:17-18*** *Now if we are children, then we are heirs—heirs of God and co-heirs with Christ,* ***if indeed we share in his sufferings in order that we may also share in his glory.*** *I consider that our present sufferings are not worth comparing with the glory that will be revealed in us. (NIV)*

His suffering for you, me and all of mankind was put on agonizing display, in the garden of Gethsemane and the Cross of Calvary—he gave his life to redeem all of us. That's authentic and irrefutable evidence of his love for all of us.

Jesus declared that the *"Greatest Commandment"* is to love the Lord your God with all of your heart, all of your soul, all of your mind and all of your strength. So, when we are called upon by whatever circumstance in our lives to deny ourself and suffer willingly for his sake, God sees and regards our voluntary suffering, as evidence of our love for him. He uses that voluntary act of suffering to secure our spiritual freedom, every time we make that choice—can you see it that way, from God's perspective? It is reciprocal—but not out of duty, like we are paying on a debt that we owe. Like we can pay God back to gain his favor…That's not it at all.

Our identity is in Christ and the bible declares that we are to be imitators of him *(Eph. 5:1)*, and to follow his example in life. Therefore, since he put his love for each of us on display as evidence, God is calling each of us to reciprocate and put our love for him on display as well.

Jesus knew that his miraculous provision of authentic, biblical freedom for all of us, was not free—that it would cost him his very life. He agonized over it, and then, he paid that ultimate price with his life on the cross. For that, our Heavenly Father resurrected and glorified him, and he sits forever at the right hand of God with all power and authority bestowed upon him.

God calls every Christian to reciprocate, in like, but very limited manner, to produce the evidence of our love for him. In fact, Jesus commands every one of us to do that—whenever a temptation to sin comes our way, that we would refuse to yield any part of ourselves to it—that we would willingly choose to deny ourselves, and suffer in our bodies, our minds and our souls, just like he did for each of us. Here's one extremely good reason why we would do that:

> **Rom. 2:9-11** *There will be trouble and distress for every human being who does evil: first for the Jew, then for the Gentile;* ***but glory, honor and peace for everyone who does good****: first for the Jew, then for the Gentile. For God does not show favoritism. (NIV)*

Every time that we choose to do that, God sees and regards that suffering as evidence of our love for him. In addition, he uses our voluntary act of suffering as a spiritual warfare tactic in two meaningful ways. Check out these two bullet points:

- **We share in his glory** – The glory documented in Romans 8:17 is unique. It is bestowed upon a Christian whenever we choose to deny ourself and suffer willingly for Christ's sake. It is both eternal, and at the same time, immediate—even though it involves suffering, we count it as a blessing, and God also adds it to our eternal account being stored up in heaven.
- **The devil's purpose & plan in our life utterly fails**—he is defeated – God uses our voluntary suffering as a mighty weapon of spiritual warfare to flog the devil and totally defeat his plan of attack upon our life. This is not to be thought of as a trivial weapon in our spiritual arsenal, not at all—our suffering in God's sight, can more accurately be compared to a very high yield nuclear missile capable of massive destruction to the devil's purpose in our lives. Don't underestimate this—in God's hands, it becomes more formidable than you can even imagine..!

Okay, I have introduced some powerful spiritual warfare tactics designed to firm up your faith and to significantly advance your effectiveness in waging this war, and I will be detailing these and adding many more throughout this book—the dominant purpose being to seriously help you avoid some kind of spiritual crisis coming upon you by reinforcing and strengthening your spiritual foundation. So, I encourage you to call upon God like he says here in Jeremiah:

> **Jer. 33:3** *Call to me and I will answer you, and will tell you great and hidden things that you have not known. (NRSV)*

These great and hidden things are all wrapped up in the person of Jesus Christ. It's all about Jesus, all the time, and you increasing your knowledge of him. That's the first reason you will seriously, and sincerely, consider denying yourself and picking up your cross to follow him every day—you do this to avoid a debilitating crisis from coming your way.

EXHILERATING JOY – THE SECOND REASON
Jesus was faced with this choice of denying himself. Scripture records what he chose:

> **Heb. 12:2** *looking to Jesus the pioneer and perfecter of our faith,* **who for the sake of the joy that was set before him endured the cross***, disregarding its shame, and has taken his seat at the right hand of the throne of God... (NSRV)*

So, what does this joy, that was set before Jesus, look like? I mean, think about it; just how desirable and compelling did that joy have to be to actually persuade Jesus to endure the agony and sheer torture of the cross? How about this...In a very broad sense, he was compelled with the exhilarating joy he would experience reconciling and restoring our relationship back to God the Father, through his Gospel by God's grace. And, absolutely destroying forever more, the law of sin & death—removing that sting separating us from fellowship with our holy God, who is a consuming fire.

To be sure, the bible expresses the abundance of that joy that was always driving Jesus, even to the point of being compelled to give up his life on the cross, taking all the sin of the world on himself. It was that unique expression of joy, filling the heart of Jesus, that compelled him to do what only he could do, for God the Father, and for all of us.

> *2 Cor. 5:21 God made Him who knew no sin to be sin on our behalf, so that we might become the righteousness of God in Him. (NASB)*

So, are we to conclude, that when we are called upon to deny ourselves, enduring hardship for God, that we will experience some kind of exhilarating joy? The short answer: ABSOLUTELY..! That being said, what does this joy, that is set before you and me, look like? The bible is absolutely prolific describing this in manifold detail—Here's a few examples:

> *John 15:11 (Jesus speaking) "These things I have spoken to you so that My joy may be in you, and that your joy may be made full. (NASB)*

Jesus himself is the personification of pure JOY that has no equal to ever be experienced in this life, since the beginning of time—he is the benchmark, and the vanguard of JOY—that distinctive reason why Christians experience such fulfillment, leading to freedom, in their lifestyles. Nothing, and no one, can ever compete with him, and his divine power, to produce that kind of JOY within each of us. Question is...do you believe that for yourself?

> *Psa. 1-3 Blessed is the man who does not walk in the counsel of the wicked or stand in the way of sinners or sit in the seat of mockers. But his delight is in the law of the LORD, and on his law he meditates day and night. He is like a tree planted by streams of water, which yields its fruit in season and whose leaf does not wither. **Whatever he does prospers.** (NIV)*
>
> *Mal. 3:10 Test me in this," says the LORD Almighty, "and see if I will not throw open the floodgates of heaven and pour out so **much blessing** that you will not have room enough for it. (NIV)*

Jesus wants to express, and to magnify his incredible love for you, by preparing you, and then giving you, the keys in your life that will unlock that kind of exhilarating JOY deep within you—providing you the greatest fulfillment that can ever be acquired, within your life. The blessing Malachi is talking about is only to be found in JESUS.

LIFE IN THE FAST LANE

On one level, *life can be summed up as a series of choices* each of us make on a daily basis. Choices to avoid things in our life that could otherwise lead to a crisis of some kind developing, and, choices to adopt, that can lead us to experience some uproarious, exhilarating joy in Christ. Life can come at you fast, and, it is always moving. I wrote about these choices being always in motion, somewhat like a "pendulum" swinging from one extreme to the other. I encouraged you to visualize this pendulum image in your mind's eye, to lock-In the concept of your mind being always active, always in motion. All that, intending to make it easy and obvious for you to **Choose Life.** Remember that? I want to build on that vision concept in this chapter. However, instead of visualizing a pendulum in your mind's eye, visualize the following picture, on the next page, of what I call the Spiritual-Highway... There is a key truth to ponder as you look at, and think about, this pic.

Notice especially that this highway has only two lanes; **Life and Death**. Remember God directing Moses to present this same choice to the young nation of Israel *(Deut. 30:19)?* Life and Death said Moses. So, once again, he challenges you and me: **Choose Life.**

Remember as well the **Accelerated Learning Technique** of using pictures visualized in your mind to lock-in key principles of truth? So, I will use the metaphor of a highway in the wilderness within this chapter, like I used a moving pendulum in the last chapter. I strongly encourage you to study well the story behind what each of these images represent, so when you visualize either of them in your imagination, you will immediately recall the principle of truth behind them. I will use this visualizing technique in your mind's eye throughout the program to optimize your ability to recall principles and precepts of truth. It is extremely effective. The following statement is often, and accurately said, *"A picture is truly worth a thousand or more words."*

This book starts off with a challenge, perhaps on a number of levels, to many of you who will study, adopt and put this program into operation. Using your mind's eye *(read: your imagination),* to visualize pictures in your mind that represent principles of truth, is likely one of those challenges to many of you. However, I want to assure you that the clinical effectiveness of this accelerated learning technique is really well established within the scientific community. Please, don't underestimate its effectiveness. *Take a look:*

This particular metaphor of using a highway to represent a choice in your life can be expanded. Here's what I mean: Your spiritual life highway has only two lanes to choose from, life or death. That's it. Take a really good look at it—especially the warning sign...*what comes to your mind?*
SPIRITUAL LIFE HIGHWAY

SPIRITUAL LIFE HIGHWAY

This technique of using **vision** to promote a change in what you believe and how you behave is not some fantasy or myth. For example, it has consistently been taught to professional athletes and business leaders alike who function at a very high level of performance. It's the language of the sub-conscious mind.

Pro athletes in baseball, football, golf and other sports, in particular, use vision every time they are in the arena of performance. Golfers stand behind the ball, BEFORE they hit it, and they visualize the path, trajectory and landing of the golf shot. They are actually *"programming the sub-conscious"* part of their brain to use the muscle memory they have perfected through years of practice. Their brain then directs the body to make that shot, just as they visualized it in their mind's eye, using their enhanced and powerful imagination. This technique of using vision to foresee some future action really works and has its origin in the bible, inspired by God, eons ago—a very powerful tactic you can and should use often. In fact, God gives us a warning to not forsake the use of vision within our life. Take a look at this from the King James Bible:

> ***Prov. 29:18*** *Where there is no vision, the people perish. (KJV)*

So, your new strategy for acquiring spiritual freedom will involve some forward-thinking techniques in knowing God and his plan for your life. This is an excellent technique you can use to visualize your response to a number of issues coming at you, throughout all of your life.

Use word pictures like this to provide a significant increase in your mind's ability to clarify goals and your response to all kinds of things that you deal with, as you move along the spiritual highway, navigating life.

THE SPIRITUAL HIGHWAY OF OUR GOD
The bible makes a special emphasis regarding the spiritual life highway image that I documented on the previous page. There is a very detailed instruction set from the Old Testament and also the New Testament. Let's take a look:

"Make straight a highway for our God"... A prophetic word from the Old Testament prophet, Isaiah. A word from the Lord directly applied to the Jews returning from exile to Israel. However, as with so many passages of God's word, this passage of scripture can also be applied to all generations of Christians who travel on the spiritual life highway of faith. Here it is:

> ***Is. 40:3-4*** *A voice of one who cries: Prepare in the wilderness the way of the Lord (clear away the obstacles);* ***make straight and smooth in the desert a highway for our God!*** *Every valley shall be lifted and filled up, and every mountain and hill shall be made low; and* ***the crooked and uneven shall be made straight*** *and level, and the rough places a plain. (AMP)*

The key principle here is God directing us to make a way for Jesus to motor down the spiritual highway of our life. *We are to prepare the way.* Clear away any obstacles that could get in his way. Make our spiritual life highway to be very straight and level. Make it very easy for Jesus to travel on, by his Holy Spirit. The New Testament documents this same principle from the book of Hebrews, that I've documented so many times throughout our study:

> **Heb. 12:1** *Therefore, since we are surrounded by such a great cloud of witnesses,* **let us throw off everything that hinders** *and the sin that so easily entangles, and let us run with perseverance the race marked out for us. (NIV)*
>
> **Heb. 12:12-13** *So then, brace up and reinvigorate and set right your slackened and weakened and drooping hands and strengthen your feeble and palsied and tottering knees, and cut through and* **make firm and plain and smooth, straight paths** *for your feet (yes, make them safe and upright and happy paths that go in the right direction), so that the lame and halting (limbs) may not be put out of joint, but rather may be cured. (AMP)*

"The race marked out for us." That race, documented here again in Heb. 12:1, is meant to describe each of us pursuing God's plan for our life as we navigate on this spiritual life highway of our faith. In support of that race, God is also counseling us in Heb. 12:12 to examine our spiritual strength, effectiveness, health and well-being. After that examination, if we find ourselves in the spiritual condition described in verse 12, then Jesus is directing us to do something very specific—he instructs each of us to, brace-up, reinvigorate and strengthen our weakened hands and our feeble and palsied and tottering knees. After reading this, imagine Jesus saying something like this to you: *So, you are seeking to acquire spiritual freedom for yourself—are you ready for that race?* What kind of shape is your spiritual vigor and vitality in? Do you need to train some more to make yourself ready? *Do you need to firm up your faith?* Jesus continues in verse 13, stipulating the reason why we should seriously consider and then do this:

"to cut through and make firm and plain and smooth, straight paths for your feet."

So, what's he talking about here?

He's saying to you and me, get ready to run..!

Once again, these scriptures are referring to making straight the spiritual highway of your life for Jesus to motor on, and for you to run the race marked out for you. You do the prep work – *purify your heart and renew your mind* – and God provides the cure and healing as needed. So, do you see all of that? Does that make reasonable sense to you? Do you agree with it, or, do you think it's silly?

Okay, I've documented some specific scriptures revealing and describing the spiritual highway of life and visualizing the race for authentic, spiritual freedom. I reiterate to you here that this visualization technique is extremely effective to renew your mind by programming the sub-conscious part of it. The more detail the better. Getting the picture? It's not silly at all.

The key principle of truth that should be getting obvious here is this: *STAY IN YOUR LANE..!* When temptations of sin, especially any consistent, besetting sin, comes your way, recall this mental exercise using your mind's eye and *refuse to change lanes*. I'll remind you often of this within the pages of this book, and life itself will also, of the peril that is always out there...So, don't go there—it simply ain't worth it. STAY IN YOUR LANE...

THE RENEWING OF YOUR MIND
Remember, this visualization technique is not like an elementary school, or some childlike experiment designed for you to daydream, or to live life in some fantasy-world, apart from reality.

Not at all, rather, it is actually, and literally, a very advanced and effective method of programming your sub-conscious mind. It further enhances and more effectively speeds-up and expedites the amount of time it takes for you to get that done. The bible provides us a very factual, accurate, logical and reasonable reason why we would not only want to program, or re-program our sub-conscious mind, but that we actually really NEED to do this. Here it is:

The condition of our spiritual freedom, and our spiritual life health and well-being is actually heavily influenced by how thorough, and how successful, we are at **renewing our mind**. The Apostle Paul wrote significantly about this, especially in the book of Romans. I strongly encourage you to memorize this following scripture and meditate on it very often. It reads like this:

> **Rom. 12:2** *Do not be conformed to this world, but be transformed by the renewing of your minds, so that you may discern what is the will of God—what is good and acceptable and perfect. (NRSV)*

Further, as you read this and begin to apply it to your life, pay particular attention to the last part, *"the will of God."* The renewing of your mind is inextricably linked to discovering and activating the will of God for your life. Christian theologians agree that the accurate interpretation of this part of Romans 12:2 would read: God's will is a singular attribute and can accurately be described as being good, **and** acceptable, **and** perfect, all at the same time, and in the same context.

God's will is always described as being good, acceptable and perfect for every person, in every circumstance, throughout all eternity. His will is good, it is acceptable, and it is perfect. God is perfect, and his will is perfect. He makes zero errors–nada–none. Believe God's Word.

SPIRITUAL WEAPONS FOR FIRM FAITH
I identified three "adversaries" from the last chapter, that are a part of our human nature—and that any of them can literally war against our efforts to establish a habit of increasing, firming up, and strengthening our faith. Here they are again:

1. Getting out of your **comfort zone.**
2. Overcoming **immediate gratification.**
3. Becoming **sufficiently content.**

I further identified that acquiring the attitude of Jesus holds the key of becoming effective, and ultimately successful, in overcoming these adversaries. We'll examine a powerful and strategic precursor that is either required, or, is often a part of faith being formed within your heart and your mind. You've just seen it documented from the last chapter on the Faith and Freedom Chart previously shown. Remember that? It first, and always, applies to God's people—to you and me, the bride of Christ. It looks like this:

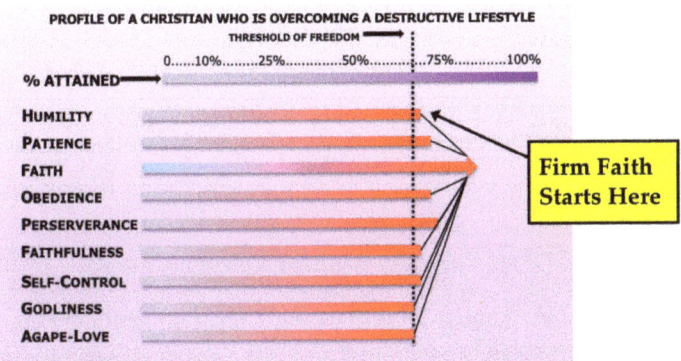

That precursor is HUMILITY. This is essential because we must first gain access to God, because Jesus himself is the author and perfecter of our faith. Without Jesus, spiritual freedom from biblical faith simply cannot happen. So, we require access to God the Father through Jesus. The following scriptures illuminates this access—first, through humility:

FIRST COMES HUMILITY
What is it? Humility is defined like this: *a state of mind well pleasing to God.*[3] Another aspect of humility reads this way: *The personal quality of being free from arrogance and pride and having an accurate estimate of one's worth.*[4] Both the Old and the New Testament of the bible are replete with examples of humility in practice. Consider well, and study the following scriptures documenting what God himself thinks about humility and the state of being humble:

> *Psa. 25:9* He guides the **humble** in what is right and teaches them his way. (NIV)

---
[3] Easton Bible Dictionary
[4] Holman Bible Dictionary

> **Is. 66:2** ... "This is the one I esteem: he who is **humble** and contrite in spirit, and trembles at my word. (NIV)
>
> **Jam. 4:6** ... That is why Scripture says: "God opposes the proud but gives grace to the **humble**." (NIV)
>
> **Matt. 23:12** For whoever exalts himself will be humbled, and **whoever humbles himself will be exalted.** (NIV)

So, pragmatically speaking, how does humility factor in as a precursor to faith? How is it used as a "gate" to access the presence of God? And, what does God do in response? The following well-known scripture reveals what God will do when you learn how to weaponize and use humility as he intends you to do:

> **2 Chr. 7:14** "IF my people, who are called by my name, will **humble themselves and pray and seek my face and turn from their wicked ways, THEN** will I hear from heaven and will forgive their sin and will heal their land." (NIV) (emphasis mine)

Previously, in earlier chapters of this book, you've read the phrase, cause and effect, quite often portrayed in the bible as... *if you – then I,* as it is here in this example. Again, both the Old and the New Testament are brimming with the use of this principle. So, believing this, **IF** I want God to hear me from heaven, and, **IF** I want my sins forgiven, and, **IF** I want to be healed *(read: to be set free)*

- **THEN**, the first action I need to accomplish is to humble myself,
- **THEN** I need to pray,
- **THEN** I need to seek God, and
- **THEN** I need to repent and turn from my wicked ways.

Think of humility being used as the gate that must be opened to the path of life that will lead you into the presence of God. You can also think of humility as the key that opens that gate.

Consider this—for God to hear you from heaven - *he must be listening, specifically to you* - when you pray. So, how can you be absolutely sure that you have his attention, and, that he really is listening to you? Here's how:

Your faith informs you that Gods' word is absolutely true, correct? That being the case, lock your brain into this scripture from the OT book of Daniel:

> **Dan. 10:12** Then he said to me, Fear not, Daniel, for *from the first day that you set your mind and heart to understand and to humble yourself before your God*, your words were heard, and I have come as a consequence of [and in response to] your words. *(AMP)*

Let's paraphrase this and unpack it a little more... The New Century Version (NCV) of the bible says this: *"Some time ago you decided to get understanding, and to humble yourself before your God.* **Since that time, God has listened to you...***"* So, what do you think? Does that word apply to you? Are you humble enough? Is God listening to you? Is your humility sincere and sufficient enough to open that gate and get God's attention?

The virtuous attributes of humility and unselfish love are not a part of our human nature—they only come from God, so, how do you convince him to give them to you? Think of it this way—there is a frame of mind that you enter into, that will always put this into motion. To be sure, God is the arbiter of examining the sufficiency and effectiveness of your humility and your faith—he will always know. But, **how can you be confident** and how can you be sure about this? I encourage you to run this scripture through your brain, prepare your mind for action and acquire the following attitude and mind-set as you ponder how humble you think you are:

> **Rom. 12:3** For by the grace given me I say to every one of you: **Do not think of yourself more highly than you ought**, but rather think of yourself with sober judgment, in accordance with the measure of faith God has given you. *(NIV)*

You will know...and, so will God – *Just speak truth in your heart—(ps: 15:2)* Fortunately for all of us, God's ways and his thoughts are way higher than ours. He is not like us—he does not grade our behavior and actions on a curve, like our school teachers do. Jesus even said the following while hanging on the cross: *"Father, forgive them, for they know not what they are doing"* (Luke 23:34).

That means that God takes into account our knowledge of him and his ways, the condition of our faith, and most importantly, the attitude and inclination of our hearts when dealing with us. And, God never deals with us impulsively, according to our sin(s), to what we actually deserve, but first, according to his loving kindness—according to his amazing grace *(Ps 25:7)*. That's his nature; that's just how he is. He is slow to anger and always abounding in grace. **He is holy, and, we are not—he is humble and we are not.**

Humility is not a quality that we are born with. Like wisdom, we must ask God to supply us with humility *(Jam. 1:5)*. Humility is a learned trait and can only be provided to us by God. Think of humility as being the opposite of pride. For example, when we humans are born, we possess and exhibit zero amounts of humility. We are totally dependent upon our parents for everything in life. We give almost nothing and take almost everything. We are totally selfish for those formative first years of life.

Then, as we learn to relate to others, and, especially to God, we begin to acquire things in life that we recognize as being beneficial and valuable. Humility is one of those virtuous values. We start out with little to no humility. We take over 95% of life stuff for our self and give little to nothing back. Then, as we grow and learn just how beneficial humility is to our way of life, and we start to exhibit and practice more of it, the percentage of selfishness in our life changes from being 95%, then 70%, then 25%, then maybe even 10% when we realize and conclude that the old popular adage is really true: **"It is far better to give, than to receive."** Just like Jesus always puts on display.

So, as you study about humility, and how it affects your faith, remember that God is always looking at and evaluating your heart—especially your heart for him.

He measures your desire to know him and the ways of his kingdom, your passion for him and your diligence in seeking him. Therefore, do not fear the thought of not having sufficient humility to access God. Trust him, that as you desire to know him more, and begin taking effective action by "Just

Showing Up," and then seeking your faith to firm up and get stronger, that he will supply all of your needs, **including sufficient humility,** to ensure that you connect with him and experience the growth and well-being of your spirit.

Further, humility, in and of itself, in addition to the influence it provides you to access God and increase the strength and vitality of your faith, provides you with incredible favor from the hand of the Lord. Consider these scriptures:

> ***1 Pet. 5:6*** *Humble yourselves, therefore, under the mighty hand of God, that He may exalt you at the proper time, (NIV)*
>
> ***Jam. 4:10*** *Humble yourselves (feeling very insignificant) in the presence of the Lord, and **He will exalt you** (He will lift you up and make your lives significant). (AMP)*
>
> ***Prov. 11:2*** *When pride comes, then comes disgrace, but with humility comes wisdom. (NIV)*

The key here again, is humility. Humble yourself before the Lord, and he will lift you up. The command *"humble yourselves"* could be translated *"allow yourselves to be humbled."* Humility avoids disgrace and leads to wisdom. So, avoid exalting yourself... Let God do it... Let God exalt you—as I'm fond of saying, **he'll do it way better than you...!** When he exalts you, the result is a blessing from him that is *"pressed down, shaken together and running over, and more than you can think or imagine!"* (Lk. 6:38 - Eph. 3:20).

This act of humbling yourself *before* God, and *before* you commit sin, is a very big-deal in context with your Freedom Strategy and Lifestyle. God wants your acquisition of freedom to succeed, and to succeed enthusiastically with great passion and intoxicating JOY..!

Jesus wants you to fervently and decisively win the spiritual war you are fighting as you struggle especially against all obstacles to your spiritual freedom.

Okay, what should you take away from this? How does this pertain to you? In context with this book, specifically in regards to you acquiring a lifestyle of spiritual freedom? Here's my answer: You will discover humility to be not just important, but very essential to your success. I therefore encourage each of you to very carefully and wisely consider just how indispensable this virtue, and weapon of spiritual warfare, will become to you. You will want your measure of humility before God to be not at all compared to a tiny rabbit-hole, but much more like a giant barn-door. *Get the picture?* So, to paraphrase several verses of scripture, from both the Old and New Testaments – God wants you to learn exactly how to **"Weaponize"** the application of both humility and patience in your life.

He wants you to gain spiritual victory **before** having to apply them to gain forgiveness, **after** you have yielded yourself and committed some destructive sin.

The bible is very clear on this distinction—**YOU HAVE A CHOICE..!**

God wants to effectually and completely convince you to learn this strategic truth that both humility and patience can be used as very effective and very powerful offensive weapons of spiritual warfare, *especially when used prior to committing sin*.

Therefore, whenever you first become aware of a temptation, even a dominant compulsion urging you to commit that besetting sin, exercise these two massive weapons of spiritual warfare, humility and patience, by dwelling on, and acting on the following: Resolutely refuse to exalt yourself and demand your own way—*by choosing to commit this sin.... Instead,* **HUMBLE** *yourself and choose not to. Decisively choose to wait upon the Lord. Think like this... I will choose to exercise* **PATIENCE**... *and not impulsiveness, before my God.*

Here's why – Here's empirical evidence – Here's reality—Matt. 23:12 states: *For whoever exalts himself will be humbled, and whoever humbles himself will be exalted*—remember, this is a law just like gravity!

NEXT COMES PATIENCE
Is. 40:31 Yet those who **wait** for the LORD
Will **gain new strength;**
They will mount up with wings like eagles,
They will run and not get tired,
They will walk and not become weary.

So, think very clearly about this, if you choose to humble yourself and exercise patience ***prior*** to yielding yourself to some besetting sin, God will honor your wisdom to make that choice and he will exalt you at the proper time, just as his word reveals:

> ***Rev. 2:3*** *and you have perseverance and have endured for My name's sake, and have not grown weary. (NIV)*
>
> ***Gal. 6:9*** *So don't get tired of doing what is good. Don't get discouraged and give up, for we will reap a harvest of blessing at the appropriate time. (NLT)*

If, on the other hand, you choose to exalt yourself and you are either unwilling, or because of your addiction, unable at the time, to exercise humility and patience prior to yielding yourself to some besetting sin, you will be going for another ride on the Yo-Yo—*"A train-wreck, with your name on it, is coming your way..."*

This ride will put you into a process, affecting all of the members of your body and mind and soul, that will get more pronounced and will worsen over time, until you actively humble yourself, seek out the Lord in prayer, then repent and turn from your wicked way(s). When you fulfill that, God will forgive you and will begin the process of restoring you.

Remember riding on the Yo-Yo? Really sucks doesn't it?

Remember also that God is specifically addressing *his people* who are riding on that Yo-Yo; *those who are called by his name*. He begins this famous scripture addressing us, that is, you and me.

Here it is again, but from the Amplified Bible Version:

> **2 Chr. 7:14** *If My people, who are called by My name, shall humble themselves, pray, seek, crave, and require of necessity My face and turn from their wicked ways, then will I hear from heaven, forgive their sin, and heal their land**. (AMP)*
>
> ** or, paraphrased to mean: **"and set them free"**

God will clearly and always honor his word irrespective of how you choose to experience the results of humbling yourself to him, either before committing the sin or afterward. So, how 'bout another weapon of spiritual warfare to put into your armory? *Check this one out:*

This is a great place right here to consider a very beneficial use of patience, in the unlikely form of **procrastination**. Usually, something that you would want to seriously avoid like the plague. But, what if you decided to procrastinate the first instance that you became aware of a temptation to sin that you usually yielded yourself to?

What if you just determined that you would simply delay your response? That you would put it off until later. Procrastination can be a very effective and beneficial form of patience. Procrastination, used in this way, can at least put you on the path to acquiring more patience.

In context with that, take a close look at the following scriptures that document patience and waiting on the Lord as a clear alternative and preference compared to acting impulsively. Especially, as you think and reason the consequences of yielding yourself to sin:

> **Psa. 27:14** *Wait for the LORD; Be strong, and let your heart take courage; Yes,* **wait** *for the LORD. (NIV)*
>
> **Psa. 37:7** *Rest in the LORD and* **wait patiently** *for Him; (NASB)*
>
> **Psa. 147:11** *The LORD favors those who fear Him, those who* **wait** *for His lovingkindness. (NIV)*

> **Lam. 3:25** *The LORD is good to those who **wait** for Him, To the person who seeks Him. (NIV)*
>
> **Is. 40:31** *Yet those who **wait** for the LORD will gain new strength; They will mount up with wings like eagles, they will run and not get tired, they will walk and not become weary. (NASB)*

The Hebrew word for "wait" from Is. 40:31 is: **qavah**, kaw-vaw´ ; a primitive root; primary definition: *to wait for: - eagerly waits for, and hopefully waits for.* This definition clearly implies the use of patience. Applying patience to your thinking and reasoning, in this context, demonstrates its use more as a spiritual weapon of offense, not defense. Without patience being used as a spiritual weapon in this way, your human nature could very probably lead you to impulsively yield yourself to *getting what you want - when you want it -* And, you would almost certainly commit sin every time you are tempted. When used like this however, patience is definitely not passive, but very active, even pro-active, along with being effective and very powerful.

FIRM FAITH - LEADING TO FAITHFULNESS - A SUMMARY
So, we begin showing up more consistently to meet with Jesus—to get to know him better than we do now. As the unsearchable riches of our knowledge of him increases, our sanctification by the Holy Spirit results in our faith becoming more firm. We are introduced to a new and powerful spiritual warfare tactic, declared in Luke 9:23: We learn that every time we choose to deny ourselves and suffer for Jesus sake, God uses that tactic to secure our spiritual freedom. The Holy Spirit of God begins showing us how to turn the virtues of humility and patience into formidable weapons of spiritual warfare. That's what sanctification does—it puts us on the right road leading us to a gate that we can open up and connect with God, in a very personal way—it defines a spiritual life highway that Jesus motors on bringing us supernatural favor, blessing, power and praise throughout our life. All of that, firming up our faith, leading to faithfulness—becoming more like Jesus…

And now, as I'm also fond of saying: ***Go and make war..!***

CHAPTER 5
FAITHFULNESS

EFFECTIVE FAITHFULNESS

So, firm faith definitely comes before Faithfulness.... And, faithfulness is an attribute of God's divine nature that Christians derive essential benefit from learning how to attain, and then sustain, with deliberate practice for the rest of their lives.

Effective faithfulness is both essential and indispensable to freedom.

Webster's Dictionary defines it like this:
Faith'ful·ness, *[noun]*
1. Full of faith, or having faith; disposed to believe, especially in the declarations and promises of God.
2. Firm in adherence to promises, oaths, contracts, treaties, or other engagements.
3. True and constant in affection or allegiance to a person to whom one is bound by a vow, by ties of love, gratitude, or honor.

Holman Bible Dictionary defines it like this:
FAITH, FAITHFULNESS
1. Contemporary English word "faith" derived from the Latin – *fides* *("fidelity")*.
2. Today, faith denotes trust. Faith does not function as a verb in contemporary English; the verb "to believe" has replaced the verb "to faith." The English noun "faithfulness" denotes trustworthiness or dependability.
3. Throughout the Scriptures faith is the trustful human response to God's self-revelation via his words and his actions. God initiates the relationship between Himself and human beings. He expects people to trust Him; failure to trust Him was in essence the first, original sin.

For the direct context of our study purposes, Faithfulness also has a distinct meaning of *Repeatability, and of Being Consistent, and of Reliable and Steady Performance*. This has a very strategic implication for all who are studying this program.

Especially for those who are afflicted with an addiction—afflicted by a besetting sin that, for a variety of reasons, they have not been able to overcome.

A STRONG SPIRITUAL FOUNDATION – THE CORNERSTONE

This chapter, entitled Faithfulness, is the third in a series of faith steps required to initially build, or, to re-build a strong spiritual foundation for oneself. Without a strong foundation, the house built on top of it will be very vulnerable to the stresses and storms of life over time. As it is with bricks and mortar, in this case, so it is with the strong foundation of your spirit required to build your life upon, that is, if you truly want your Christian lifestyle to be one of freedom. Every spiritual foundation, just like a physical buildings' foundation, requires a Cornerstone to be solidly in place. The cornerstone will effectively anchor the foundation to ensure that it is structurally sound and sufficiently strong to build upon. And, so it is with every Christian's spiritual foundation:

> ***Eph. 2:20*** *You are built upon the foundation of the apostles and prophets with Christ Jesus Himself the chief Cornerstone. (AMP)*
>
> ***1 Pet. 2:6*** *For thus it stands in Scripture: Behold, I am laying in Zion a chosen (honored), precious chief Cornerstone, and he who believes in Him (who adheres to, trusts in, and relies on Him) shall never be disappointed or put to shame. (AMP)*

The New Testament book of Matthew records the incredibly pragmatic reason why Jesus Christ himself fulfills these passages of scripture. He literally is that anchor for every Christian's spiritual foundation, and, for very good reason— reminding you here again, also from the Amplified Bible, that Jesus himself spoke this timeless scriptural truth when he walked the earth:

> ***Matt. 7:24-25*** *Jesus speaking: "So everyone who hears these words of Mine and acts upon them (obeying them) will be like a sensible (prudent, practical, wise) man who built his house upon the rock. And the rain fell and the floods came and the winds blew and beat against that house; yet it did not fall, because it had been founded on the rock." (AMP)*
>
> ***Matt. 7:26-27*** *"And everyone who hears these words of Mine and does not do them will be like a stupid (foolish) man who built his house upon the sand. And the rain fell and the floods came and the winds blew and beat against that house, and it fell—and great and complete was the fall of it." (AMP)*

Essentially, a spiritual foundation that would be considered by biblical standards to be sufficiently strong enough to successfully weather the storms of life has two basic common denominators, each one contributing to building up your faithfulness. Those two were presented to you in the last chapter. Let's add some detail and unpack them a little more.

KNOWLEDGE IS POWER – OR, IS IT?
We are talking about knowledge and action. Remember again that well-known adage that says: *Knowledge is Power...* Let's provide some beneficial detail that will be effective in firming up your faith and making it even stronger. Generally speaking, the phrase knowledge is power, means to infer an advantage one has over others when attaining an education. But, knowledge, in and of itself, is only the first step in the process of acquiring power from it.

The fact is that effective power only results from knowledge when a very solid understanding of that knowledge, combined with the application of that knowledge, begins to exist. There is a *synergy* [5] of both knowledge and action that must be present if effective power, especially the spiritual power required to secure and maintain personal freedom, is going to be produced and sustained. In addition, authentic and efficacious spiritual freedom is also "synergetic" in that it requires **a relational component** - *through an effective relationship with the person of Jesus Christ,* **and an academic component** -

---

[5] *"Synergy"* - *Defined as the interaction or cooperation of two or more parts to produce a combined effect greater than the sum of their separate effects.*

through an effective understanding and application of God's word – in order to be functional and effective. Both are essential. So, what are we to learn and conclude from this?

- Knowledge, by itself, will not provide any useful spiritual power.
- Knowledge acquired, through an effective relationship with Jesus Christ, is the beginning of spiritual power.
- Knowledge acquired and applied, through an effective relationship with Jesus Christ, results in the production and demonstration of – ***effective*** – spiritual power.

Further, and to paraphrase the point – *You can memorize and recite the entire Bible and/or the Encyclopedia Britannica, but, without an effective relationship with Jesus, and without the wisdom that comes from experiencing the result of understanding and applying otherwise useful biblical knowledge – there will be no spiritual power.* **That is none... nada... zero... spiritual power will be produced within you.**

You will be smarter, academically... you can win a lot of money playing on Jeopardy... but **you will not be any wiser or any closer to acquiring the authentic, effective spiritual power you need to master the besetting sin in your life.**

Now, with the building of our spiritual foundation detailed a little more, let's open up some of the attributes of faithfulness that are so relevant and strategic to gaining spiritual power and freedom. So, you begin increasing the unsearchable riches of your knowledge of Christ in your life.

Okay, what's next:

Here's what's next: *Put your gift of faith, and initial knowledge, into effective operation within your life.* Remember that old adage: **You must use-it or lose-it?** It rings true with your faith. Should you fail to use it with some consistency, atrophy will set-in and your faith will grow dim. That's just how it works. Let's take a closer look: Remember, the bible establishes and teaches what faith actually is, and how it is formed, from a couple of biblical perspectives:

> **Heb. 11:1** *Now faith is the assurance of things hoped for, the conviction of things not seen. (NASB)*

Same scripture—slightly different perspective from the Amplified Bible:

> **Heb. 11:1** *Now FAITH is the assurance (the confirmation, the title deed) of the things (we) hope for, being the proof of things (we) do not see and the conviction of their reality (faith perceiving as real fact what is not revealed to the senses). (AMP)*

HOPE – TRANSFORMED INTO FAITH

The bible establishes a link here between hope and faith. Faith can be developed from hope, and, hope can be transformed into faith. So, how does this work, and why is it relevant and important?

Secular dictionaries and contemporary thinking define hope as nothing more than wishful-thinking. However, the Greek word for hope is *"elpis,"* and it denotes, *"confident expectation of good"* or *"anticipation,"* not just wishful-thinking.

Hope is consequently an expectation or belief – *read:* hope transformed into faith – in the fulfillment of God's promises. Biblical hope is hope in *what God will do in the future*.[6] The following scripture is a favorite of mine:

> **Is. 40:31** *… but those who hope in the LORD will renew their strength. They will soar on wings like eagles; they will run and not grow weary; they will walk and not be faint. (NIV)*

A very practical and pragmatic example of how hope is transformed into a working faith. Hope, in this scripture, and in this context can be paraphrased to mean; *I have a beginning desire that develops into a sincere hope that the Lord will……*

---

[6] *Holman Bible Dictionary*

1. Renew my strength
2. Enable and empower me to *"soar on wings like an Eagle"*
3. Enable and empower me to *"run and not grow weary"*
4. Enable and empower me to *"walk and not be faint"*

This scripture in Isaiah describes a godly person, or a youth who might normally be considered very strong, but who is currently experiencing a struggle with weakness, in some form. Could be mental anguish, like discouragement or perhaps depression, or something similar… even a besetting sin affliction.

This scripture also implies a previous experience or history of the Lord providing for them a significant and more than sufficient strength for navigating the struggles of life. So, they desire to have that strength back, **"to have it renewed."**

At the initial stage of this desire, they do not yet believe that this will actually happen, so, they *"hope"* that it will. If their desire and hope is strong enough, they will progress or move it to the next level of taking action through prayer- they will pray that God will give them what they have been hoping for. At some point, or rather, *"in the fullness of Gods' time,"* and *if they do not give up*, Jesus will impart a living faith into their hearts and minds. They will be renewed, enabled and empowered.

When Jesus does that, they no longer need to hope for God's answer - **they have it.** Through a working and firm faith, once they actually believe it, they now know that they have what they initially just hoped for. They OWN-IT… They know it will happen. It now is just a matter of time. *That's what firm faith in action, faith put into operation, looks like…* THAT'S WHAT IT DOES!

So, as you can see by this scriptural example, faith is a present and continuing reality of your life, lived out day-by-day. It is not simply a virtue sometimes practiced in antiquity. It is a living thing, a way of life for the Christian. Remember again, this essential axiom of your Chrisitan lifestyle:

Faith is to the spirit what blood is to the body—**IT IS LIFE..!**

It can, and very often does, begin as a small desire or a dream to achieve or an experience in your life that initially, is thought to be impossible—but, you would really like to have it or experience it - **think:** *Your Spiritual Freedom.* From that beginning, it can, and quite often does, for the Christian, turn into a living reality through the faith that Jesus provides, firms-up and perfects within each of us who believe, over time.

FAITH, SPIRITUAL HEALTH AND FREEDOM
The bible establishes and teaches how faith is developed. Very basically, it begins by hearing the words of Christ. It can start out with a dream, desire or hope as just described, or, Jesus can impart it to you by his Holy Spirit whenever you encounter Gods' word, through reading or studying the bible— even through someone simply talking about his word, through a pastors' sermon at church, hearing the word on the radio or TV, and through a myriad of other ways that God can impart to you. The bible documents the origin of faith in this scripture:

> **Rom. 10:17** *So faith comes from hearing, and hearing by the word of Christ. (NASB)*

An additional insight into faith and God's word:

> **Matt. 4:4** *Jesus answered, "It is written: 'Man does not live on bread alone, but on every word that comes from the mouth of God.'" (NIV)*

These scriptural axioms of truth determine that our spiritual strength, health and well-being is inextricably linked to our faith and belief in God's word. Especially those words directed personally at each of us. Therefore, you can rightly conclude that a strong spiritual foundation requires a firm faith in Gods' word, as documented in the bible, and also, that your faith needs to be very active. In addition, your ability to consistently resist the devil and his evil schemes are inextricably linked to the ***evidence of your faith.*** Perhaps one of the best examples of that evidence comes from the testimony [7] of a very well-known Christian by the name of Josh McDowell. I've documented that testimony in Addendum I, at the end of this chapter, for your reference. I encourage you to read it and adopt that clear evidence to base your own faith upon. That strong evidence will magnify your faith for a very good reason. After reading those words, ask yourself these questions: Just how firm do you think your faith is? How faithful is your actual behavior to the commands of Christ? Think this through.

EXAMINE, EVALUATE AND TEST YOUR FAITH

Okay, what comes next? How about this, before we move on: You need to sincerely assess the condition of your faith. I encourage you here to apply some godly wisdom and discipline. Don't just reason your way into this, or, try this assessment by yourself with only your intellect and smarts being used. Don't just think about it. That will never work. Always remember, it is following your instincts, understanding, reason and emotion, and not God, that has almost certainly influenced, or even caused, the condition you are in.

That process must change for you to develop a strategy whereby you are actually enabled to acquire spiritual freedom. So, first, ask God, and then give him your assent while you are in a posture of sincere and earnest prayer to search your heart according to scripture. Memorize the following scripture and pray it often as God follows through, over time, to answer your prayer.

> ***Psa. 139:23*** *Search me [thoroughly], O God, and know my heart! Try me and know my thoughts! And see if there is any wicked or hurtful way in me, and lead me in the way everlasting." (AMP)*

This will take time—many sessions of prayer. Remember, God is wanting you to first learn FAITHFULNESS starting out by just beginning to show-up. *Take a look at this process—**be patient with yourself**—exercise wisdom:*

Next, over multiple prayer sessions, as you begin this process of assessment and evaluation, ask the Lord to help you examine the condition of your faith.

---

[7] **ADDENDUM I:** *"Evidence for Faith" An updated account of the massive evidence to be found within the Christian faith.*

Ask in prayer that he would reveal evidence of your faith, starting with your initial saving faith, that you know Jesus is exactly who the bible says he is, in exactly the same way that you know who you are—and that his work on the cross is absolutely complete, applied personally for you, and that you also believe you are indeed forgiven of all your sins and that you have eternal life. Make sure you really believe all of that and do not have any doubts about it.

Then, examine what you believe about your sanctification - **read:** *You're learning how to become less selfish and more effective in adopting and following the commands of Christ, and his Gospel, as you live out your life.*

Sincerely, and realistically, think this through. Can you see the evidence in your life that God is shaping you and changing you into the image of Christ over time? A good exercise: Have you experienced a change in your spiritual attitude and behavior over the last month—over the last year? Check out these two perspectives from the NIV and AMP:

> *2Cor. 13:5 Examine yourselves to see whether you are in the faith; test yourselves. Do you not realize that Christ Jesus is in you—unless, of course, you fail the test? (NIV)*
>
> *2Cor. 13:5 Examine and test and evaluate your own selves to see whether you are holding to your faith and showing the proper fruits of it. Test and prove yourselves (not Christ). Do you not yourselves realize and know (thoroughly by an ever-increasing experience) that Jesus Christ is in you—unless you are (counterfeits) disapproved on trial and rejected? (AMP)*

We simply cannot trust ourselves and our reasoning abilities to function like a compass that always points to the north, like I wrote earlier. The mind simply does not work that way. When we are searching for, and seeking the truth for our lives, our conclusions from reasoning will only be valid when they are in agreement with God's word through the bible.

That is the primary reason God instructs each of us to *examine ourselves to be sure we are in the faith*. Until you learn to accurately do this, you will be severely hampered to grow further in your spiritual health and faith. This examination requires you to **skillfully use Humility and Patience as weapons**, now that you know exactly how to do that. Don't be foolish, and don't rush, or be short-sighted about this process. On the one hand, be brutal with yourself in believing and adopting what God reveals about the condition of your faith and your heart as you apply pertinent scriptures. On the other hand, just be sober minded and be extremely thankful to God for loving you enough to reveal the truth to you. And, trust him completely. He will not permit anything to come upon you that you cannot bear or hold up under – *(1Cor. 10:13 – Acts 15:10)*.

Remember well, once again, these words: *our actual behavior reveals the working condition of our faith* so, examine and evaluate the effectiveness of your faith, not by how you feel, and not so much by what you think, but, mostly, or almost exclusively, by how you act, what you do, and how you behave, over time—that's where truth resides, and that's where your faith should be.

This appraisal often proves to be one of the most important elements that changes your life for good as you look back on it. So, embrace the truth with joy. It is the truth, revealed in multiple areas of your life that will ultimately set you free. Therefore, cooperate with the Holy Spirit as he motors down your Spiritual Life Highway to change you from the inside out. Practice often *visualizing yourself, staying in your own lane*, on that highway. See yourself also, in your mind's eye, considering, but then – *refusing to change lanes* – **Always Choose Life....!** Once you can and do accept, believe, and adopt this truth about your own heart, and the condition of your faith, which absolutely determines and governs your will, judgments and actions, you need to ask God, the great physician, to do something within you and for you:

> **Psa. 51:10** "Create in me a pure heart, O God and renew a steadfast spirit within me." (NIV)
>
> **Ezek. 36:26** "I will give you a new heart and put a new spirit in you; I will remove from you your heart of stone and give you a heart of flesh." (NIV)

Got it down? OK, you have been connecting with God in prayer on multiple occasions, and you are convinced that he is answering your prayers to change your heart. Now, memorize, add and pray this scripture in your prayer and devotional time with God, declaring it often:

> ***Psa. 119:10-11*** *"I seek you with all my heart; do not let me stray from your commands." I have hidden your word in my heart that I might not sin against you. (NIV)*

GUARD YOUR HEART WITH ALL VIGILANCE
Once God begins to set you free, and creates in you a clean and pure heart, you need to consistently pray that God will enable you to keep your heart clean and pure, preferably on a daily basis, but certainly as consistently as possible for you. Think, meditate and pray often on this scripture, again, from Proverbs:

> ***Pro. 4:23*** *Keep and guard your heart with all vigilance and above all that you guard, for out of it flow the springs of life. (AMP)*

You are now consistently connecting with God, and, you are increasingly believing what God's word says about acquiring and exhibiting faithfulness, and what the bible declares about your heart and your mind. So, to close out this chapter, what are some really helpful, beneficial and effective ways to optimize and increase your level of FAITHFULNESS? Try these:

For those of you young in the faith, just starting out, do this:
1. Read and study the Book of John, memorizing John 15.
2. Read and study the Book of Proverbs and Psalms. Pray and ask the Holy Spirit to point out scriptural passages to memorize. Store his word in your heart (Ps. 119:11).
3. Read the entire bible from start to finish. Pray and ask the Holy Spirit to point out chapters and scriptural passages to study. I can suggest the NIV or NASB versions of the bible, at least to start out with.

For those of you who have walked with God for some time, and are familiar with the bible, do this:
1. Read and study the Book of Romans. Memorize chapter 6. Pray and ask the Holy Spirit to point out scriptural passages to memorize from Chapters 2, 7 and 8. *Especially Rom. 7:19, 24 and 25.* Focus on learning and applying the grace of God to yourself and your lifestyle as you study these particular passages of scripture in Romans.
2. Read and study the Book of Ephesians and Colossians. Pray and ask the Holy Spirit to point out scriptural passages to memorize.
3. Memorize and declare out loud often in prayer: 2Cor. 10:3-5; Dan. 11:32; Rom. 8:37; Phil. 4:13; Phil. 4:8 Ps. 18:1, 2, 16-19, 28-36, Ps. 91 and Heb. 12:1,2

For everyone:
1. Find, commit, or re-commit to a bible teaching, evangelical church.

These last 5 pages or so, from a spiritual growth standpoint, are considered to be fairly heavy, or weighty, in regards to adopting and putting into consistent operation. Especially for every Christian whose life is at a place of needing to effectively confront any wickedness or evil at work within their own life. This is Spiritual Warfare. This is serious stuff indeed...!

The principles and precepts of biblical truth documented in these pages, are clearly intended to deliberately challenge you, by design. But, also to encourage you, via the building up of your faith, over time. It may very well be easy for you to grow weary and lose heart the first time that you read over these pages, thinking that this is way too much for you to consider alongside everything else in your life. However, you are never alone in your mission...

So, never forget—God himself, in a very personal way through Jesus, has a firm grip on you, and will never fail you. Read it again:

> ***1 Pet. 5:10*** *And after you have suffered for a little while, the God of all grace, who called you to His eternal glory in Christ, will Himself perfect, confirm, strengthen and establish you. (NASB)*

Let these comforting words from Psalm 18 also encourage and uplift you as you think about and consider a number of prospective and challenging changes that are likely to be bearing down on you about now:

> ***Psa. 18:32-34*** *It is God who arms me with strength and makes my way perfect. He makes my feet like the feet of a deer; he enables me to stand on the heights. He trains my hands for battle; my arms can bend a bow of bronze. (NIV)*

The next chapter will examine both constructive and destructive lifestyles. We will be applying how faith influences, and quite often determines, what kind of lifestyle we develop for ourselves.

But first, to end this chapter, I encourage you to read through Addendum I, **Evidence for the Christian Faith, on the next page.**

ADDENDUM 1
EVIDENCE FOR THE CHRISTIAN FAITH

ADDENDUM 1
THE EVDENCE FOR THE CHRISTIAN FAITH
By Josh McDowell - Published April 08, 2018 - FoxNews.com

My life growing up was a struggle. When I walked into college, I carried a heavy burden of years of hurt and bitterness. I was mad at my father for beating my mother. I was angry at a man who worked on our farm and sexually abused me from ages 6 to 13. All of this led me to really despise God, religion and anything to do with the church. I was the last person in the world who you would expect to become a Christian.

When some young believing students at school challenged me to investigate the evidence for Christianity intellectually, I was shocked. Specifically, they challenged me to investigate the evidence for the resurrection. I thought it was a joke. In fact, I thought it would be easy to marshal the evidence disproving the claims of Christ. Since I like a good challenge, I accepted their offer.

I left the university and traveled across the United States, Europe and the Middle East to study ancient manuscripts and gather the evidence against Christianity. After months of study, I returned to a small library in England. I leaned back in my chair, cupped my hands on the back of my head and said **"It's true. It really is true."**

I returned to the university and couldn't sleep. The evidence for Christianity was stronger than all the years of my pain and skepticism that kept me from believing it. I knew that if I was going to be honest, I could not remain a skeptic. The historical evidence really indicated that Jesus died, was buried, and rose on the third day. Needless to say, my research had taken quite an unexpected turn. I set out to disprove the historical resurrection of Jesus but ended up becoming a follower of Christ.

I first published my research in 1972 in the book "Evidence That Demands a Verdict," which has since been printed over 4 million times in 44 languages.

The historical evidence for Christianity today is like a tsunami. And yet, the amount of evidence we have engulfs the kind that led me to believe in Christ over five decades ago. The textual, archaeological and manuscript evidence is increasing regularly.

The waves keep crashing as more and more things are being discovered. Because of this, my son Sean and I recently teamed up to revise "Evidence That Demands a Verdict" with all of the latest discoveries that bear upon one verdict: Jesus Christ has risen from the dead in confirmation that he is God. This is obviously a radical claim to make today. After all, many smart people disagree with me. How do we know the claims of Christ are not "fake news?"

My challenge for you is to consider the evidence for yourself. According to the Apostle Paul, if Christ did not rise from the dead, then Christianity is false, and Christians are to be pitied *(1 Corinthians 15:14, 17)*. But if Jesus did rise, then Christianity is true. The evidence is there, if you are willing to consider it. After 50 years of studying it, I can tell you that this tsunami has not let up.

Working with Campus Crusade for Christ and founding the youth outreach Josh McDowell Ministry, Josh McDowell has shared the gospel with more than 25 million people in 125 countries. He is the author or co-author of 148 books, including "Evidence That Demands a Verdict."

Question to my FRP readers – **So, what do you think?**

PART 3
FREEDOM STRATEGY & LIFE ACTION PLAN

The initial words of freedom, from the Introduction, to the last chapter, describe Part 3 really well—here it is:

This book has been leading up to a specific freedom strategy and life action plan that you need to determine, develop and put into effective operation. Right? Isn't that it? Therefore, my research has led me to layout a series of obstacles throughout this book that need to be personally confronted and overcome by you, to get this done. These obstacles are clearly standing in your way and must be identified and effectively dealt with, for that to happen. This is personal with Jesus, and he means it to be personal with you—your freedom strategy and life-action-plan is unique to you, because you are unique to him. That's why you won't find a 7-step, or 12-step, or any other step plan here. So, I just encourage you here, to calibrate your thinking, and planning, to anticipate something that I write about, coming up in chapter 7. I paraphrase a wonderful statement that Jesus spoke in Matthew 16—he said this about you: **"I will build YOU, and the gates of hell will not prevail against YOU."** *Ponder this phrase as we begin chapter 6...*

Apply these last five chapters to be the fertilizer of your new Freedom Strategy & Life-Action-Plan.

CHAPTER 6
LIFECYCLES

CONSEQUENCES - A STUDY IN CONTRASTS

This chapter adds additional layers and levels to help you respond to the universal mandate that God has declared, in Hebrews 12:1 & 2, for every Christian to believe in, and to abide by. I begin this chapter continuing to focus on our faith, on the choices that we make, and how they influence our lifestyles, both for good and not so good. These day-by-day choices end up determining the habits we will develop from the core-values and comfort-zones that make up the spiritual foundation of our life. That's the key reason I have started this chapter with all the expanded detail about the choices we make, how important they are, and what influences them, for the most part.

We'll be focusing our attention on the *consequences of those choices—* especially those that can lead us to a destructive lifestyle, contrasted with those choices leading to an abundant, and constructive lifestyle. That's the path Jesus wants all of us to clearly recognize, to know really well, and then to follow tenaciously. I encourage you to prepare your mind for exactly that.

My FRP in this chapter, begins with significant details regarding the *Destructive Cycle of Life* that is produced within a Christian, when the love of yielding to, and following after, the evil desires of the heart exceed the desire to love and follow after the Lord Jesus Christ, and his commands. I will answer this question: **What can I expect to happen to me if I consistently choose this destructive kind of lifestyle?**

In contrast, we will then examine what it looks like to experience the *Constructive and Rewarding Cycle of Life* when a Christian decides to love God more than loving the fulfillment from yielding oneself to the temporary pleasures of sin—or, from developing a mind-set seeking to escape from the rigors and struggles that the reality of life can often bring.

Christ has set us free, therefore we are free to choose whatever we desire in life for the most part, however, not all of these choices are really healthy and good for us—we are to apply wisdom and assess each choice to determine whether we can expect it to be beneficial or not. Jesus wants us, and teaches us here that, to be forewarned is to be forearmed.

FOREWARNED AND FOREARMED – THE GATES OF LIFE
Jesus was always forearmed with the truth that governed every choice that he made in life, to be that vanguard example for each of us to emulate and follow. He thought and reasoned his way into every choice that he made. Jesus left nothing to chance; He never "gambles" with our welfare. He knew the spiritual law of sowing and reaping, and that every choice he made would be subject to the consequences of that law, just as it is with each of us, today.

On one hand, the results of that law can be very blunt and even brutal with some choices we determine to make—on the other hand, it can also be exceedingly wonderful and rewarding, depending of course, on what we choose to believe and to act upon, moment by moment throughout the day, every day. We'll be looking at some scriptures coming up that I documented from previous chapters, however, I want to assess them, and how they relate to our freedom, from a different perspective.

Regarding of being – *forewarned and forearmed* – Jesus had this to say:

> **Matt. 7:13-15** *Enter through the narrow gate; for wide is the gate and spacious and broad is the way that leads away to destruction, and many are those who are entering through it.*
>
> *But the gate is narrow (contracted by pressure) and the way is straitened** and compressed that leads away to life, and few are those who find it. (AMP)*
>
> ** *"Make straight the highway"* – Remember this one?

Jesus is providing us here in these particular scriptures, another level of his unique, prescient, and pragmatic provisions of truth. He is revealing a very beneficial insight and perspective into the level of difficulty, or, said another way, the relative ease of making choices that lead to either *a Constructive Cycle of Life, or, to a Destructive Cycle of Life.*

He is simply contrasting how relatively easy it is to make choices that can lead to a destructive lifecycle, vs how difficult it can be to make choices that can lead to a beneficial, rewarding, and constructive lifecycle.

Why is that gate so narrow that Jesus reveals in Matt. 7:13?

Take another look at this:

> **Luke 9:23** *Then he (Jesus) said to them all: "If anyone would come after me, he must deny himself and take up his cross daily and follow me. (NIV)*

Jesus reveals here, one of the most damaging attributes of our human nature—we are all selfish and we almost always choose the easiest path, irrespective of the consequences of that choice. Most people, even Christians, are prone to follow that easiest path, or choice, in life.

In fact, Jesus documents that there are many who open that *wide-gate* and enter that *wide-path*, even though it leads to destruction—ironically, even when they absolutely know that it leads to some form of destruction. He then contrasts the wide gate with *a narrow one that leads to life*, and reveals to us that *few are those who find it*, because it's just so hard and difficult to oppose our deep-rooted selfishness at times. That indictment from Jesus, regarding the finite weakness of our human nature, is documented really well here in the book of Isaiah:

> **Is. 55:8-9** *For My thoughts are not your thoughts, neither are your ways My ways, says the Lord. For as the heavens are higher than the earth, so are My ways higher than your ways and My thoughts than your thoughts. (AMP)*

Jesus is teaching us here to, *consider, and then to count the cost*, of the consequences of each action we choose to make in our life every day, especially the hard choices when they show up. Each of us will reap whatever we sow through the choices that we make, apart from Gods' grace. No exceptions...

> **Gal. 6:7-8** *Do not be deceived: God cannot be mocked. A man reaps what he sows. The one who sows to please his sinful nature, from that nature will reap destruction; the one who sows to please the Spirit, from the Spirit will reap eternal life. (NIV)*

We are all accountable. That inescapable contrast between those attributes of our human nature, compared to those attributes of God's divine nature clearly reveal just how desperate every Christian should be to acquire that attitude of Christ. To learn to think at least a little like Jesus, so we can escape the corruption that comes upon all those who enter that wide gate leading to destruction. Consider the clear example, here again, of how Jesus thought about, and responded to, the mission that God the Father sent him to perform and complete:

> **Heb. 12:2** *Let us fix our eyes on Jesus, the author and perfecter of our faith, who for the joy set before him endured the cross, scorning its shame, and sat down at the right hand of the throne of God. (NIV)*

Counting the Cost - Jesus thought long and hard about the cost he was about to pay. He agonized over it in the garden of Gethsemane, asking God the Father to take this cup from him if possible *(Matt. 26)*. He even asked his disciples to pray with him about it—remember that? The actions of Christ in the garden, and his forthcoming crucifixion, confirms that Jesus was indeed, counting the cost he would have to pay, for our spiritual freedom.

COUNTING THE COST – WHAT ARE YOU WILLING TO PAY?

He compared that agonizing cost with what he would receive for completing the mission that God the Father had given him. He weighed out the return he could expect to receive from both alternatives.

On the one hand, Jesus had the option to reject the will and plan of God the Father. He really could have been spared his death on the cross; however, this is what he had to say about that choice:

> **Matt. 26:53-54** *(Jesus Speaking) Do you think I cannot call on my Father, and he will at once put at my disposal more than twelve legions of angels? But how then would the Scriptures be fulfilled that say it must happen in this way?" (NIV)*

On the other hand, for Jesus, unlike each of us, there really was no competition between his two choices. Here's why:

Jesus bound and committed himself and his will to these prophetic declarations: *"I have come to do your will, O God" (Heb. 10:7)* and, *"I always do what pleases him" (John 8:29)* and the following well known scriptures:

> **John 12:27** *(Jesus Speaking) - "Now my heart is troubled, and what shall I say? 'Father, save me from this hour'? No, it was for this very reason I came to this hour. (NIV)*
>
> **John 10:15 and 18** *(Jesus Speaking) - "Just as the Father knows me and I know the Father—and I lay down my life for the sheep. No one takes it from me, but I lay it down of my own accord. I have authority to lay it down and authority to take it up again. This command I received from my Father." (NIV)*

Jesus determined that the intense and exhilarating joy he would receive by acting upon his love of God and his love of us, and his prophetic compulsion to do the will of the Father, completely negated any and all other choices.

Oh, that we could be that wise, insightful and determined...

Because Jesus loved God and loved us to such a fervent degree, he compelled himself to be the prophetic instrument of God the Fathers' plan of salvation establishing the Gospel of Christ:

> ***John 3:16*** *(Jesus Speaking) "For God so loved the world, that He gave His only begotten Son, that whoever believes in Him shall not perish, but have eternal life." (NASB)*

That's how and why Jesus counted the cost, and decided to endure the cross. He endured the unspeakable agony of the cross because, **God so loved.** The love that Jesus has validated for God the Father and for each of us is perpetual, eternal, is always in effect, always in motion, and will never fail *(1Cor. 13)*. So, like Jesus, we are to think about it, and then, count the cost. If we decide to wisely stay in our lane, ***choosing life,*** that choice will clearly be a beneficial one and we can expect to receive a fulfilling and rewarding return from our Father in Heaven. Conversely, if we decide to change lanes, ***choosing destruction,*** that choice will clearly be a detrimental one and we can expect to receive a return that includes trouble and distress, apart from God's grace. Sounds really simple doesn't it?

That's because it really is, just that simple...

So, *be forewarned and forearmed* to exercise wisdom and think deliberately, long and hard about the certainty of that return you will receive from the daily, moment by moment choices that you make. Be sure that the consequences of those choices will be beneficial and rewarding to you, and all that you value and hold dear.

The question continues to persist—why do Christians in conflict with the struggles of life so often choose a path leading them to trouble and distress, instead of choosing a path leading them to joy and fulfillment? Here's some of the most prevalent reasons I have learned from the bible, from my own experience, and from researching a large number of Christian case histories over many years:

1. **Temptations** - We are tempted to sin, either inwardly from our own sinful desires, or, outwardly from demonic forces of evil and wickedness.

2. **Pain** - We experience different kinds of pain as we navigate life. For many, the struggles of life pile up and take their toll. We all will

face seasons of life that are difficult, by design. Dealing with those realities of life, for some of us, and at different times, tempts us to want to withdraw from the reality of life—just to get some relief; a respite from the tension and pressures of life. At some point, the emotional and mental strain and stress can become so great that we become desperate for immediate relief, so, we medicate ourselves—to relieve that pain, we try to withdraw from reality through booze and alcohol, some form of drug abuse, overeating and binging on food, expressing anger, yielding to sexual immorality like pornography, or other related expressions of sinful behavior. The pain can make us want to escape and get away from it, so, we recoil and look for immediate relief. We medicate.

3. **Pleasure** – We are drawn to the temporary pleasure experienced when yielding ourselves to sin. At some point if we are unwilling, or unable (addiction), to control our behavior and repent, we become a lover of pleasure, more than a lover of God, as the bible documents:

> *2 Tim. 3:4 Traitors, heady, high minded, lovers of pleasures more than lovers of God; (KJV)*

4. **Boredom** – Believe it or not, many Christians simply choose some expression of sin because they get easily bored with their tedium of life. They become indifferent to the realities and accountabilities of life and cease caring about spiritual life stuff and relationships with God and people; they escape reality through sin.

Some of these causes of sinful behavior documented here adversely influence many Christians navigating life, however, one or more of them can even dominate their thoughts, actions and behavior.

How about you? Are you influenced by any of these, or others? Are you actually dominated by any of them at this point in your life? Let's take a closer, and very sobering look at this:

SIN CAUSES DEATH TO SHOW-UP

Okay, take a good look at this—*get a really good grip on it*—the bible documents this truth in the following two scriptures:

> ***Ezek. 18:4*** *(God speaking) For all people are mine to judge—both parents and children alike. And this is my rule: The person who sins will be the one who dies. (NLT)*
>
> ***Rom. 6:23*** *For the wages of sin is death, but the gift of God is eternal life in Christ Jesus our Lord. (NIV)*

Here's the rub – **Whenever we sin, we begin to die, on every level...**
The following Key Principle clearly documents this consequence of sin:

> ***Key #10*** *- Whenever we sin,* ***we begin to die...*** *We begin reverting back to behaving through the instincts of our human nature. This decline of life will continue on all levels until we humble ourselves and repent.*

On every level? Really—what does that mean, in practical terms?

The death you begin to experience in your life, on every level, when you yield yourself to sin, is not generally immediate, but, **the effects** *of that death experience do begin immediately* upon committing that sin, and worsen over time until you repent. The following outline documents some of what can be expected:

What happens to us when we sin? ***The immediate consequences...***

1. The precious faith we have in God gets "dull" and begins to dissipate and die off.
2. Our active fellowship with Jesus by his Holy Spirit is "cut off." *(Jesus will not hang out with you closely again until you sincerely confess and repent of that sin)*
3. Your desire and diligence in seeking God and his kingdom will diminish.

4. The ability of our minds to think clearly begins to decline. We become "Double-Minded" - Unstable in all of our ways.
5. The stress and struggles of life become more evident and consequential. Your vocational work becomes more difficult and less productive and enjoyable.

   5.1 Want some proof? Remember the curse that God put on Adam when he sinned in the Garden of Eden? God said this: *"Cursed is the ground because of you; In toil you will eat of it all the days of your life."* This curse will once again be magnified, worsened, and more influential in your life.
6. The Yoke of Christ, and his provision of abundant life to you is no longer available until you sincerely repent. As a consequence of that, life will become more burdensome and your load will be heavier. Debilitating stress in, and on, your life will increase.

   6.1 So, instead of throwing off everything that hinders and the sin that so easily entices, as God mandates you to do in Hebrews 12:1, you will actually be throwing off the Yoke of Christ, and his provision of abundant life—and that my friend, will really suck. You need to seriously consider and think about this loss that you will certainly bring upon yourself. **This is a really bad deal for you—don't do it.** Refuse to trade your precious fellowship with Christ for some temporary sinful pleasure - You can have one or the other, but, you cannot have both at the same time. Consistently choosing sin over the fellowship of Christ is a terrible transaction that can wreck your life if you fail to stop it. Burn this principle of truth deep into your brain, and, never forget it. What you sow, you will reap, and—YOU DO NOT WANT TO REAP THIS—avoid it at all cost.
7. You will not be able to care about life like you want to, and know that you should. You will become more indifferent about life and relationships, even those that are dear to you. Your ability to THRIVE in the enjoyment and fulfillment of your life will really begin to fade—you'll regret it.

8. You will begin to be more isolated from meaningful and strategic relationships.
9. You will begin to experience a loss of intimacy, respect, admiration and joy from all relationships, especially those meaningful and dear to you.
10. Your susceptibility of being easily-deceived into thinking that you can manage the consequences of your sin will increase—especially, how long sin may grip you. Truth is, once you yield yourself to that sin, you lose your God-given ability to control what happens next. You will become a slave-to-sin—just like the bible says you will—because you will lose the usual control and management of your lifestyle. These unexpected-circumstances and unforeseen-results can absolutely HAMMER your life.

   10.1 My research over many, many years has sadly uncovered numerous case histories of godly men and women who have had to endure an unexpected and unforeseen season of mental and spiritual anguish—losing significant control over the usual thoughts and behavior of their lifestyle. Some have not been brought back to their senses for many months and even years—like the prodigal, all because they failed to heed God's warning. **These consequences are spiritually discerned**—*you can't feel it happening like you can if you hit your thumb with a hammer*—it just doesn't work that way. God lovingly warns us to exercise godly wisdom, discipline, resolve and control over our bodies and our minds throughout the bible. I encourage you to review and study what can happen if you fail to heed the many warnings that Jesus has provided us, as he lovingly shepherds us through life.

Therefore, once again, if you think that I'm intentionally trying to *Scare the Hell out of You*—**you'd be right!** Here's a couple of very good reasons why:

> *1 Th. 4:4* "*that each of you should learn to control his own body in a way that is holy and honorable.*" *(NIV)*

> *Gal. 6:7-8* *Don't be misled. Remember that you can't ignore God and get away with it. You will always reap what you sow! Those who live only to satisfy their own sinful desires will harvest the consequences of decay and death. But those who live to please the Spirit will harvest everlasting life from the Spirit. (NLT)*

There are sins of commission, even very pre-meditated and deliberate sins of commission we can be tempted to commit. There are also sins of omission and others that we can easily be attracted to, originating from evil desires that come from the wickedness of our own hearts, or from temptations outside of ourselves. These consequences are very real and are enforced through Gods' – *Law of Sowing and Reaping* and his *Law of Sin and Death* – We are all accountable to his laws—no different from gravity or electricity—every one of us…

But, all of us are not as responsible as we should be – **How about you?**

Okay, let's pause here for a word of encouragement. The consequences of yielding yourself to sin can be a really heavy topic that can weigh you down significantly if you're not careful. So, let not your heart be troubled over these last few pages, and you can look forward in a few more pages to exploring a lot of detail about Gods' grace that always abounds more than any of your sin abounds. His love for you covers a multitude of sins so keep a Gods' eye view and perspective on this. Be *God-Conscious* way more than being *Sin-Conscious*.

THE DESTRUCTIVE LIFECYCLE – A DILEMMA
Remember, the destructive lifecycle is compared to experiencing life as if you were riding a Yo-Yo, going up and down, but never, or rarely, moving forward. The bible also speaks to this Lifecycle Yo-Yo that we can become trapped in— Remember these two….?

> *Rom. 7:15* *I do not understand what I do. For what I want to do I do not do, but what I hate I do. (NIV)*

> **Rom. 7:18-19** *I know that nothing good lives in me, that is, in my sinful nature. For I have the desire to do what is good, but I cannot carry it out. For what I do is not the good I want to do; no, the evil I do not want to do—this I keep on doing. (NIV)*

The Apostle Paul is speaking here of the law of sin and death at work within him, and within each Christian as a part of our human nature. We are all born with, and have to deal with, that law as a part of our nature throughout our entire life here on Earth. We really are sinners by birth and by choice. That law sets up an ongoing tension and conflict within our hearts and minds often producing a very real competition between our own selfish will and desires, against God's good and perfect will for our life.

So, here we are again wondering, where to turn?

> **Rom. 7:24-25** *What a wretched man I am! Who will rescue me from this body of death? Thanks be to God—**through Jesus Christ our Lord**. (NIV)*

This passage of scripture gives us great hope and insight into our destructive lifecycle of death dilemma, and, what can be done about it. The apostle Paul, inspired by the Holy Spirit of God, identified this dilemma and inscribed it here, into the book of Romans.

Putting words to his anguish of knowing what to do, but, realizing that there was nothing within himself that could possibly carry out his desire to perform or produce it—and that he needed rescue from outside of himself, namely, through the person of Jesus Christ our Lord. So, be very encouraged here because Paul wrote this as a practicing Christian disciple, just like you and me.

Further, God took some 20 years of transforming Paul's heart, renewing his mind, and refining and perfecting his ministry ***after his salvation experience,*** before the Lord had him prepared to write these words in a letter to the Romans—later becoming the famous New Testament book of the same name.

So, Paul, almost certainly, wrote this timeless scriptural passage describing his own personal dilemma trying to overcome a spiritual issue, or issues, that he was, or had been, experiencing. In addition, and especially for our example, this scriptural passage also applies to Christian disciples like you and me, struggling to overcome a besetting sin issue in our own lives, that we are challenged with. God clearly wants all generations of Christian disciples to be encouraged, and to never give up on this pursuit of freedom—that's exactly why he sent Jesus.

Further, Paul provides us some additional, and very pertinent detail, describing his experience seeking the freedom that Christ has provided all of us. *Check this out:*

> ***Phil. 3:12*** *(Paul Speaking) Not that I have already obtained all this, or have already been made perfect, but I press on to take hold of that for which Christ Jesus took hold of me. (NIV)*

Paul is further establishing here that – he is pressing on to take hold of that for which Christ Jesus took hold of him. So, the question is often asked...

"What is Paul after here; what exactly, is he pursuing?"

The documented answer(s) to that question from many well-regarded bible commentaries are many. However, it must be certain here that Paul is describing a "life-journey" of some kind, and, at the very least, that **he is definitely in pursuit of the freedom that Christ has made available to him and every Christian** – That much is certain.

Therefore, take these encouraging words from the Apostle Paul into account and be very patient with yourself and with this learning process. It takes time, sometimes a lot of time, but, the result in your new life of freedom is immensely worth the investment you will make to acquire it. God will never quit or give up on you, so, commit to never, ever, give up on him, or give up on yourself and your mission in this life to acquire and sustain a lifestyle of authentic, personal, spiritual freedom. I encourage you, once again, to add this perspective from Paul's writings here to your own pursuit of spiritual freedom as you seek to avoid, or prevent, a destructive lifestyle taking a hold of you. Now, let's develop another perspective.

SUFFICIENT KNOWLEDGE – THE DEVIL AND THE NATURE OF SIN
God wants you to be wise and to understand the devil's tactics to steal, kill and destroy everything good and everything godly in your life. Especially your faith in God. This is personal. You need to understand and believe that. God wants to make you a blessing to his kingdom and a very real threat to hell. So, check this out:

Sin will come at you and will attack you, in one of two general ways:

1. **Directly from your adversary, the devil and/or his demons.** The forces of evil are extremely skilled and adept at devising schemes, temptations and compulsions designed to deceive and entrap you into yielding yourself to commit sin, especially a besetting sin.
2. **Directly from the wickedness stored up within your own heart.** This comes from your own human nature to rebel against God, refusing to submit and comply to his will and to his wonderful plan for your life—and also, from you corrupting your mind, with the effect of loving sinful pleasure more than loving God.

Okay, acquire what you really need to know about your adversary. Then, add this biblical knowledge to your spiritual arsenal. Then, learn how to weaponize it and put it into action. It will often come to you in the form of a spiritual transaction. If you are looking for it—*if you are vigilant*—you will detect it: God delights in giving good gifts to you *(Jam. 1:17 and Ps. 103:5)*. The devil works to take all those good things and gifts away from you. Reads like this:

> ***John 10:10*** *"The thief (the devil) comes only to steal, and kill, and destroy; I (Jesus) came that they might have life and might have it abundantly. (NASB)*

> *1 Pet 5:8* "Be self-controlled and alert. Your enemy the devil prowls around like a roaring lion looking for someone to devour. (NASB)
> *Someone Like YOU……!* (Remember this one?)

I reiterate here again on purpose; Never forget, that this is personal. These scriptures inform you that the devil, your adversary, your enemy, is always active, is very tenacious, and has a plan to harm you in any and every way that he can. However, God has something to say about that:

> *2 Cor. 2:11* in order that Satan might not outwit us. For we are not unaware of his schemes. (NIV)
>
> *2 Cor. 2:11* To keep Satan from getting the advantage over us; for we are not ignorant of his wiles and intentions. (AMP)
>
> *Eph. 4:27* and do not give the devil an opportunity. (NIV)
>
> *2 Tim. 2:26* and that they will come to their senses and escape from the trap of the devil, who has taken them captive to do his will. (NIV)
>
> *Psa. 91:3* That's right—he rescues you from hidden traps, shields you from deadly hazards. (NRSV)

The bible documents the fact that God does not want any of us to be unaware or ignorant of the devil's schemes, plans and traps that he intends to use against us as he opposes every good thing that God provides us. Consider the following points to add to your knowledge that expand and detail these biblical precepts of truth. Like this one again—*do not give the devil an opportunity*—an old Jewish proverb puts it this way: *A bird can land in your hair, but, you do not have to let it make a nest!*

The most pragmatic explanation reads like this: A temptation can come upon you at any time, but, you do not have to allow that temptation to gain any advantage over you, and you therefore have no obligation to yield yourself in submission, compliance or obedience. Absolutely none at all. You literally are FREE, but you have to learn how to acquire and "Walk" in your freedom. Remember key scriptures like this: 1 Pet. 5:8…. *"be disciplined, be alert"*

> **1 Pet. 5:8** *Discipline yourselves, keep alert. Like a roaring lion your adversary the devil prowls around, looking for someone to devour. (NRSV)*
>
> **Rom. 12:3** *For by the grace given me I say to every one of you: Do not think of yourself more highly than you ought, but rather think of yourself with sober judgment, in accordance with the measure of faith God has given you. (NIV)*

In context with that, remember also one of my previous Key Principles:

Do not think that becoming Easily Deceived could not happen to you. Refuse to think that way. Instead, realize that we are easily susceptible to being deceived and deluded about God's will in our lives at any point in time. That is why we need a Shepherd in the first place, and that is why our need for Jesus, His Grace and His Truth is DESPERATE.

Always Remember – Apart from him, you can do nothing - *(John 15:5)*

Your adversary, the devil knows this about you and your human nature and he will exploit this every time you give him an opportunity to do so. Therefore, be very sober minded about the true nature of sin—particularly, besetting sin. *Check this out:*

- *Yielding yourself to sin* will take you where you do not want to go…
- *Yielding yourself to sin* will cost you more than you think you ought to pay…
- *Yielding yourself to sin* will cost you more freedom than you think you ought to lose…
- *Yielding yourself to sin* will result in an increase in the susceptibility of your becoming significantly deceived, and suffering an immediate loss of managing and controlling most circumstances in your life—you will, once again, become a slave to that sin…
- **You will spend way more time immersed in the grip of sin than you ever thought you would…**

Got all those bullet-points down? Count the cost—*it just ain't worth it..!* However, as you count that cost, always keep the following in perspective:

Where sin abounds, grace abounds all the more. (Rom. 5:20)

Sin Cannot Take You Where Grace Cannot Find and Restore You.

You simply cannot out-sin the grace of God. It is virtually impossible. The Gospel of Christ is that powerful, and God really is that good, because his love for you will never fail. Okay, let's unpack this destructive lifecycle predicament just a little more. Remembering the following phrase from chapter 3: *"All it takes for evil to prosper is for good men to do nothing."* A couple of very similar biblical proverbs state it this way:

> **Prov. 6:9-11** *How long will you lie there, you sluggard? When will you get up from your sleep? A little sleep, a little slumber, a little folding of the hands to rest... and* **poverty will come on you like a bandit** *and scarcity like an armed man. (NIV)*
>
> **Prov. 24:32-34** *I applied my heart to what I observed and learned a lesson from what I saw: A little sleep, a little slumber, a little folding of the hands to rest—and* **poverty will come on you like a bandit** *and scarcity like an armed man. (NIV)*

What do we conclude from this? That if we fail to learn this lesson, if we observe correctly that we are trapped in a destructive behavior, but, we are not willing or able to take any action, that is, <u>any effective action</u>, then the evil we seek to avoid will, in fact, continue to overtake us, every time.

The result: We are held fast to the destructive Yo-Yo lifecycle. This in turn leads us back to the beginning—***just how well do you know Jesus?***

Here it is again:

> *Dan. 11:32 the people who* **know their God** *will display strength and take action. (NASB)*

CONSEQUENCES – RESULTS OF DISOBEDIENCE vs OBEDIENCE

The consequences of obeying and also disobeying God's word and his commands are spelled out very clearly throughout both the Old and the New Testaments of the bible. These consequences do not happen in a random manner, or, by coincidence. They are all governed intentionally and put into operation and force by God's precise laws over all creation, both, physical and spiritual.

The following scripture may very well be regarded as the most prominent and, perhaps the most dominant of spiritual laws *(Law of Sowing and Reaping)*, that governs both good and evil consequences, especially in context with your freedom:

> *Gal. 6:7-8 Don't be deceived: God is not mocked. For **whatever a man sows he will also reap**, because the one who sows to his flesh will reap corruption from the flesh, but the one who sows to the Spirit will reap eternal life from the Spirit. (HCSBS)*

In addition, the following scripture may very well be regarded as the most prominent declaration of these consequences, both for good and evil:

> *Rom. 2:9-11 There will be trouble and distress for every human being who does evil: first for the Jew, then for the Gentile; but glory, honor and peace for everyone who does good: first for the Jew, then for the Gentile. For God does not show favoritism. (NIV)*

Remember this really well... These two scriptures function as spiritual LAWS; they are exact and pragmatic. They truly govern our spiritual, moral behavior in exactly the same way that physical laws govern the cosmos, like gravity and electricity. Should you violate them, you can expect to experience the consequences, both for good and for evil, apart from Gods' grace.

However, God has provided a way that the consequences of violating these spiritual laws can actually be *mitigated or modified, and even nullified.*

That specific provision is through God's GRACE, and his GRACE ALONE.

As Christians, God does not judge us, or grade us on a curve, like so many teachers and college professors do. Through his grace, he always has the option to deal with us according to his lovingkindness, and not according to our sin and iniquity *(refer: Ps. 103:10).*

He can, and very often does, override the sometimes-painful consequences of **trouble and distress** *- (Rom. 2:9)* when we commit sin and do evil. Even when that sin is pre-meditated and/or deliberate. His loving-kindness and his goodness really are that great, through his grace, because HIS LOVE FOR US NEVER FAILS!

However, each of us make mistakes, commit sin and fail quite often. The bible coins this well-known phrase to describe this truth about our propensity to sin:

All of us like sheep have gone astray *(refer: Is. 53:6 and 1Pet. 2:25).* So, when we do, God will use all manner of things in our life to instruct us in obeying his word and learning his ways; even from the consequences of our own inclination to be easily enticed by sin and wickedness. Check this out:

> *Jer. 2:17, 19* Have you not brought this on yourselves by forsaking the LORD your God when he led you in the way? Your wickedness will punish you; your backsliding will rebuke you. Consider then and realize how evil and bitter it is for you when you forsake the LORD your God and have no awe of me, declares the Lord, the LORD Almighty. (NIV)
>
> *Jer. 2:19* Your own wickedness shall chasten and correct you, and your backslidings and desertion of faith shall reprove you. Know therefore and recognize that this is an evil and bitter thing: (first,) you have forsaken the Lord your God; (second,) you are indifferent to Me and the fear of Me is not in you, says the Lord of hosts. (AMP)

Certainly, the first step required to overcome and master the sin in your life, is to be made aware of it. That is precisely what the Law-of-God does *(refer: Rom. 7:7)*. Know this—our loving God wants you to become very aware of, and very adept at, learning from your mistakes. Develop this tactic as a functional part of your new Action-Plan. It goes something like this:

Consider every mistake that you make from now on to be an opportunity that you can learn from. Think of the mistake as one of your new virtual teachers. Think and reason all the ways that caused you to make that mistake—*especially if that mistake caused you to yield yourself to a besetting sin*. Refuse to gloss over it, put it out of your mind and just move-on. Instead, deliberately refuse to put it out of your mind and intentionally place considerable and significant value on the experience.

You will learn best when you learn within the *"Arena of Performance."* This is where life actually happens—this is where *"The Rubber Meets the Road."* Think of what it was that triggered you, in the first place, to condition your mind to begin the process of yielding yourself to this sin.

DO NOT LOSE OR WASTE THIS OPPORTUNITY TO LEARN—it will only come around once. It is really valuable for you to begin recognizing what triggers your sinful behavior *as early in the process as possible.* Become very aware of this. Play it back over and over again in your imagination, in your mind's eye.

The sooner you learn to recognize this initial trigger, or triggers, the more effective your response to resist it, or them, will be. The key principle here, is that every time you purposely think and dwell upon these triggers, you will be instructing your sub-conscious mind that it needs to be renewed. That it must be re-programmed. Simple as that. That's one of the ways your sub-conscious mind works. The more you deliberately think and dwell upon the what and why of these triggers, the more malleable and open to change your sub-conscious mind becomes.

In the same way, **writing down these triggers** is a very effective method of programming your sub-conscious mind. Understanding these programming principles and acting upon them consistently is like hitting a stand-up single in a baseball game. It puts you in the game, or in the race. You're now on first base—you can effectively make some notable and rewarding progress to renew your mind. *Stay in the race—stay in your lane...*

It would be so wonderful if only we could just learn by reading about the consequences of disobedience and obedience in the bible and then always choose and put into consistent behavior the wonderful consequences of obedience. However, life just doesn't work that way. We are all born with a very selfish human nature. So, God has purposely included struggle against that selfish nature to be a very real and prevalent part of life. Primarily, so we can LEARN through that process. One indispensable precept of learning to overcome and avoid the consequences of disobedience is first to understand each part of the process that cause it to happen in the first place, especially, the very beginning of it. *Got that?*

ADVANCED LEARNING – RENEW YOUR MIND
Learning, by having to experience the consequences of your disobedience, through your own wickedness, even when the grace of God is abundantly provided you in the process, is definitely not God's first choice of instructing you and me. The bible provides you a much better, much more desirable, and much more effective way for you to learn.

Read, ponder and study this:

> ***Rom. 12:2** Do not conform any longer to the pattern of this world but **be transformed by the renewing of your mind**. Then you will be able to test and approve what God's will is—his good, pleasing and perfect will. (NIV)*

God clearly wants you and me learning how to avoid the consequences of disobedience by learning how to renew our own minds. *Set yourself on that course*—it's absolutely essential that you do that. The program code that you need to use has already been given to you by God. It is found in the bible—it is in fact the very, but specific and particular, Word of God – His particular and personal message to you, revealed by the Holy Spirit of God with exactly the content and context needed to renew your unique mind. That renewing of your mind is a major key objective of this program of mine, in both books and within my website action-plan—to show you exactly how to do that.

An incredible and effective aid to that mind-renewal process is readily available to you. So, take note of this very key and strategic precept of truth and spiritual warfare tactic. This principle and precept of truth is yet another offensive tactic of spiritual warfare that you should acquire and adopt for yourself. Here it is:

> **Key #11** - *God in his wisdom and sovereignty has carefully hidden within the consequences of obedience and disobedience an "abundance" of clues and keys and tactics to help you develop your own freedom strategy.*

Those consequences are literally pregnant with truth and tactics that God wants to reveal and teach to you by his Holy Spirit. And, God means for you to discover them for yourself. He knows the joy that you will experience each time that you discover, learn and adopt one of them to the development of your own freedom strategy, and, he purposely wants you to experience that joy. He has intentionally designed your mind to respond to that joy. It is the joy of that learning process that he wants you to recognize within the consequences you experience in life—to propel you towards the freedom you are so desperate to acquire. Therefore, put this tactic into operation every time that you experience a consequence of your obedience and/or your disobedience.

Remember to STOP, THINK, and REASON. Take your personal experience of that consequence to Jesus and ask him in prayer to reveal what he has hidden in that experience that he wants you to see—that he wants you to know—that he wants you to learn from and act upon.

> **Jer. 33:3** *'Call to Me and I will answer you, and I will tell you great and mighty things, which you do not know.' (NASB)*

Don't let this pass. Once again, tenaciously resist the impulse to just move on. Do not allow yourself to drift anymore. Pay Attention—check out a very clear evidence from scripture that documents this message from God, by his Holy Spirit, that he wants you to know and that *he wants you to activate:*

Here it is:

> **Prov. 25:2** *It is the glory of God to conceal things, but the glory of kings** is to search things out. (NRSV)*
>
> ** *The meaning of Kings in this context is* <u>One who takes dominion</u> - *from Gen. 1:28 This is directed squarely at you and me.*

Remember a very significant fact documented earlier in this program: God has deliberately designed life to be a struggle at times. He has intentionally done this because he knows that this struggle will make us stronger.

Therefore, life, including the searching out of truth, is not intended to be easy, but sometimes very hard, requiring extensive work and effort— sometimes taking years to find and experience that particular truth that God knows is needed to renew our mind and set us free from addiction, besetting sin and a destructive lifecycle.

So, get serious, and live your life intentionally - *"in the moment"* - in reality, with great purpose. Sincerely resist how easy it has been for your mind to wander and to drift away from reality. FIX YOUR EYES ON JESUS - *(Heb. 12:2).* There is "GOLD" hidden within each consequence experienced from obedience and also from disobedience for you to discover and learn from, and be rewarded by—but, you have to get in there and mine it for yourself. You have to work at it and search it out. You need to function like a king who takes dominion over the sphere of influence that God has given in all areas of life. Here is that first evidence from scripture, that documents this message from God, by his Holy Spirit, that he wants you to know and that he wants you to apply in your life to Take Dominion - *Just do it...*

Spoken by God to Adam and Eve...

> **Gen. 1:28** *God blessed them, and God said to them, "Be fruitful and multiply, and fill the earth and subdue it; and **have dominion** over the fish of the sea and over the birds of the air and **over every living thing** that moves upon the earth." (NRSV)*
>
> *This mandate from God to take dominion over all life, including our own life, especially our minds, is still valid and remains in force today for every human being—**it's an attitude.***

Spoken by God to Cain...

> **Gen. 4:7** *If you do what is right, will you not be accepted? But if you do not do what is right, sin is crouching at your door; it desires to have you, but **you must master it.**" (NIV)*
>
> *This mandate from God to master the sin in your life, is still valid and remains in force today for every human being—**it's a mindset.***

These mandates from God are still in effect and remain absolutely valid today, and he expects each of us to put them into practice. So, **Take Dominion.** That dominion will come to you as an actual mind-set that you will experience every time that you successfully acquire the tenacious attitude, and yoke of Christ. That's what it looks like—you'll want to do this, and you'll come to cherish it...That's how you will recognize it.

Take on his yoke to completely avoid a destructive lifecycle producing trouble, distress, anxiety, frustration, little to no growth of character and integrity, no true peace in your soul, no vision or clear direction for your life, and so on. Refuse to be like a high-performance athlete being forced to just *Run-in-Place*, unable to *Run in the Race*. It almost always comes down to a simple choice—so, think about that—CHOOSE LIFE..!

The first part of this chapter has been focusing upon the consequences experienced from a *destructive lifecycle*—what you really want to avoid. We will now compare that to living life **yoked to Christ within a constructive lifecycle**—what you really want to acquire for yourself.

CONSTRUCTIVE LIFECYCLE - ABUNDANT LIFE THROUGH CHRIST
When the Holy Spirit of God comes to indwell you at salvation, and begins producing the image of God within you, your life is literally changed forever. You will never be the same again. As your new life, or, as the case may be, your renewed life in God unfolds, his Holy Spirit begins to reveal truth to you about life in general—and, about life in his Kingdom.

But especially, he begins teaching you about the *unsearchable riches of the knowledge of Jesus.* He wants to increase that knowledge within you, on a daily basis—every day that you will seek him, and allow him, to do just that. He will teach you about the destruction that sin causes in your life. God abhors and hates sin, and, he will teach you to hate it like he does—that is, if and when you sincerely determine to know and follow Jesus—not perfectly, but sincerely, and earnestly. To know Christ like he wants you to know him, more deeply, and, because of that knowledge, to follow the commands of Christ with love, intensity, diligence and effectiveness. *You up for that?*

There is an abundant life that Jesus offers each of his believers, but, *that kind of life is conditional.* God delights in rewarding his children, and, the bible documents that *he gives good gifts so that our youth is renewed like the eagle - (Psa. 103:5).* Many of God's gifts are simply given to us, like salvation, that cannot be earned any other way.

However, the abundant life that Jesus offers us, in this context, is an actual lifestyle, a new way of living - *it's like the Christian life on spiritual steroids -* That kind of lifestyle has a cost, and requires something from us—that is, if we expect to maintain that kind of lifestyle over time. If we truly desire and seek the spiritual freedom that God includes as a part of this abundant life in Christ, then God will challenge us, and oblige us to produce the evidence that this kind of lifestyle in Christ requires of us. Not always out-of-duty, but sincerely and authentically, **out of our love for God**—even when we don't feel like it. We first fall in love with him, and because of that love, we then choose and determine to serve him. This evidence is produced by us, not by chance, but by choice. We truly choose our way into this constructive lifestyle that we experience, however, Jesus still does the heavy lifting.

TAKE ON THE YOKE OF CHRIST AND THE ARMOR OF GOD
Once we become born again, Jesus offers all his believers an abundant lifestyle that effectively "transcends" our human nature *when we are yoked to him*. We become yoked to Christ by living our life in cooperation with, and dependence upon him. Abundant life in Christ is what God considers to be the default and normal spiritual lifestyle for every Christian.

God looks upon that kind of everyday lifestyle as being completely normal. It cannot be accurately described as *just getting by, or, just surviving in life*—not at all; God provides everything needed for life, in abundance *(2 Pet. 1:3)*. Not perfect life, but normal life that can often include struggle. The yoke of Christ is also linked to the condition of your faith; there is an ebb and flow to it, just like there is with faith. That yoke also includes the *"Armor of God"* providing abundant protection of your spiritual life, health and well-being *(Eph. 6:10-17)*.

Further, that yoke acquires the attitude of Christ in you that is mandated by God to put into effective operation so you can think more like Jesus, and less like the world. That's what is meant by God providing everything. Further, it is conditioned by what your core-values are, and by the choices you make. For instance, whenever you choose to sin, especially choosing deliberate, besetting sin, you will be effectively throwing the yoke of Christ off of yourself. You will be folding your tent and throwing your spiritual sword in the dirt. It's a mind-set that can come upon you—an attitude of opposing God. That's what happens to you when you *"Get it Backwards."* Here's what I mean by that:

Taking on the Yoke of Christ will always lead you to a constructive lifestyle, in turn enabling you to submit yourself to God and resist the devil (Jam. 4:7). However, *a destructive lifestyle will conversely lead you to get that backwards*—to do just the opposite—***you end up submitting to the devil and resisting God.*** You will go for another ride on the Yo-Yo *(Rom. 7:18-19)*. See the difference?

Therefore, you can clearly comprehend the contrast in lifestyles—right? And, you are learning that God has given you some very powerful and offensive weapons of spiritual warfare.

You know about humility and patience and are learning how to use them effectively as powerful weapons of spiritual warfare. You are understanding the wonderful benefit of refusing to exalt yourself by deliberately choosing to sin; instead, you choose to humble yourself and wait upon God to exalt you, and to rescue and protect you from all evil *(Ps. 91:14)*.

You are learning to actively and effectively use godly vision through the imagination formed in your mind's eye. Using this vision as a weapon of spiritual warfare, *you can see yourself motoring down your spiritual life highway,* choosing to STAY IN YOUR LANE. You are maintaining the good health and well-being of your soul and spirit, as well as your body and mind, as you consistently refuse to CHANGE LANES—and, you understand the peril you can face anytime you choose to change lanes.

Okay, now take a look at this—the Greek word for abundant from the original language in the bible is: *"perissea,"* meaning - *to be more than enough, be left over, be present in abundance, be abundant, abound, excel; exceeding the usual number or size, extraordinary, abundant, profuse, superfluous, fullness...*

You get the meaning...

Let's unpack this a little more. The abundance of life that Jesus provides arrives to us on many levels. This abundant life from Jesus is also the subject of a myriad of books on theology, philosophy, self-help, etc. published down through the ages. However, in this program, we focus on how this abundant life in Christ influences and affects our spiritual freedom. So, what about this contrast: What can we expect to experience once we actually begin acquiring and sustaining the personal spiritual freedom that comes from a constructive lifecycle?

CONSEQUENCES - LIVING THE CONSTRUCTIVE LIFESTYLE
To begin a consistent abundant life experience, that eventually will lead us to the freedom we desperately desire and need, we must learn to trust Jesus with the direction and welfare of our lives, exclusively. There is a myriad of really beneficial and rewarding reasons that we should learn to trust Jesus,

on every level of our lives and with every aspect of our lives. These spiritual life saving benefits can be experienced as a consequence of acquiring, adopting and abiding in the abundant life that Jesus provides you through a constructive lifecycle. Not all at once, but over time, and throughout a lifetime. So, I encourage you to consider, rejoice over, and study the following list of attributes Jesus makes available whenever needed as you learn to navigate life as a new, or renewed disciple of Christ. You really need this power filled lifestyle because Jesus said, *"In this life, you will have trouble."* - *(John 16:33).*

1. **Hope—Leading to Faith** - The truth is, that before some of you can even develop, or re-acquire, even the smallest desire to begin moving your life back into a positive direction with God, all you have to hold onto is some level of hope that this is even feasible for you—even possible for you.

    Does this describe your life experience in some way? Can you grip the reality of a future where your life opens up, and you're actually enabled to walk in newness of life—seeing yourself walking in and by the Spirit and not doubting God so much like you have been? If that rings a bell with you my friend, the beginning of the abundant life experience that Jesus offers you right now starts with HOPE. Authentic, tangible and genuine hope that you can begin to believe in, and actually wrap your head around. If these words are speaking to you, it is about ACTION… not good intentions… not lip service…. but deliberate and effective action that can turn your hope into authentic faith—that's the evidence God is looking for in you—that's what leads to obedience for you, and God knows it—putting wheels on your faith leading you to that elusive freedom.

2. **Spiritual Power—Order out of Chaos** - Establishing, or restoring, significant control over the usual thoughts, choices, and behavior of your lifestyle. The authentic, spiritual power to control, order, or reorder your thoughts more methodically and more effectively— acquiring that elusive biblical freedom that you are looking for from

Christ—that you desperately need, and, that you cannot acquire anywhere else.

> ***Acts 1:8*** *but you shall receive **POWER** when the Holy Spirit has come upon you…. (NASB) (emphasis mine….)*
>
> ***John 14:12*** *"Truly, truly, I say to you, he who believes in Me, the works that I do shall he do also; and greater works than these shall he do; because I go to the Father. (NASB)*

3. Transformation—A new heart and a path of renewal for your mind

Jesus provides an amazing and miraculous transformation in your life that cannot be achieved any other way. Whether it's salvation, or a new act of repentance—Jesus will rejoice over you with gladness. He knows absolutely everything, and he can do virtually anything…! The reality of your condition does not, and simply cannot, hinder or obstruct God in the slightest. He is supernatural and omnipotent. He already has exactly what you need, and, he longs to give it to you. Can you get ahold of this? It's irrefutably true, because Jesus said he would do, exactly that - ***If you'll do this…Then I'll do that.*** He said it—he means it.

Therefore, it simply does not matter one whit of how impossible your situation may look to you right now. Nothing, absolutely nothing, is impossible for God (Luke 1:37). Should God determine, or, better yet, when God determines, unlike you, he is able to speak FREEDOM into your life at any time of his choosing. ***Your part is to actually believe it.***

Logically speaking, if God can create light, when and where there was no light, he can also create freedom in your life, where there was no freedom—where it did not exist before. He does this all the time—every day. What do you think? Can that be true? Does God actually do that today? ***Would he do that for you?***

4. A Strong Spiritual Foundation—Leading to a Balanced Lifestyle -

God is not like you and me. He is not natural; he is supernatural and God is Spirit—he made each of us in his image. Okay, let's take a closer look at this—remember, we are created with a body, mind, soul and spirit. Restating that a more accurate way:

We "<u>are</u>" spirit – and, we "<u>have</u>" a body and a mind.

Our body, mind, soul and spirit are functionally interrelated and integrated with each other. Should any one of them break down or suffer dysfunction, the others are affected. Most people work at strengthening their bodies and their minds, but inadvertently ignore the crucial importance of the health and well-being of their own soul and spirit. That's what this program is all about; this is another abundant-life attribute that Jesus offers every believer—learning how to enhance and optimize the human soul and spirit to develop and maintain a very high-performance lifestyle, in addition to prospering in your vocation and your physical, mental and emotional health and well-being. The first of my Key Principles in this program reads like this:

> ***Key #1*** – *It is the health and well-being of the soul and spirit, not the body or mind, that is directly linked to achieving and maintaining spiritual freedom.*

One cannot achieve and maintain personal, spiritual freedom by being just physically, mentally and emotionally fit, strong and healthy. We are all building our lives upon our spiritual foundation, such as it is. Jesus offers you a very strong and formidable spiritual foundation to build your life upon. You want authentic biblical freedom? That kind of foundation is absolutely essential—so, don't ever let it become optional with you...

5. **Spiritual Effectiveness—Leading to a more Fruitful Lifestyle** – The abundant lifestyle Jesus provides you includes consistent growth

and spiritual strength as you continue to hone in and develop godly habits and increased levels of spiritual discipline. God will always reward your discipline and diligence seeking him. Consider these words:

> **John 15:5** *(Jesus Speaking)* *"I am the vine; you are the branches. If a man remains in me and I in him, he will bear much fruit; apart from me you can do nothing." (NIV)*
>
> **John 15:8** *(Jesus Speaking)* *"This is to my Father's glory, that you bear much fruit, showing yourselves to be my disciples." (NIV)*
>
> **John 15:1, 2** *(Jesus Speaking)* *"I am the true vine, and my Father is the gardener. He cuts off every branch in me that bears no fruit, while every branch that does bear fruit he prunes so that it will be even more fruitful. (NIV)*
>
> **Phil. 1:6** *being confident of this, that he who began a good work in you will carry it on to completion until the day of Christ Jesus. (NIV)*

There are many other attributes of the abundant life provided by Jesus that we will explore and focus time and study upon throughout the remainder of this program. However, the key principle at this point is for you to easily contrast what you can expect to happen when you ride the Yo-Yo and experience a destructive cycle of life, compared to what you can expect to happen when you choose to take the Yoke of Christ upon yourself and experience a constructive cycle of life. Okay, let's summarize what this chapter has been focused on:

LIFECYCLES SUMMARY - A STUDY IN CONTRASTS
So now let's summarize this contrast of life cycles being sure that your understanding is "abundantly" clear:

DESTRUCTIVE LIFE CYCLE CONSEQUENCES
1. The precious faith we have in God gets "dull" and begins to die.
2. Our active fellowship with Jesus by His Holy Spirit is "cut off"
3. Your desire and diligence in seeking God and His kingdom will diminish.

4. The ability of our minds to think clearly begins to decline. We become "Double-Minded" – Unstable in all of our ways.
5. The stress & struggles of life become more evident and consequential.
6. The Yoke of Christ, and His provision of ABUNDANT LIFE to you is no longer available until you sincerely repent.
7. You are no longer able to care about life like you know you should and Your ability to "THRIVE" in the enjoyment and fulfillment of your life begins to fade.
8. You are more isolated from meaningful and strategic relationships.
9. You experience a loss of intimacy, respect, admiration and joy from all relationships, especially those valuable and dear to you.
10. Your susceptibility of being "Easily-Deceived" into thinking that you can "Manage" the consequences of your sin... Especially, how long sin may grip you. Truth is, once you yield yourself to that sin, you lose your God-given ability to control what happens next. You will become a "Slave to Sin" because you will lose the usual control & management of your lifestyle. These "Unexpected-Circumstances" and "Unforeseen-Results" can absolutely HAMMER your life.

CONSTRUCTIVE LIFE CYCLE CONSEQUENCES

1. **Hope**—*Leading to Faith* – Before you can obey God, you have to believe God.
2. **Spiritual Power**—*Order out of Chaos* – Establishing, or restoring, authentic, spiritual power to control, order, or reorder your thoughts more methodically and more effectively.
3. **Transformation**—*A new heart and a path of renewal for your mind* – Jesus provides an amazing and miraculous transformation in your life that cannot be achieved any other way.
4. **A Strong Spiritual Foundation**—*Leading to a Balanced Lifestyle* – Learning how to enhance and optimize the human soul and spirit to develop and maintain a very high-performance lifestyle, in addition to prospering in your vocation and your physical, mental and emotional health and well-being.

5. Spiritual Effectiveness—*Leading to a more Fruitful Lifestyle* - The abundant lifestyle Jesus provides you includes consistent growth and effective spiritual strength.

Now do yourself a favor. Go back over both lists and lock each point into your memory, especially those that specifically pertain to you. I encourage you to take the extra step of writing these specific points down on paper—to further imprint them into your sub-conscious minds. As you do so, be sure to remind yourself that each of these life cycle attributes come from the bible and are therefore, absolutely true. Refuse to gloss over this. You need the highest return on your time and energy that you can get—refuse to spin-your-wheels anymore.

Make this count.

Consider well, the impact of your choices upon your life and the life of your loved ones, family and friends who love you and care about you, and, the influence of your life upon them. Deeply think about all the ways that your choices impact your life, both your past and present life, and your future life, considering these two contrasting lifecycles. Once again, *"You will be weaving these lifecycle attributes into your freedom strategy and life-action-plan"* if in fact, you are going to be successful.

The good news, is that the devil, his demons, and all his evil ways will not be able to stop you from acquiring this authentic, biblical freedom that Christ is revealing, and offering you, right now... Here's Jesus again reminding you of this powerful, and indisputable truth:

> ***John 10:10*** *(Jesus Speaking) The thief comes only in order to steal and kill and destroy. I came that they may have and enjoy life, and have it in abundance (to the full, till it overflows). (AMP)*

Godspeed to you now as you push back against every obstacle along that authentic, spiritual freedom journey you have with Jesus. ***Go & Make War...***

CHAPTER 7
OBEDIENCE THROUGH FAITH

PERSPECTIVE
Throughout the pages and chapters of this book I have endeavored to focus substantial and specific attention on the subject of spiritual freedom. The bible says this, about that: *"It is, and was, for FREEDOM, that Christ has set us free."* Therefore, after you reading six chapters of this book, I know, that you know, just how true these words penned in Galatians 5:1, by the Apostle Paul really are—however, there's more. Here's the rest of what Paul had to say in this scripture. *"Stand firm, then, and do not let yourselves be burdened again by a yoke of slavery."*

Chapter 1 starts out developing a chronicle designed to challenge every reader, especially those who are struggling with, or beginning to be influenced by, some kind of difficult life issue, or any consistent sin in their life. The opening paragraph is copied here, FYR:

"The first part of this challenge that you face is to consider, to focus your thinking, and then believe something different about yourself, about God, and how life works than what you have been believing."

That challenge is squarely focused at the condition of your faith...

In addition, throughout the pages and chapters of this book, I have assembled an essential and indispensable series of principles and axioms of truth, from scripture and other freedom related sources. Each of these have been selected to become integral offensive and defensive weapons of spiritual warfare, that will form your spiritual armory. Each of you will be needing these weapons as you pursue your new lifestyle of spiritual freedom. Here in chapter 7, we start pulling all this together...

I've written 3 chapters specifically focusing attention on your faith—*that begs a question...* why would I dedicate a full third of my book on this subject of faith? What's faith got to do with spiritual freedom? Here the answer: *It is your faith that works like a catalyst* to combine all of these axioms of truth into a formidable spiritual warfare juggernaut. ***The working faith that you acquire and maintain, will become that massive spiritual war steamroller you will be needing, to get this done.***

Jesus calls on every one of us to fulfill Hebrews 12:1, and the many other commands that he has documented throughout the bible. So, by now, you fully realize—you have obstacles to overcome...

However, conducting abundant research over the years, I have discovered that there are only a relatively small number of these obstacles that have a significant and prevailing influence on a Christian's pursuit of acquiring a lifestyle of spiritual freedom.

Perhaps the chief issue among them is obedience, or, the lack of it....

Most Christians logically equate and link their spiritual freedom with their ability and effectiveness to obey God and his word, at least at some level. How about you? Can you agree with that? For your reference here, I restate the following, to focus your attention:

> "Find out what God wants from you.... **and give it to him.**"

> "Find out what Spiritual Freedom will cost you, **and pay that price.**"

Remember those two from earlier chapters? Life and death – good and bad – right and wrong. Many directions to consider. Every time that you say yes to one of these life choices, you are saying no to all the other options you are considering. That makes **NO** a choice, and means **YES** is a responsibility. A distinction that really matters. Wouldn't you agree?

EVIDENCE OF A GODLY LIFE

Okay, we left the last chapter thinking about our behavior, and, how that behavior determines the quality of our life, for the most part. I began to detail some of the consequences of a destructive lifestyle and also a constructive lifestyle. We started unpacking the spiritual law of sowing and reaping, examining some of those consequences. Woven through most of these chapters, I've developed and documented, in a number of different ways, this very key, essential and strategic principle of truth:

> *Key #12* - *It is your actions and your behavior, put on consistent display over time, that truly produce and reveal the evidence of what you actually believe and highly value in your life.*

This key axiom holds true in your life substantially more than what your good intentions are, and what your hopes and dreams would look like.

This is where **obedience through faith** *comes in.*

Jesus said, *"You will know them by their fruits"* - By what they do and how they live. This chapter is all about what the evidence of a godly lifestyle should really look like. Assessing your current level of obedience—*what you are actually able to put into operation within your life right now*, compared to what you know for certain needs to be challenged, changed and developed deep within your heart, your soul, and your mind.

Therefore, I've assembled a sequence of these specific scriptural references, principles and precepts to help *"focus your faith"* more clearly and effectively. Focusing your faith will aid you in identifying and developing your freedom strategy and life action plan, as you move forward in this study. Jesus always focused his faith to accomplish the will of our Heavenly Father—especially when his faith and obedience were tested severely. *Check it out:*

Recall back in Chapter 6, I documented a beginning mandate recorded in Gen. 1:28 that God gave Adam and Eve, and by extension, to each of us, that we should all take dominion and subdue every living thing, including ourselves, and **especially our minds**. I'm paraphrasing here in context, and with specific regards to spiritual freedom, including numerous scripture references from all throughout the bible.

So, how effective was Jesus when he put this mandate into practice within his own life, during his incarnation here on Earth? *Let's take a look.*

Turns out that Jesus developed all-inclusive effectiveness in his life as he learned and perfected obedience through his faith, and perfectly obeyed this mandate—every time that he was tested. Through perfect obedience he displayed his tenacious attitude and exercised it often. Evidence? Yes indeed, abundant evidence. Look at this narrative from Matthew 4:

> **Matt. 4:1** *Then Jesus was led (guided) by the (Holy) Spirit into the wilderness (desert) to be tempted (tested and tried) by the devil. (AMP)*

This passage goes on to record Jesus being tempted and put to the test by the devil for 40 days and 40 nights to determine if he could be broken by yielding to some kind of sin. In each temptation that Satan hurled at him, Jesus refuted the devil putting his formidable attitude on display, declaring that **"IT IS WRITTEN."**

Remember back in Genesis 3:1 when the devil challenged and tested Eve with the statement, *Hath God said?* He tried that with Jesus in the desert and failed miserably every time. You can just picture Jesus getting in the devil's face with an attitude stating,

"Yes Satan, God hath said, and, **IT IS WRITTEN..!"**

The evidence from numerous passages of scripture inform us that Jesus developed, displayed and maintained a resolute attitude and used it again and again whenever his Father's will and his mission was being challenged. Take a good look at this one again:

> **Matt. 16:18** *(Jesus speaking) I will build my church, and the gates of Hades will not prevail against it. (NRSV)*

Jesus has a personal message here, that he wants you to hear, one more time; this same scripture reference from Matthew, paraphrased to read:

I will build you, and the gates of Hades will not prevail against you.

What do you think of that? Can you believe that Jesus is focusing this paraphrase right at you? Do you think that Jesus is vested with determination for your attitude to be like his? Have this same attitude in you that was also in Christ Jesus. What do you think—do you agree?

Perhaps the best, or one of the most applicable books of all that I researched on this subject of attitude was written by pioneering psychologist Angela Duckworth. That book she authored is entitled, *Grit*. [8]

Her extensive research in the clinical fields of behavior psychology and her subsequent hypothesis that what really drives achievement is not genius, talent or advanced education, but a special blend of passion and long-term perseverance. She coined the term, *"GRIT."* She also researched numerous men and women leaders within the business world, education, sports and related vocations and discovered the identical and dominant trait that identified their success was also a very focused, and determined, GRIT—way more than anything else that they could attribute to their success. Each of them were highly motivated—they were not going to be deterred in any way.

That's also the measure of Christ's attitude—but on steroids, at an exponentially higher level than any of us can ever attain. In that context, and more to the point, Jesus is determined to develop and build a similar attitude in you—the kind of grit that will fortify, and reinforce your faith. You ready for that? Will you cooperate? Will you follow him? Will you develop an attitude and sufficient faith to obey him more consistently?

---

[8] *"Grit"* - Publisher: Simon and Schuster; New York, 2016

That kind of grit is what the apostle Paul is documenting here in Heb. 12:1, that I refer to over and over again throughout this book. Here it is again:

> **Heb. 12:1** *Therefore, since we are surrounded by such a great cloud of witnesses, let us throw off everything that hinders and the sin that so easily entangles, and let us run with perseverance** the race marked out for us. (NIV)*
>
> ** *Dogged Determination*
>
> *Stubborn Endurance*
>
> **GRIT** - *"There's no quit in him"* - *"He refuses to buckle"*

Okay, I know you're all in to go after this. What's next? How do you put on display and apply your new found and developing attitude effectively? Here it is: You focus that dogged determination of yours to take on the Yoke of Christ, like I stated way back in the first chapter.

Once again, Jesus said it like this:

> **Matt. 11:29** *(Jesus speaking)* **Take my yoke upon you** *and learn from me, for I am gentle and humble in heart, and you will find rest for your souls. (NIV)*

Remember again what Jesus said in John 15, *"Apart from me, you can do nothing."* You need to be yoked to Christ like an ox is yoked to his master. Please don't misunderstand this statement. An ox is often referred to as a dumb animal. Jesus is not inferring this likeness to you and me at all. Far from it—the purpose of that yoke on the ox is to harness and focus all the power and might that the ox can bring to bear on whatever purpose the master wants accomplished. That yoke helps the ox focus his power and strength right where the master wants it to go...

And, most importantly, the yoke fitted to the ox is made of wood but the yoke of Christ for you and me is completely derived from our love of God, from our attitude, and how we choose to display it. And further, so it is with you, me and Jesus. You determine to take on his attitude and his yoke for the purpose of thinking more like him, acting more like him, and obeying him through your faith that he authors, strengthens and perfects in you. *Then, all you need is spiritual power.* And, you too shall receive that same spiritual power that enabled Jesus to defeat the devil in the desert. That same spiritual power you've been missing, after that the Holy Spirit has come upon you:

> **Acts 1:8** *But you shall receive* **power** *(ability, efficiency, and might) when the Holy Spirit has come upon you (AMP)*

Okay, your faith journey continues by increasing the unsearchable riches of your knowledge of Jesus. You continue learning his ways, that will more easily move your mind into a state of action, thereby enabling you to reliably, and consistently, acquire his attitude—at every opportunity. By doing that, you are made ready to exercise Gen. 1:28 to *take dominion and subdue your body, mind, soul, and spirit to display strength and take action* according to that knowledge you have acquired in him.

Got that... So, you take what kind of action—and, to do what?

How about this—especially for those of you seeking a new, or restored lifestyle of freedom—you exercise, take effective action, and fulfill the following scripture:

> **James 4:7** *Submit yourselves, then, to God. Resist the devil, and he will flee from you. (NIV)*

Okay, I Got it... So, how exactly do I accomplish that? What's next?

SPIRITUAL WARFARE – FORMIDABLE TACTICS
Whether you are just wanting to know Christ a little better, or, you want to stop *"riding the Yo-Yo"* as much as you do—or, you know if something significant and definite doesn't change within your heart and your mind,

you are headed for a crisis. Every Christian, seeking a lifestyle of freedom, is absolutely required to learn how to.....

Wage war against the principalities and powers of darkness and the spiritual forces of wickedness.

This is detailed in Ephesians 6:12. We are all born into this spiritual warfare that we have no control over—however, as born-again Christians, we absolutely have a choice to determine how we will respond to it.

So, this last scripture here, from James 4:7, is staring you right in the face. Take a good look at it again. We began unpacking this scripture in earlier chapters, and continue here with a slightly different perspective. James is revealing here, a *"fork-in-the-road"* challenge that every Christian must deal with, every time they are tempted to sin in some way. Especially that category of sin that is consistently debilitating our lives, either addicting us to it, or leading us in that direction. Always remember in context to this, what God spoke to Cain, way back in Genesis 4:7, *"sin is crouching at your door; it desires to have you, but **you must master it.**"* This is among the first, and very powerful tactics to think about using, as you wage war against that sin in your life.

> *Remember what God said to Cain...*
> ***because he is saying the same thing to you..!***

Cain chose not to exercise his responsibility before God and ended up murdering his brother Abel. A very costly choice indeed. God showed him the road to freedom, it was clearly in his grasp, but, he chose not to take it. Cain knew that he should submit himself to God and resist the sin that the devil wanted him to commit—especially since God himself warned Cain to repent and to master that sin of extreme anger that was hammering his soul. Fast forward a few thousand years and God inspired the Apostle James to write the spiritual prescription that Cain should have adopted and adhered to, right here in James 4:7. Here's what Cain would likely say if he could have been interviewed by Fox News, or CNN way back when:

CNN Reporter:
"Hey Cain, you failed big time—you allowed your anger to get completely out of control. Now, you have forfeited that freedom you should have been cherishing in your life, and, you cannot get it back. How does that make you feel?"

Cain:
"This really sucks... I completely failed to realize just how crappy I would feel if I murdered my brother Abel—especially knowing that I really did have the opportunity to prevent this from happening in the first place. Wow! What an exceedingly foolish, and incredibly destructive, and utterly stupid choice that I have made. I really regret it and wish I could go back and do it over again. However, I am now confronted with the fact that some choices and decisions simply cannot be reversed—so, yeah, I feel like crap."

Take a look at the following, related, case history I recently researched:
A very famous celebrity, who is a well-known singer & actor, had an incredible experience, similar to the biblical account of the Prodigal Son—it was like an epiphany for him... Truly, a come to Jesus moment. At the time, he was 38 years old and had just experienced an alcohol and drug binge, that he was on, for several days. He was busted—physically and mentally bewildered, wasted, and exhausted.

The Holy Spirit of God showed up and miraculously revealed where the path that he was on would lead him. Like the prodigal, he was brought to his senses as God revealed the truth to him, and the reality of how he was living, and what that could cost him. That's the first time anything like that ever happened to him and it totally changed the rest of his life. He was raised as a Christian, and this intervention of God brought a deep conviction upon him. God brought to his mind the lifestyles of a number of his friends and acquaintances, and what they experienced. A number of them had been living like him for years and they ended up dying at a very young age—and worse, they lost, or forfeited, their marriages, their work, their financial wealth and everything else that they valued in their life. They lost it all.

However, a few of them came to their senses, responded to God, repented of their destructive lifestyles and were prospering in their lives again. He said this after experiencing God in such a personal way:

"God literally scared the hell out of me."

He knew right then that he had to get right with the Lord or, some impending crisis was almost certain to come upon him—he said he could see it so clearly in his mind's eye, and knew that it was inevitable, unless he dealt with it right away. That supernatural intervention by Jesus literally, and immediately, changed his life and it has never been the same ever since. He repented of his sin, got plugged back into church and the Christian lifestyle, and he's been thriving ever since.

Here's the key thing—**he heeded Gods' warning**, he displayed strength, he took effective action, and that ended up setting him free. God warned him with two axioms of truth—two tactics of spiritual freedom that are firmly anchored in these words I wrote to begin chapter 3—Faith:

"BEFORE YOU CAN OBEY GOD – YOU HAVE TO BELIEVE GOD"

So, BELIEVE THIS...! The bible boldly declares that we shall know the truth and the truth will set us, and make us, free—it says so, right here:

> ***John 8:32** and you will know the truth, and the truth will make you free." (NRSV)*

Following here, are two tactics and strategic axioms of truth that God used to scare the hell out of this celebrity, and many others like him, that my research has led me to study, over many years. So, I encourage you to see these following two principles of truth as both a warning that God gives us, and also, an encouragement that he wants us to receive, that we are growing spiritually in the nurture and admonition of the Lord—increasing the unsearchable riches of our knowledge of Jesus. Doing that, I next encourage you to develop here, an accurate perspective about **the timing of your actions...**

Ask yourself this question: Am I ready to take immediate action right now, like this celebrity, or, am I thinking that God is only wanting me to add these two principles of truth to my spiritual warfare armory right now, as he continues to renew my mind—two choices; repent immediately, or wait upon the Lord for his perfect timing. Think this through, then take action.

One thing is certain—these two principles of truth, that I am parsing here, can enable you to rise up and produce sufficient spiritual grit, and effective faith, to overcome a pattern, or season, of consistent, debilitating sin. I strongly encourage you to load these into your brain and act decisively on them:

The first truth—a warning from God

1. My Keynote #10 declares this axiom of truth: *"Whenever you sin, you begin to die."* The death you begin to experience in your life, on every level, when you yield yourself to sin, is not generally immediate, but, the effects of that death experience do begin immediately upon committing that sin, and worsen over time until you repent. Refer to that list of immediate consequences I documented earlier in the last chapter.

2. It is the application, and the timing, of this particular truth that I bring to your attention. Every time that you yield yourself to this kind of sin, all of the 10+ consequences that I listed are activated and put into operation—you will be experiencing all of them, to some degree. You will be plundered, and that's a fact. These consequences are very harmful to you and your loved ones—*that's why God warns you.* He does not want you to experience any of them. He wants you to exercise wisdom and avoid them all.

3. Here's another key truth that God wants you to see – *These consequences do not reset back to zero every time*, when you are brought back to your senses and you repent. That's strictly up to God, by his grace. That's what is so insidious about them—they can continue to accumulate and keep getting worse the more that you consistently

yield to the nemesis of sin. While you are in the grip of it, the devil is actively at work plundering you—he will steal everything of value that you have and hold dear, and when he has completed ripping you off, he'll kill you. That's what he'll continue to do, until you determine to repent, call out to Jesus, and stop him.

4. In addition, and equally insidious, is the fact that you may not even be aware of this happening to you, to the degree that it is, especially when you are in the grip of a debilitating sin like this—you can't feel it, like you can when you hit your thumb with a hammer. It just doesn't work that way—it is spiritual. The usual control that you have over issues of life will absolutely diminish, and deteriorate, over time, and, you'll hardly be aware that it is happening to you. That's why you cannot effectively manage your sin for very long - **you are not in charge** - Jesus is.

5. That explains why so many alcoholics and drug addicts have to hit the bottom, losing almost everything that they value, before they begin to understand what is happening to them. It's a spiritual problem, and, our human nature simply lacks the attributes to fix it—we can be so easily deceived, unable to assess what is actually going on. Therefore, until you effectively come to your senses and repent, this will, almost certainly, just keep getting worse in your life.

The second truth—another warning from God

1. If you continue failing to heed these first warnings that the Holy Spirit of God will be revealing to you - at some point in time - you will absolutely experience what the home page of my website boldly declares, **"There is a CRISIS in the church."** That is as certain as the next sunrise—it is absolute—that's always where this kind of experience with besetting sin will lead anyone, and every one, who consistently yields themselves to it. It's just a matter of time before a crisis develops and comes upon you.

2. Here's another attribute of this truth that is absolute—*every crisis that a Christian will ever experience begins as a thought*—usually some kind of temptation. Over time, unless it is effectively dealt with, it will develop into a bad and harmful habit. The longer it is in operation, the more entrenched it becomes, and, the harder it is to overcome and get rid of.

3. However, the opposite of that principle is also true—*every avoidance of a crisis that a Christian will ever experience, also begins as a thought*. A thought leading to an effective freedom strategy and life-action-plan. I am purposely stating a plan here, because your new experience of authentic, biblical freedom does not begin as an event. It is a definite process, and, almost always involves a span of time, and, that time span is exclusively determined by God. He can, and sometimes does, deliver us miraculously in an instant of time. I've experienced him doing that, along with a multitude of other believers, throughout history. Therefore, whether Jesus determines to set you free in an instant of time, or, he puts you on a path of working out your salvation with fear and trembling, over a span of time—*your spiritual freedom is absolutely certain.*

It's just a matter of time—*his time, not yours.* He is sovereign, you are not. So, what do we conclude from these two axioms of truth? Here's my take on it— our part first, is to study and meditate on these two principles, until we truly believe them, and we stand ready to adopt them into our lifestyle. Almost half of this book is focused on this—on believing what God has said in his word. Therefore, I reiterate once again - *before you can Obey God, you have to Believe God.* That's why the bible declares these following axioms of truth so boldly:

> *Prov. 9:10 The reverent and worshipful fear of the Lord is the beginning (the chief and choice part) of Wisdom, and the knowledge of the Holy One is insight and understanding.." (AMP)*
>
> *Prov. 1:7 The fear of the LORD is the beginning of knowledge, but fools despise wisdom and discipline. (NIV)*

The wise Christian fears the Lord for the right reasons. He doesn't fear the Lords' reprisal, judgement, or wrath—the Gospel effectively removes that fear from the Christian. The wise Christian fears the Lord because he knows that what God has said will absolutely come to pass, apart from his grace—he knows Gods' word is absolutely, and irrevocably, true. That's exactly why Jesus – your Lord, Savior, and life coach mandates you to believe all that he has spoken. It's that fear of the Lord where godly wisdom, reverence, discipline, and resolve begin.

Therefore, receive these two tactical principles of truth with wisdom and reverence. Exercise godly control over the members of your body, including your mind, and refuse to act impulsively. Take your time and be careful that you don't get out over your skis, setting yourself up for failure. Let these two axioms of truth become an active part of your thoughts - meditate on them very often, until you own them, and they become a functional part of your identity in Christ. That's where you will find the path to spiritual freedom. What do you think...sound right to you?

SPIRITUAL WARFARE – LIFE IN THE FAST LANE
Sometimes life comes at you so fast that you quickly have to get yourself out of the way. When you are getting shot at, the best tactic might very well be to duck-and-run. That's what Cain wished he would have done when he began losing control of his anger. That's the spiritual warfare tactic that Joseph applied when Potiphar's wife attempted to get him to compromise his integrity—she tried to seduce him. Study Genesis 39 - Check out what he did:

> *Gen. 39:12 She caught him by his cloak and said, "Come to bed with me!" But **he left his cloak in her hand and ran out of the house.** (NIV)*

Turns out that Joseph was enabled by God - slowly, over time - to exercise that kind of spiritual warfare tactic—a kind of ***spiritual fire insurance.*** God enabled him to immediately flee and get himself out of there—he hardly had to even think about it. God had prepared and trained Joseph for this kind of response by instilling in him the spiritual gift and attribute of *self-control*—a very powerful spiritual warfare tactic that Joseph acquired, by investing a lot of his daily time, just getting to know God.

Over time, those formidable attributes of Gods' divine nature just began to rub off on Joseph—the more he got to know God, the better he liked God, and Joseph actually started going out-of-his-way to spend even more time in his presence. That was really smart. That was really wise.

None of us can simply acquire this kind of self-control over impulses, by an act of our will. I can tell you that this kind of spiritual warfare tactic is not an intrinsic attribute of our human nature at all, like it is Gods' divine nature. God, and God alone, is the supplier and purveyor of all these powerful spiritual warfare tactics—he makes them available exclusively to us, through Jesus. It is this lack of impulse-control that is at the forefront of so many hurtful choices, that believers are having to deal with just navigating ordinary life—this lack of impulse-control is almost always the first ***"trigger"*** that must be confronted and effectively overcome within the Christian lifestyle, as we pursue that elusive spiritual freedom for ourselves or loved ones.

Further, your response to whatever particular struggle in life—be it spiritual, medical, financial, or other that you may be facing, is always predicated on just how well you know and relate to God our Father, through Jesus—our Lord, Savior, best friend, and life coach. The more that you know him, the better equipped you will be to prevail over those life and freedom sucking bandits that come our way from time-to-time.

SPIRITUAL WARFARE – RENEWING AND PROGRAMMING OUR MINDS
There is a specific, and formidable, spiritual code that God has given to all believers, for the renewing of their minds. James 4:7 is one of them. God intends each of us to use this scripture, and many others, to program our sub-conscious minds, in a similar way that a computer engineer programs a line of software code into a computer application. Think of your mind, pragmatically speaking, in this way, as a *biological computer*. Jesus is the engineer who writes the code, and the Holy Spirit makes it actually come

alive within every Christian who chooses to believe that it is a valid word of God, thereby making it absolutely true.

This scripture is just a word on a page, until the Holy Spirit makes it miraculously come alive. The words in scripture are actually *"pregnant"* with spiritual power, and our faith is the switch, or the catalyst, that God can use to activate that spiritual power he has embedded within his word. Our faith in his word is used by the Holy Spirit to transform the passive, stored, spiritual energy he has embedded within his word, into active, kinetic, spiritual energy & power, made alive by him and put into operation, to carry out his purpose for it, within our life. He *"breathes life"* into his word, making it come alive and perform his perfect will.

James is revealing here in this scripture a very profound and powerful clue from God designed to challenge and to change our usual, and almost always impulsive, response to temptation. First, James 4:7 begins with a choice that we all have available; *Submit yourself to God...* Let's see what that really means—think and reason your way through this.

You apply your knowledge of Jesus – **what would he do** – you acquire his attitude – **how would he think** – then **you take dominion and subdue your mind.**

That is literally what it means to submit yourself – <u>before</u> – you submit to God. You instruct your mind, that you are going to do what Jesus did in the Garden of Gethsemane—you determine Gods' will to be done, above your own—just like Jesus did. You have first of all, humbled yourself and then, having done that, you go ahead and take that following action and submit yourself to God.

> Let's take a detailed look at **"submitting to God"**...
> It's a military term meaning—**your war with God is over...**
> you agree to stop fighting him, **you lay down all your weapons...**
> and **you actually surrender to him.**

However, this is different...this is spiritual warfare, and, there's some really good news—*check it out:*

Because Jesus wins, he makes you the winner also, and not the loser—Jesus gets a victory, and so do you. In warfare fought here on Earth, when you surrender, you get pummelled—you get hammered—you get locked up—you lose your freedom...

However, in spiritual warfare, when you surrender yourself to God, you win—you get the victory—you actually gain your freedom—you seriously rejoice—because you experience the unique, *life-giving-freedom* through obedience, that only comes from Jesus. You put a huge smile on his face... This is his *Win—Win* reward that he bestows upon you.

This is how you get it... **You deliberately choose to humble yourself and surrender your will to Jesus** by first, denying yourself, and then, to take his yoke upon yourself, instead of yours—choosing to follow him, instead of following your own understanding like you usually do. That's the challenge, isn't it? That very specific choice is known as *where-the-rubber-meets-the-road from James 4:7*. So, are you, at this point in your life—in this study, willing to do that?

Further, it answers and determines your response to Key #12 documented earlier; What have you conditioned & programmed your mind to believe in more, and, what do you really value more—following your own understanding, or, following the commands of Christ?

Very simple, very profound, and absolutely true—it actually defines the first action God is wanting you, and directing you, to take. That literally means that you must first put yourself under sufficient control, and then next, you submit yourself to God - **before** - you can even have the remotest hope or chance of effectively resisting the devil. If all you bring into this fight with the devil is your will and your intellect, you are doomed to failure. That's exactly why Jesus said these famous words in John chapter 15: **"Apart from me you can do nothing."**

So, I encourage you here to pause, and to think your way through this process, to harness your mind, putting it under control, so that you are even able then, to submit yourself to God. It is clearly a paradox—you surrender yourself, but, you don't lose... You actually win. You acquire, or, you maintain, the spiritual freedom that Christ has provided for you. Take your time here—this is a two-step process. Refuse to rush it—you really need to own this.

Okay, you've submitted yourself to God. The next step of James 4:7 directs you to *"resist the devil."* Pay close attention here—like I just said before, don't ever try to resist the devil - **before** - you have effectively taken dominion over your own mind and then submitted yourself to God. The devil will crush you every time you try that. No man can effectively resist the devil without the spiritual power of God being applied.

Christians struggling with besetting sin(s) and various addictions often get this scripture out of sequence. Many believers get it backwards. I documented something similar in the last chapter. Instead of first submitting themselves to God, they end up first submitting themselves to the devil, thereby yielding themselves to sin, and that causes them to actively resist God. Remember that destructive lifestyle issue? Another paradox! And, we end up fleeing from God, because he has no fellowship with the presence of sin.

God promises to never leave you, nor forsake you, but your sin will separate you from fellowship with him, every time. So, be on the alert for these **"triggers"** showing up in your life.

It often begins something like this:

For an alcoholic, it could be hearing the sound of ice cubes tumbling into a glass, or a cold beer commercial on TV... A drug addict could be experiencing the welling up of stress, thinking about what a wonderful relief a joint, or a hit from some other drug would be right about now... Or, someone just lusting after a piece of lemon cream pie to temporarily satisfy that excessive, abusive hunger craving... Or, it could also be another form of lust with some bewildered Christian being tempted by an old pattern or series of immoral, angry or thoughts of getting even—of getting vengeance over someone.

It can even get much worse, with thoughts leading to a strong compulsion, yielding to another session of viewing pornography, committing adultery, or some other form of sexual immorality. The list goes on and on—many, if not most of these besetting sins, that can easily lead a Christian to addiction and bondage, if not corrected, fall under the category documented here, from the Amplified Bible:

> *2 Tim. 3:4...They will be lovers of sensual pleasures and vain amusements more than, and rather than, lovers of God. (AMP)*

For some of you, this really stings doesn't it?

Many of us have been there at various times in our life. At the time that any of these temptations or compulsions start, the wise Christian will remember God's conversation with Cain - **"sin is crouching at your door; it desires to have you, but you must master it."** What a paradox indeed! A paradox, but, not a surprise to God. Way back in Genesis 3:8, the Lord God was walking in the garden of Eden and called out to Adam, saying, *"where are you?"* And, as Paul Harvey was so famous for saying, *"you know the rest of the story."*

God knew the rest of the story as well, that sin would separate him from the creation that he loved so much. Further, God knew that there would be seasons of life where his people, down through the ages, would continue choosing to experience being *"lovers of pleasure more than being lovers of God."* Being so easily enticed to sin. So, what did the Lord God do about that paradox? And, *"you know the rest of that story"* as well... He sent Jesus to fix the sin problem, filling him with a ferocious resolve, and an unassailable attitude, and the rest is history! And, what did Jesus do? Here it is again, boldly declared in Galatians 5:1, **"It was, and is, for FREEDOM that Christ has set us FREE."** And further, Jesus mandates every believer of his, to have that same kind of attitude.

Always remember, God is saying that exact same thing to you and me today, every time any of us are tempted to sin, that he said to Cain—God hasn't changed, and the nature of sin has not changed either, in all these thousands of years since the time of Cain. Whatever the expression of consistent sin that is hammering your life may be, it is no different than the sin of uncontrolled anger that was hammering Cain's life.

That rampant anger dominating Cain ended up costing him a life of freedom *that could have been,* had he only learned how to control it. So, how about you? I know these are some hard words to hear for some of you, however, I also encourage you with the following axiom of God and his grace:

> *Sin cannot take you where the mercy, grace and loving kindness of God cannot find you, rescue you, deliver you, and then heal and restore you to a fulfilling, abundant life of purpose and well-being – You simply cannot out-sin the Grace of God.*

This axiom is absolutely true and valid for you, even though it's also true that your adversary, the devil, is prowling about seeking to plunder, destroy and even to kill you if he can *(John 10:10-1Pet. 5:8).*

However, God also has a lot to say about that, throughout the entire bible:

Something like this:

> *"If you truly desire a lifestyle of spiritual freedom, and put the Gospel of Jesus into effective operation within your life, the devil and all of his demons will not be able to stop you from acquiring that desire of your heart."*

SPIRITUAL WARFARE – PRINCIPLED TACTICS

A few passing thoughts for you to ponder about the need for every Christian to take dominion over and subdue their mind; and, to do this in a way that maximizes their potential and opportunities to experience that abundant lifestyle of freedom that Jesus has made possible to all of us in his Gospel. Check out the following eloquent words:

Our nations' famous WWII General, Douglas MacArthur, as Supreme Allied Commander in Japan, put this life revealing poem from Samuel Ullman, simply entitled, **"Youth"** on his office wall. I paraphrase a part of it here that is exceptionally appropriate to the context of this chapter:

*"**Youth** is not so much a time of life; as it is a state of mind; it is a matter of the will, a quality of the imagination, a vigor of the emotions; it is the freshness of the deep springs of life that spring up from the heart.*

***Youth** means a temperamental predominance of courage over timidity of the appetite, for adventure over the love of ease. This often exists in a man of sixty more than a boy of twenty. Nobody grows old merely by a number of years. We grow old by deserting our ideals.*

***Years** may wrinkle the skin, but to give up enthusiasm wrinkles the soul. Worry, fear, self-distrust bows the heart and turns the spirit back to dust. Whether sixty or sixteen, there is in every human being's heart the lure of wonder, the unfailing child-like appetite of what's next, and the joy of the game of living."*
Samuel Ullman; 1840 - 1924

Obedience through faith, and mastery over sin, will require you to be both impatient and patient, at the same time. The impatience of allowing yourself to waste precious time and delay beneficial action that you could otherwise put-on display immediately.

And, the patience and wisdom to delay immediate gratification, waiting instead for your good works to accumulate, and then trusting God, your new comfort-zone and your new life action plan to get you there.

Over time, your habits become deep-seated. Your belief system, core values and comfort-zone harden. It's easy to get comfortable. The longer you wait, the more deeply embedded you get in your current lifestyle. You line up with that? So, I remind you of what I have written:

Complacency is a fierce enemy...

So, in the God's eye view of your life, and as I wrote in chapter 1 of this book, it is not very meaningful just how successful or unsuccessful you are right at this particular moment. Whether the habits within your current comfort-zone are putting you on the path toward success, is far more important and instructive. Therefore, **your current trajectory in life matters substantially more than what your current results may reveal.**

Begs the question: Where are your current habits likely to lead you through this next month, next year, next decade?

Do you need to make some changes? What do you think?

We all develop some kind of a routine we call our comfort-zone that I talk about a lot in this book. We all can tell when we are functioning at our best throughout the day.

That's the time span when your brain is functioning really well at peak performance. Rarely does that time span exceed somewhere between 1 and 3 hours for most of us. So, an essential question for you to ask yourself is: *Who is currently getting that peak-performance time from you?* The best time from your brain every day—who or what currently gets that?

Who or what are you giving it to? *Jesus…? Weed…? A six pack?*

Remember these words…? You get the picture.

A lifestyle is not an outcome, it is a dynamic, living process. For this reason, all of your energy should go into building godly habits, that can supercharge your comfort-zone—not making better goals or chasing better results. So, to paraphrase many axioms in the bible—Don't just sit there, **DO SOMETHING!**

New goals do not deliver optimum results.

New lifestyles do.

The determined commitment you make to God and yourself, that you will tenaciously maintain the pursuit of increasing your knowledge of Jesus, and the consistent fellowship with his Holy Spirit, will almost certainly end up being the most rewarding habit that you will ever form and put into operation within your lifetime...

And, with the success of that habit, will come that elusive obedience to you, through faith—that's the hallmark of your upward calling in Christ.

That's where you will soar on wings like an eagle..!

CHAPTER 8
FREEDOM TACTICS

SPIRITUAL WARFARE – ADVANCED TACTICS

Your initial tactics of fighting this spiritual war begins by bringing your own mind under control—taking dominion over it, and then subduing it, to put you into conformance with God's word. That's the safe place for you to be. You first prepare and renew your mind, just getting it ready to effectively submit to God. Then, when you believe that you're ready, you begin doing that with all of your heart. You humble yourself, submit your mind, your will, and all that you are, to God and his will, his word, and his plan for your life. **Take on that Yoke of Christ!**

Remember, from last chapter, to do all of that, just preparing yourself, - way before - you develop your plan to resist the devil. Here's another one of my strategic keys to help you remember that, and to put it into perspective as a functional part of your new comfort-zone.

> *Key #13 - To master consistent, besetting sin in your life, it is better and much more effective to **turn on the light** rather than, or certainly before, you fight the darkness. **Actively pursue knowing and obeying Jesus** and the unsearchable richness of his fellowship. Do that, way sooner, and way more, than actively resisting the devil, by trying to manage and control your own sin. Do that effectively, and the darkness of that habitual sin will begin to diminish and fall away.*

Okay, earlier in this program, and throughout both of my books, I document a teaching technique that Jesus used a lot when he spoke. *Stories and parables*—he would often relate stories and parables to his disciples making it much more effective for them to remember, and then to easily recall, what Jesus was teaching them. Jesus did this very deliberately because he knew that telling a story about something would more effectively engage the disciple's imagination. I wrote about this, in an earlier chapter, documenting that age-old idiom that says, *"A picture is worth a thousand words."* Remember that?

Let's take another run at it – *More detail from a different perspective...*

Remember the pendulum image from chapter 3? What do you think of when you recall seeing the image of that pendulum in your mind's eye? Something about the ability of your sub-conscious mind to think really good and beneficial thoughts in one direction of the pendulum, leading to life, then swing all the way opposite and think of selfish and evil thoughts that can lead to death. Sound about right to you? I encourage you to go back and refresh your memory of that principle of truth I identified with the mental image of that swinging pendulum, if you need to. Further, let's add some more detail here to make the image in your mind's eye even more effective for your life. *Looks like this:*

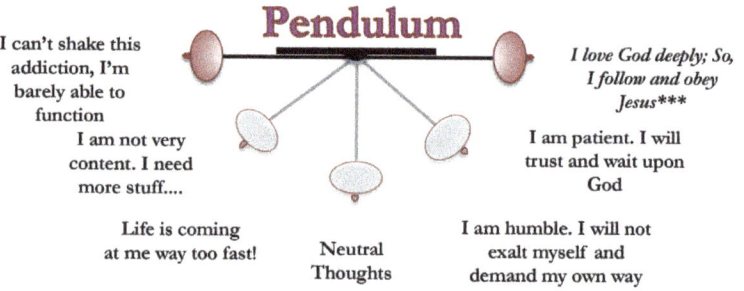

***–*This is where you want your mind to go...*

Notice once again the contrasting choices that lead to life on one side of the swinging pendulum, and death on the other. Contrasting choices—remember that? Let's take another look at that verse from the book of Matthew we documented earlier:

> **Matt. 7:13-14** *(Jesus Speaking)* "Enter through the narrow gate; for the gate is wide and the road is easy that leads to destruction, and there are many who take it.

> For **the gate is narrow and the road is hard that leads to life**, and there are few who find it. (NIV)

Life and Death—God used Moses to start all this by simply declaring this contrasting choice, back in Deut. 30:19, to the young nation of Israel, encouraging each of them to Choose Life. Jesus adds more detail to this same contrasting choice here in Matthew 7—he adds a road, or a series of roads, to be thought of as pathways leading to life:

> **Acts 2:28** You have made known to me the paths of life; you will fill me with joy in your presence. (NIV)

So, whenever you are tempted a little bit, or even vigorously compelled to commit a sin, especially a premeditated, besetting sin that you are clearly struggling to overcome—whenever those first thoughts hit you, do this:

Immediately, ***STOP and THINK—DON'T ACT - NOT YET...***

Instead, let's take the advanced tactic of using vision to reprogram and renew your mind, to a significant higher level of effectiveness—start by counting the cost of your action, knowing that the wages of sin will be paid to you in some form or another if and when you yield yourself and commit that sin. Do this... ***STOP*** - then ***THINK*** - the following thought:

If I yield myself to this sin, that I really, and strongly, desire to commit right now, I will be doing the exact and the extreme opposite of what I really should be doing. (Rom. 7:15-23)

Instead of **humbling myself**, I will actually be **exalting myself**, and thereby opening myself up to experience significant risk, trouble and distress—so, don't let yourself go there...Refuse to change lanes...

Perhaps another image, with more detail, will illuminate what God is clearly wanting you to know from Matthew 7:13-14, as you consider taking another ride on the Yo-Yo. *Check this out:*

Two Gates

Wide

I'm addicted...... Life sucks.

I am selfish...

Life is coming at me way too fast...!

Death

If I open and go through this wide gate, I will end up being like a bull with a ring in his nose. I will be led down the path of death for another visit with the grim reaper. I will forfeit the usual control of my life and I will become a slave to that sin...
(Rom. 6:16)

Narrow

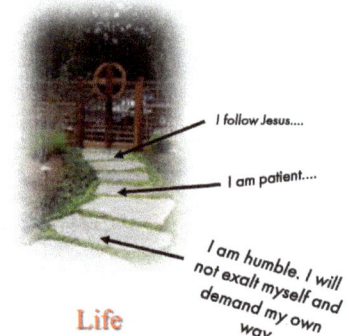

I follow Jesus....

I am patient....

I am humble. I will not exalt myself and demand my own way

Life

If I open and go through this narrow gate, life will be full, abundant and good. I will be choosing to love and follow Christ as he fulfills his word in my life to set me free and keep me free. I will become a slave to righteousness in him...I
(Rom. 6:18)

I also encourage you right here to load the previous image of the swinging pendulum into your mind and ponder the message it reveals to you. Your brain is certainly capable of leading you in either direction, for good, or for evil. So, don't let your brain go numb here. It is truly your choice—the ball is in your court. This represents that **Fork-in-the-Road** challenge I write about so often throughout this program.

Every time that foreboding temptation comes your way, you would do well to remind yourself that you are running in a very competitive race, and, that you are actually competing with, and against, **Your Old-Self.** Hebrews 12:1. Remember what it says?

That **nemesis** *that you often face is the wickedness within your own heart.*

Well, what do you think? Is the Holy Spirit getting through to you? Made up your mind yet? When you get to that fork-in-the-road, Jesus is standing tall, right there in the middle of that fork—right between those gates. He stands between those two gates, clearly pointing out to you, which path to take. Which gate to open and go through. He is not willing to see you fail. He makes intercession for you. And, God has provided the following strategic scripture as a spiritual prescription to all of that so, load this deep into your brain...

A virtual synopsis of - **what to do and how to handle** - every temptation. Here again, is this prescription of his, for your spiritual path of life:

> *2 Chr. 7:14 If my people, who are called by my name, will humble themselves and pray and seek my face and turn from their wicked ways, then will I hear from heaven and will forgive their sin and will heal their land. (NIV)*

Therefore, Jesus implores you now to go ahead and weaponize your humility, and make it operational. Put it on display. Refuse to believe and resign yourself that you cannot prevail over this sin that has kicked you're butt so many times. Stop believing that lie. God said this about that: *"For lack of vision my people perish."*

So, like the old adage said: **don't just stand there, do something...!**

Do this - Activate and use your imagination, your mind's eye, to visualize those two gates from Matthew 7. The wide one and the narrow one. Next, look at those two pathways leading up to each of those two gates. Further, ponder the phrases from both sides as you walk the path toward each gate. Take it all in... *Got it?*

Okay, now contemplate and think the issue through, while you are still on the path, prior to arriving at those two gates. Count the cost - **before** - you get there and end up making a foolish and stupid choice to yield yourself to that besetting sin, and suffer the consequences. Instead, apply the grace and wisdom that Christ gives you to consider what will, or certainly could, happen to you - **after** - you make that choice and yield yourself to that sin.

Count the Cost! Once you open the wide gate especially, yielding yourself to that sin, you'll be taking a ride on the Yo-Yo again. Life for you will suck...

This is a really good time for you to do something that you'd never do intentionally—this is where you **procrastinate – on purpose.** You need to war against seeking after that immediate-gratification that is a result of allowing yourself to get out of control and become double-minded. Remember that the bible declares a double minded man to be unstable in all his ways *(Jam. 1:8)*. Don't go there. Stay in your lane. Capture those bad thoughts—replace them with good thoughts. You can do this!

So, I say again, procrastinate and delay that attitude from coming upon you. That is not the attitude you want to acquire. Instead, do this—*acquire his attitude:*

When you acquire the attitude of Christ effectively, this is what happens:

> *2 Cor. 10:5 We demolish arguments and every pretension that sets itself up against the knowledge of God.....and we take captive every thought to make it obedient to Christ. (NIV)*

Jesus is revealing here, in a very wonderful and even merciful way, that he has already exposed what can, or will, happen to you, if you choose to go through the wrong gate and jump on the Yo-Yo. He has clearly exposed what you will reap, BEFORE you make that choice. Remember, *being forewarned is being forearmed.*

So, as you consider which path to take, and why you would take it, and which gate to open, you can actually ***preview*** what is likely to happen, or, what could happen, for good or not-so-good, depending upon which gate you choose to go through. Be deliberate—***use these tactics.***

Weaponized Tactics - Always beginning with humility and thinking just like Jesus, you take on his attitude. Copied here from chapter 3, take another look:

Attitude of Jesus - Learn from him. Specifically, learn how to *"weaponize"* your humility, patience, contentment, perseverance and your faithfulness, resulting in you becoming less selfish than you are now.

There is an old American adage that was taught to me years ago that serves as an apt example of putting this truth into action; putting your attitude on display; goes like this:

> *There is only one reason that organized crime networks do not easily operate within the FBI main headquarters in America... That reason.......*
>
> *The FBI leadership -* **WILL NOT LET THEM...!!!**

The very same thing holds true regarding you letting the devil and / or wicked thoughts operate within your own mind. Jesus absolutely never allowed this in his mind—nor should you.

Develop therefore, that same mind set and attitude. Determine to no longer allow evil that kind of access... *Take Dominion... Subdue Your Brain... Put your attitude on display!*

PARABLE OF THE STOLEN CAR
How about this—another related example from normal, everyday life that I have named, *The Parable of the Stolen Car.* Imagine yourself at rest in your home and you notice a car thief trying to get into and steal your car parked outside. What would you do?

The difference in your response to the devil sending a thief to steal your car, compared to the devil personally stealing some of your spiritual faith, joy, and effectiveness, has everything to do with **how and where you place your values in life.** What do you value and why? Ever think about that? I'll come back to this parable of the stolen car in a few pages, but first, let's look at your values a little more.

The bible is replete with examples of how and where to place your values—of what should be highly valuable and precious to you—of those things in your life that you would definitely CHOOSE TO FIGHT FOR.

The most precious and valuable gift that you can receive from God, or anybody else for that matter, by far, by leaps and bounds, is the unsearchable riches of the knowledge of Jesus—and also, how you put that knowledge into effective action within your life. It's documented throughout the bible and this FRP. *That knowledge of Jesus becomes the **compass** of your very life—it is the fertilizer of your faith.*

So, I encourage each of you to do some more critical-thinking about this, and apply sufficient logic and reason to place a value upon your desire to acquire a constructive, abundant, and higher performance, higher fulfillment, lifestyle. What really matters is to establish how personally valuable you believe it will be, if and when you actually do acquire, and begin to experience, living out this abundant, constructive, and high-performance, kind of lifestyle. **Put a value on it.** Take some action—Inform your mind...What would this really mean to you? How valuable is it, especially compared to other life goals you may have? Think this through—how bad do you really want this?

This process of taking the time to accurately assess and evaluate your thoughts, feelings, and values about acquiring this kind of very desirable lifestyle for yourself, if done correctly, will assist you mightily to develop and establish that **effective attitude**—which you must consider to be absolutely essential, and not optional.

You know by now that this attitude is not acquired as a one-time event... No, no... you will find yourself seeking to acquire, and then maintain, this attitude of Christ, often times on a daily basis—sometimes over & over. You'll need to invest a lot of time getting to know Jesus and relating to him—and, you'll need to know the reason why, because it is going to cost you something. This endeavor is not always easy, and, in fact, sometimes very elusive and difficult to attain. Some days you will roar...! Other days you will strike out and fail miserably—*but, you'll get up again...*

However, as you learn to effectively acquire and put this attitude of Christ in operation within your life, you will increasingly come to value it very highly. At some point, if you do this effectively, it can exceed the value of every other experience you hold dear in your life.

This acquired attitude is one of the unsearchable riches you will come to value and cherish as your knowledge of Jesus increases. When done correctly, **you will indeed FIGHT to maintain this attitude** and you will resist the devil every time he comes to try and take it away from you. In addition, the riches that come to you through the increased knowledge of Jesus are acquired not by sight, touch or feel, but only by faith. So, you will not "see" the devil when he comes to steal your faith or other spiritual gift that God has given you, like you see a thief stealing your car, but you can learn to become incredibly sensitive and aware within your spirit, *whenever the devil comes prowling around,* ***seeking to devour you.*** *(1 Pet. 5:8).*

Therefore, as you learn to grow into and experience your physical life, you learn to acquire and place a value upon, all of the things you want and need to support your lifestyle, right? You navigate your life by your human senses. If you see someone trying to get into and steal your car, you will be highly motivated to respond, probably in immediate fashion, to stop that thief from stealing your car. However, and mark this well—*your response will be directly contingent upon the value* you have placed on that car.

If it doesn't mean much to you... if you place little value on it... then, most likely, you may not try to stop the thief from stealing it; especially, if you think the thief might just punch you out! On the other hand, if you place a significant and high value on it, you may even risk your life resisting, opposing and trying to stop the thief from stealing what belongs to you. You will take dominion over, and you will subdue that sucker, or try to...! *Isn't that right..? What do you think?*

In contrast, but also somewhat similar, as you learn to grow into and experience your spiritual life, you will also learn to acquire and place a value upon, all of the things you want and need to support your spiritual lifestyle.

You navigate your spiritual life at times, by your human senses, but mostly by your faith in Jesus, by your prayer life, which in turn is also contingent upon your knowledge of him. If you sense an impending spiritual warfare threat or attack, you will be highly motivated to respond also, but in direct proportion to the sensitivity and relative strength of your faith.

You may not feel or see, or even be physically aware that some spiritual event may be coming your way, but when your faith is sufficiently strong, you will connect with God and know what to do—you'll know how to respond. Jesus will make sure of that—He always has your back. He is always faithful to you, even when you are not to him. In fact, the bible documents that—*His faithfulness will be your shield and rampart so that you will not fear (Ps. 91:4).*

With that spiritual sensitivity in mind, you might wake up some morning and sense that you just do not "feel" like spending time with God in prayer and devotion, or you find yourself becoming "easily bothered or even angered" by something that would normally not affect you very much, or you experience other similar outlooks—*don't blow this off—pay attention.*

When something along those lines happen, then, you need to consider that those feelings and bad attitudes **may not be coincidental at all, but may very well be the devil intentionally at work trying to steal some good gifts that God intends for you to have and use.** Good gifts from God, like peace, joy and a well-ordered mind that he intends for you to put into operation that day or week to make your life more effective and rewarding.

Good gifts, like progressing in your efforts to acquire that attitude that is in Christ Jesus, thereby providing you power to overcome these spiritual warfare attacks that you cannot obtain anywhere else. Check this scripture out:

> ***1 Pet. 5:8*** *Be serious! Be alert! Your adversary the Devil is prowling around like a roaring lion, looking for anyone he can devour. (HCSB)*

HE'S LOOKING FOR YOU...!!!

Remember that one? Further, as you grow and mature spiritually, what you learn to value becomes more distant from your human senses and much closer to your spiritual faith in God through Christ. The bible states that even your good name, your reputation, the integrity of your moral character is to be **valued much higher** than things you acquire in your physical life, even precious possessions like silver and gold—*here it is again, FYR.*

> **Prov. 22:1** *A good name is more desirable than great riches; to be esteemed is better than silver or gold. (NASB)*

Okay, I trust that by now a fairly clear mandate is being developed within each of you studying this program, to focus your attention on what has been documented in these last few and forthcoming pages—even if you have lost a myriad of spiritual battles in the past resulting in the significant hammering of your faith, esteem, or even dignity, in addition to losing financial assets like income, savings, your house, your car, etc. **Be encouraged**...The bible tells us that God is able to *"Make-Up what the Locust has eaten."*

Check this scripture out:

> **Joel 2:25-26** *And I will restore or replace for you the years that the locust has eaten... And you shall eat in plenty and be satisfied and praise the name of the Lord, your God, who has dealt wondrously with you. (AMP)*

So, don't let yourself think that your case is just too bleak—that God can never make up what you had before; that life can never be the same—REFUSE TO THINK LIKE THAT. It just isn't true - Here's the truth: God really is able, and God can fulfill this scripture in you! He does it all the time. *Just give him something to work with—get this thing started.* Take that next step to change. Just decide, and then commit, and then, DO IT...! Seek Jesus with a newly applied diligence and ask him to restore or replace the tenacious zeal and motivation that you may have had before, and that you certainly need right now.

SPIRITUAL WEAPONS - BE SINCERE - BE AUTHENTIC

Further, with some of you reading this book who know Jesus to a certain extent and have walked with him for a longer period of time, my research involving many case histories reveal a very profound confirmation of some words that Jesus spoke from the book of Revelation. Jesus is not talking about, or looking for lip-service here—no, *he is wanting to see some evidence from you.*

And, like the prodigal son, Jesus and your heavenly Father are tenderly calling out to you, saying, *"Come home my son, my daughter... I really miss you..."*

> *Rev. 2:4-5 "Yet I hold this against you: You have forsaken your first love. Remember the height from which you have fallen!* **Repent and do the things you did at first."** *(NIV)*

Simple, true and very profound... For some of you, these few paragraphs, and this scripture spoken by Jesus himself, is really ALL YOU NEED TO HEAR. You know very well, deep down in your soul, the Holy Spirit of God is speaking to you—beckoning you to just come home. Therefore, today if you indeed hear his voice, refuse to harden your heart and do pay heed and follow after what he is saying to you.

Jesus is calling you back to renew that first time you fell in love with him. He wants that love from you kindled again but, in the form of sincere, authentic evidence, beginning with a changed heart that you seek from him with a newfound diligence and sincere desire. For many of you who are experiencing a besetting sin of some kind, you have hardened your heart and caused your first love of Jesus to grow cold and ineffective. You've just stopped caring so much about life, like you used to. You know so very well if that has happened to you, and is true in your life... and, so does Jesus—he knows.

The remedy is just as simple, true and profound as it always has been: **Humble yourself and repent** and begin doing the things with Jesus that you did at first... demonstrating your love of God through your relationship with Jesus.

Do those things again faithfully, with diligence, and God will also show up again faithfully to reward you—pressed down, shaken together, running over, with more than you can think, ask or imagine...

He will pour out a blessing that you can hardly contain. That's what his law of giving in the bible records: Give, and it will be given to you. *"A good measure, pressed down, shaken together and running over, will be poured into your lap."* *(Luke 6:38-NIV)*. In this case meaning that you give the best of your life, and your love to Jesus, as often as you can, at every opportunity.

SPIRITUAL WEAPONS - NEVER, EVER GIVE UP
I have been made aware of many, many people, over the years that I have been researching for this FRP, both inside and outside of the Church, who have experienced what they consider to be an absolutely devastating, and even un-recoverable, sense of ever being able to attain an authentic lifestyle of freedom. Some think it now to be impossible for them. They have literally tried and failed miserably so many times. That specific inspiration they need to gather themselves up and prepare their minds for action again, even just one more time, seems so far out of reach for them.

So, refuse to let that happen to you. Refuse to despair... *Let these words encourage you:*

> ***Prov. 24:16*** *for though a righteous man falls seven times,* he rises again... (NIV)*

> * *Take note that Jesus didn't say he only falls once or twice,* ***he said 7 times***—*he knows all of our weaknesses and anticipates every fall we make.*

> ***Luke 18:1*** *Then Jesus told his disciples a parable to show them that they should always pray and* ***not give up****. (NIV)*
>
> ***Gal. 6:9*** *Let us not become weary in doing good, for at the proper time we will reap a harvest if we* ***do not give up****. (NIV)*

Rather, let God, by his Holy Spirit encourage you through these scriptures. They are the Word of God; therefore, they are absolutely and empirically true for every Christian, but especially now for you, at your point of need. Further, consider, study, believe and adopt for yourself the following axiom of truth also from God's word to be applied directly to you and all of your current circumstances:

> **Phil. 1:6** *And I am convinced and sure of this very thing, that He who began a good work in you will continue until the day of Jesus Christ (right up to the time of His return), developing (that good work) and* **perfecting and bringing it to full completion in you.** *(AMP)*

No matter what your circumstance, no matter how many years, or even decades you have been afflicted and held fast in bondage to this sin; NO MATTER WHAT... God has not given up on you and definitely does not want you to give up on yourself, on him or his word. He has made a way for you. He really has—*It's out there for you to grab...*

Therefore, settle this in your mind and commit or re-commit to acquiring the faith you need to give this freedom thing another shot... But this time, a different shot, a more viable and even a certain shot. **YOU CAN DO THIS...**

Okay, remember the **Parable of the Stolen Car?** Think and respond in like manner as if someone is trying to steal your highly valuable car. Your Mercedes, your Corvette, your whatever. You know if that was happening, you would go out and try to stop that thief with everything you have. You would DISPLAY STRENGTH... you would TAKE ACTION... because that is what the people who know their God are taught and trained to do by the Holy Spirit, as he shows you how to *"Overcome the World" (John 4:4)* by making you *"More Than A Conqueror" (Rom. 8:37)* through him who loves you.

Truth is, for many of you at this point, it's relatively easy for the devil to steal away your zeal for God, and to dull your faith. He has his boot on your neck! So, a strategic and formidable key to winning this spiritual warfare battle is to be objective and more pragmatic in your thinking and assessment.

When you first become aware that your desire for God, and those things in your life that you highly value become weak, don't go there. Refuse to accept your identity as being a victim—that's not your identity so, reject it and do not let it get attached to you, in any way. That's what the devil wants you to believe about yourself, but, that is an absolute lie for any Christian. You are definitely not a victim! Your identity is in Christ, you belong to him, and, he will complete this good work that he has begun within you.

Jesus is making you to be - **More than a Conqueror in Him.**

May not feel like it right now, but, nonetheless, **it is absolutely true.**

So then, simply do what I encouraged you to do just a couple of pages ago—pray and ask God to restore and replace that desire and zeal that has been ripped off, and take that very same action each and every time you become aware that your faith is not sufficient. CHALLENGE IT—doesn't really matter what caused you to experience a loss like that. Just **display strength and take action and get it back.** This give and take struggle is a part of spiritual warfare, and it can occur at any time, several times a week or even several times a day.

The devil is very motivated to keep his boot on your neck, to keep you from being effective in God's kingdom and he will keep trying to steal every good gift that God has given you, especially your desire to know, follow and obey Jesus. But, at some point in this struggle, the following situation will begin to happen:

> ***James 4:7-8*** *Submit yourselves, then, to God. Resist the devil, and he will flee from you. Come near to God and he will come near to you. (NIV)*

Your desire to draw closer to God, like the strength of your faith, is closely linked to the condition of your heart. When God sees that you are sincerely inclining and opening your heart to draw closer to him, He will act on your behalf and will begin frustrating the devils' strategy to plunder you of every good thing God has given you.

However, before you take any action resisting the devil, remember first to submit yourself to God effectively. That's when **God can enable you to effectively resist the devil**—Satan and his minions will have to flee from you.

This scripture is absolutely true, and it has been experienced not only by myself, many times, but by a vast multitude of God's people down through the ages; especially those who have been under siege to some addiction and besetting sin. It is pragmatic and Jesus wants you to know and experience how he makes this scripture come alive within you.

It often happens like this:

At some point in time, and, in some cases, perhaps a lot of time, you will realize and experience that **you have crossed that amazing threshold** whereby your desire for that comfortable, besetting sin you've grown so used to, clearly begins to fall away, and your desire for Jesus begins to definitely increase.

What a day that will be for you...! The truth of this scripture will be validated in your life because you believed this word to be true and you have consistently displayed strength and have acted to prove it. And, here's how that begins: **You decide** whether or not you will surrender your will to God by choosing to humble yourself and wait upon the Lord whenever temptation comes your way. When you consistently choose that action, you will begin to experience winning more spiritual battles than you lose. When that process begins to grip you, and it really will happen *if you just simply refuse to give up*—you refuse to fold your tent and throw your sword in the dirt, like you used to do when tempted.

At that point, you will cross the threshold—that line in the sand—that new border you have set up, and you will successfully resist the devil, and guess what? **The devil will have to flee from you.** He simply has no choice. The choice and the action of this process is initiated and controlled by you... The timing and the power of this process is determined and controlled by Jesus, remembering here, once again, that *"apart from Jesus, you can do nothing."*

So, once more, this scripture from James 4:7 reveals a two-part spiritual warfare tactic that God has provided, and I'll remind you of very often. Sometimes focusing your attention and action on one, sometimes the other, and sometimes on both at the same time. Jesus will always lead you and point the way.

SEEK CHRIST – BEFORE A CRISIS DEVELOPS
Throughout the many years of researching this FRP, I sought out an answer to this common question of almost everyone who was being hammered by, or heavily influenced by, some kind of debilitating sin or addiction:

What is it that caused you to finally challenge yourself to humble out and repent of your besetting sin, addiction, or almost addiction?

Great question isn't it? The vast majority said - *it was a crisis* - of some kind. They believed God's word, that a crisis would result if they failed to repent, either sooner, or later—they knew they were pushing their luck, and that it was coming, that it would really happen—that it was inevitable. They knew that certainty made them extremely vulnerable.

Therefore, this FRP and both of my books have been written with a primary mission of documenting to any Christian, exactly how that crisis can be effectively, and successfully, averted. That primary mission will require a Christian to effectively CONFRONT and OVERCOME, whatever is causing the lead-up to that crisis. That being the case, here's another pertinent question:

Why - *do so many Christians put-off and delay this confrontation?*

Why? Sadly, here's the answer: A large number of Christians simply become *lovers of pleasure more than lovers of God*. You've heard this before in previous chapters. The struggles of life cause them to harden their hearts, and, as a result of that, many end up *forsaking their first love of God (Rev. 2:4)*. Turns out that loving sinful pleasure is easy—and, loving God can be really hard. The bible says it like it is—sometimes, very candidly. I bluntly paraphrase again what Jesus said here from John 14:15:

If you love me, you will obey what I command – ***If you don't, you won't.***

Once again, these words can really STING. God's word, and his truth, cuts through every excuse we may declare, and lays bare the true condition of our hearts. Your obedience is always conditioned by your faith in, and your love of, Jesus.

I've endeavored to document the many answers to this question of confronting evil and wickedness in your life throughout every chapter of my book and every session of the action-plan on my website. Truth is, the dominant cause comes from our own *selfishness*, and it is this attribute that causes so much grief, trouble and distress to come into our lives. Truth is, consistent selfishness put on display, can and will, eventually, lead-up to a crisis—that is, unless it is effectively confronted, subdued and corrected.

The bible informs us that – ***we all like sheep have gone astray*** – *(Is. 53:6)*. We want our own way, our hearts can be exceedingly wicked, and this causes us to clash with God, and to outright rebel against him, his laws, and his way of life more often than any of us would like to admit. Isn't that right? He knows the wickedness of the human heart, and that we all can be easily enticed to rebel against him and sin, at any time, throughout all the days of our life. He has also faithfully and truthfully revealed the consequences of our sin and rebellion throughout the pages of the bible. So, we are totally without excuse, just like the bible tells us – *(Rom. 1:20). Isn't that Right? Don't you agree?*

Therefore, apart from God's grace, the wages of our sin are always paid. However, in context with the veracity of his laws, God certainly does not want any of us to perish, but he wants all of us to come to repentance *(2 Pet. 3:9)*. **That's why he has warned us to guard our hearts and avoid the consequences of sin, in the first place.** He sent us a shepherd named Jesus, to show each of us exactly how to get that done.

Jesus, as you all know, has come to give us life, and life more abundant that includes the spiritual freedom we all crave. He is determined to shepherd each of us into a lifestyle that is abundant, rewarding and enjoyable. In addition, he is equally determined to show us exactly **how to avoid a crisis** that will surely happen, at some point in our life, if we fail to develop a lifestyle that includes effective repentance, whenever warranted.

Therefore, God is appealing to you here, in this program, and throughout the bible, to exercise wisdom, logic and sound reasoning to believe and adopt the fact that a crisis of some kind will surely be coming your way if you fail to heed his many compassionate warnings. Remember this:

> *Rev. 3:20 Here I am! I stand at the door and knock. If anyone hears my voice and opens the door, I will come in and eat with him, and he with me. (NIV)*

Even though the Lord is speaking here to the 7 churches in Revelation, he also makes this offer personally to you, every day of your life. He certainly wants you to open that door, but further, **he wants you to keep it open throughout the entire day.** Anytime, and every time that you commit, a consistent, besetting sin, you are effectively slamming that door shut in his face. Jesus does not want you to do that anymore. He wants you to learn how to effectively avert a crisis that will always show up, at some point, with any expression of consistent sin in your life.

So, I encourage you to remember, and consider the parable of the Prodigal Son, as recorded in Luke 15: 11 through 32, but take particular note from this scripture in the middle of the story:

Luke 15:17 – When he came to his senses....

Now, prior to coming to his senses, the prodigal had squandered all the riches from his inheritance on wild living. Who knows how long that took? However, after having done that, *a significant crisis came upon him* when he could no longer finance that kind of rebellious lifestyle, and, he found himself out of bucks and out of spiritual gas. Fortunately for him, and also for each of us who fall into the same category, this is the message of repentance that the Holy Spirit of God put into his mind:

> **Luke 15:18** *I will set out and go back to my father and say to him: Father, I have sinned against heaven and against you... (NIV)*

So, when you come to your senses after riding the Yo-Yo for a while, you confess your sin and repent of it, then, by the grace of God, Jesus will open that door again to you, over and over, throughout the rest of your entire life, if that is what it takes for him to get through to you. He really is that good and loving, and his Gospel really is that powerful and strong—his love never fails.

Some of you have been riding that Yo-Yo for over a decade. You've been running from God, or, you have simply given up on trying to run the race anymore that God has marked out for you *(Heb. 12:1)*.

That begs another question for you to consider. Are you getting tired of this destructive lifestyle yet? Are you ready to come back home to Abba Father now, or, will you wait for that crisis, or another crisis, to come upon you?

Always remember, you have this choice to confront your besetting sin issue(s) right now, or, like so many other Christians, you can choose to procrastinate and delay the inevitable until that crisis shows up.

However, at that time, the crisis will **FORCE** you to deal with it.

At that time, the choice you have right now will be gone. God clearly is saying to you, don't wait for that to happen. Jesus has given you freedom to make that choice, so, save yourself a lot of grief, and determine to make that choice soon. That's why the bible declares - **Today, if you hear his voice, do not harden your hearts.** God does not want that crisis coming upon you.

Remember as well, from many previous sections of this FRP, that *God has intentionally designed life to be* **hard** at times. He wants it that way because he knows when we struggle with it, *that very struggle will make us* **stronger**. I encourage you to apply some effective logic and reason to this...

God makes it clear that even though the normal life experience for every Christian will be hard at times, God also makes it clear for any Christian, who gets trapped into yielding themselves to some kind of consistent sin, their lives will be exponentially way more difficult and even harder. So, it is consistent sin in your life that becomes the difficult taskmaster, not God.

In addition, God will not violate your free will. So, remember again, the longer you wait to display strength and take effective action to get yourself free, the more entrenched besetting sins and addictions become. It will be way easier to confront the issue(s) now, rather than next week, or next month, or year, or decade! *The longer you wait—the higher the cost.* Remember this well-known axiom as well, from a previous section: *"The only thing necessary for the triumph of evil is for **good men to do nothing.**"*

I remind you – Complacency is a deadly enemy...!

Okay, enough said. Next, I want to close out this chapter with a challenge to those of you not currently experiencing a debilitating crisis in your spiritual life. A major intent of this chapter has been to make all of you very aware of the struggle that God has deliberately designed into navigating life. Especially through the myriad of contrasting choices we, as Christians, must contend with on a daily basis. This struggle of life can often lead to a crisis, and, sometimes that crisis even comes by way of God himself. Remember, when God finds a weakness in something, or someone, he shakes it. He wants to ensure that we are made aware of any weakness within our spiritual health and well-being, especially our faith. *He does that on purpose - **so, we can get it fixed...***

Therefore, the challenge is to begin thinking and planning the rest of your life to develop more of a *long-term view of life—the Gods' eye view of life—*rather than a very limited, short-term view.

WALKING IN AND BY THE SPIRIT

To actually adopt this longer-term attitude and point-of-view, and put it into operation within your life, will require that you earnestly advance your spiritual life skills learning to walk-in-and-by-the-spirit, way more effectively than you do now. *Consider this:*

One of the first things we learn in life, just after we are born, is to walk with our bodies on a weak little pair of legs that do not know what to do, where to go, or how to get there. We soon discover that those weak little legs have to go through an arduous training process, and be put into consistent operation, requiring a lot of patience and practice. We fall down, we hit the floor, we bounce our heads off tables & walls, causing bumps & bruises, and, as a consequence, we experience significant pain at times.

This process of learning to walk with our bodies goes on for at least several months, and for some of us, can take a couple of years. But, at some point, we work through all the difficulties, and pass a threshold where walking actually becomes effortless—we no longer have to even think about how to walk—we just do it.

And, so it is, with sometimes amazing similarity – learning to walk in and by the Spirit. This is where your initial experience of spiritual freedom advances to the pinnacle of living life to the highest and most rewarding fulfillment possible.

> ***Gal. 5:16-17*** *So I say, live by the Spirit, and you will not gratify the desires of the sinful nature. For the sinful nature desires what is contrary to the Spirit, and the Spirit what is contrary to the sinful nature. They are in conflict with each other, so that you do not do what you want. (NIV)*

Irrespective of how old you are, or how complicated your current life might be, you need to develop and establish for yourself, through Jesus, **a powerful juggernaut of a spiritual foundation.** You really need that to fulfill what Jesus said, in Matt. 7:24-27. However, you will first need to fulfill Gods' word here in Galatians 5:16-17—just like in your physical life, **you must learn to walk, before you can run...**

The bible is teaching and admonishing us to abide in Christ, with his word richly abiding in us, and then learn to walk in and by the spirit, in such a way that we will not carry out the evil desires that can well up from within our own hearts and minds. This process can take years and even decades for some of us—I'm not exaggerating here—there are many case histories of wonderful men and women believers who have literally walked with God for decades, but, who have not yet mastered walking-in-the-spirit with confidence and stability—they're still learning. In fact, it turns out that a significant number of them do not sincerely begin learning how to **"Walk in and by the Spirit,"** until a crisis comes upon them—that's when they start in earnest. However, God doesn't want you to wait for that crisis to show up...

Regarding spiritual freedom, It is truly said,

"Necessity is the Mother of Invention."

God knows that when the intensity of your determination to acquire spiritual freedom rises to a level of being absolutely necessary for you, and is no longer just an option, you'll be like - *"a dog with a bone"* - you'll seek after this like Edison did when he invented the light bulb...after he failed over 1,000 times to make it happen—he was *"doggedly-determined"* to do it. He never quit—he just kept working at it. That was his mind-set. He considered that invention to be absolutely necessary for him and his life, but, it took a fair amount time before he actually succeeded...

That's a fact, so, be very patient with yourself and with your God. Take the long-view thinking about how absolutely wonderful you will feel knowing that you just fulfilled Matthew 7:24-27, and that door Christ has opened up to you at the beginning of your day is still wide open. Think and ponder a while on that, knowing that you will have just averted another ride on the Yo-Yo, and have also made the face of Jesus smile and shine upon you.

Godspeed My Friend – Time To Ramp It Up....!

CHAPTER 9
FREEDOM THROUGH GRACE

OUTLOOK......
This book has been leading up to a specific freedom strategy and life action plan that you need to determine, develop and put into effective operation. Therefore, my research has led me to layout a series of obstacles throughout this book that need to be personally confronted and overcome by you, to get this done. These obstacles are clearly standing in your way and must be identified and effectively dealt with, for that to happen. This is personal with Jesus, and he means it to be personal with you—your freedom strategy and life-action-plan is unique to you, because you are unique to him. That's why you won't find a 7-step, or 12-step, or any other step plan here. So, I just encourage you here, once again, to calibrate your thinking, and planning, to recall something that I wrote back in chapter 7. I paraphrased a wonderful statement that Jesus spoke in Matthew 16—he said this about you: ***"I will build YOU, and the gates of hell will not prevail against YOU."***

So, that looks like a great place to start this last chapter... Let's go there—we left off chapter 8 focusing our minds on learning how to walk in and by the Spirit. I documented what Jesus inspired the Apostle Paul to write about that from the bible in Galatians 5:16-17. Here it is again, for your reference, but this time, from the Amplified Bible version:

> *Gal. 5:16-17 But I say, walk and live [habitually] in the [Holy] Spirit [responsive to and controlled and guided by the Spirit]; then you will certainly not gratify the cravings and desires of the flesh (of human nature without God). For the desires of the flesh are opposed to the [Holy] Spirit, and the [desires of the] Spirit are opposed to the flesh (godless human nature); for these are antagonistic to each other [continually withstanding and in conflict with each other], so that you are not free but are prevented from doing what you desire to do. (AMP)*

I love the Amplified Bible version because it will often provide a *"how-to"* glimpse into something God is revealing to us—something specific he wants us to focus our minds on, learn everything about, and then to adopt, own, and make operational in our lives.

In this particular case, Jesus is telling every believer, who is learning what it means to follow after him, that they must make this process a powerful HABIT in their day-to-day living experience. I'm writing again here, about your comfort-zone, remember that? We all have one, and, I've written something about it in almost every chapter of this book.

Your existing habits—all the good ones, and all the bad ones, determine what your existing comfort-zone looks like, and how it functions. So, Jesus is saying here in this scripture, to *"make walking in the Spirit an essential habit"* and put it at the forefront of your comfort-zone. A habit—much like brushing your teeth, driving your car, walking down the sidewalk, or in this case, ***you walk in - and live by - the Holy Spirit***. You deliberately, and strategically, develop a consistent, daily routine to build this one into your most formidable habit— this is the one you make absolutely essential, and you never let it become optional and ordinary, like some of the others. You make it the most highly valued of all your habits within your comfort-zone.

You want authentic, spiritual freedom? This is the habit that will get you there. So, the following question comes up a lot from my research—what makes this particular habit so unique, and, what's the most effective way to develop it? There's one strategic scripture that answers the first part of that question really well. Here it is:

> *2 Cor. 3:17 Now the Lord is the Spirit, and **where the Spirit of the Lord is, there is freedom**. (NIV)*

You want authentic, spiritual freedom? Practice immersing yourself in the presence of the Lord—ask and pray often that God would reveal the presence of his Holy Spirit to you. The bible is filled with many virtuous reasons and benefits why you should do this. One of the most rewarding, especially for any believer who may be struggling with some kind of sinful behavior, is this; the presence of God – and the presence of sin – cannot coexist—they cannot occupy the same place. It's virtually impossible. When you are in the presence of the Lord, you simply, and wonderfully, cannot commit sin. So, that's a colossal reason to make spending abundant time in his presence, a life time habit of yours. Wouldn't you agree? Let's get that started…

The core-values that you believe in and adopt for your life make up all of your good, virtuous and godly habits. Therefore, the cornerstone and bedrock of those particular core-values that make up this habit of walking and living in and by, the Spirit, are all centered on LOVE—on how you put it on display and express it in your life, as an integral part of your Christian lifestyle. Here's how it is expressed in the bible:

The Greatest Commandment of Christ

> ***Luke 10:27*** *He answered: "'**Love the Lord your God** with all your heart and with all your soul and with all your strength and with all your mind'; and, '**Love your neighbor as yourself.**'" (NIV)*

The Greatest Characteristic of a Christian

> ***John 13:35*** *By this everyone will know that you are my disciples, if you have love for one another." (NRSV)*

Love is Greater than Knowledge, and even Faith

> ***1 Cor. 13:2*** *If I have the gift of prophecy and can fathom all mysteries and all knowledge, and if I have a faith that can move mountains, but have not love, I am nothing. (NIV)*

Love is Greater than Charity

> ***1 Cor. 13:3*** *If I give all I possess to the poor and surrender my body to the flames, but have not love, I gain nothing. (NIV)*

Love Magnifies and Weaponizes Humility, Kindness and Patience

> *1 Cor. 13:4* Love is patient, love is kind. It does not envy, it does not boast, it is not proud. (NIV)

Love is the Antithesis of Pride, Anger and Selfishness

> *1 Cor. 13:5* It is not rude, it is not self-seeking, it is not easily angered, it keeps no record of wrongs. (NIV)

Love is the Arbiter of Truth

> *1 Cor. 13:6* Love does not delight in evil but rejoices with the truth. (NIV)

Love is Eternal

> *1 Cor. 13:7* It always protects, always trusts, always hopes, always perseveres. (NIV)

Love is the Catalyst of All Godly Virtue

> *Gal. 5:22-23* But the fruit of the Spirit is love, joy, peace, patience, kindness, goodness, faithfulness, gentleness and self-control. Against such things there is no law. (NIV)

Love is the Greatest of All Godly Virtue

> *1 Cor. 13:13* And now these three remain: faith, hope and love. But the greatest of these is love. (NIV)

These core-values that literally define the characteristics of unconditional love are all uniquely personified in the person of Jesus Christ. No other human being can even come close to realizing this expression of unconditional love in their lifestyles like Christ, however, Almighty God does not mandate that we must all hold fast to that standard—not at all.

He knows, and personally identifies with our weaknesses through Jesus, however, he does mandate that we deliberately focus our lives, and pattern the expression of our living, on this standard of unconditional love as defined in the bible—it is how **we are to target our behavior.** We can never perfectly comply our lives to this standard, but, he does expect us to earnestly comply with it—to try, and try really hard, every day that we are able.

Therefore, I encourage you to adopt these attributes of unconditional love that I list here, as your own set of core-values, and use them to develop your new habits, into your new comfort-zone, and eventually, into your new abundant and constructive lifestyle. God is love, we are made in his image, and he inspires us, and even reasons with us, to navigate life by his Spirit.

That's what God is meaning in these wonderful scriptures:

> ***Eph. 5:10*** *trying to learn what is pleasing to the Lord. (NASB)*
>
> ***Is. 1:18*** *"Come now, let us reason together," says the LORD. "Though your sins are like scarlet, they shall be as white as snow; though they are red as crimson, they shall be like wool." (NIV)*
>
> ***Matt. 12:20*** *He will not crush those who are weak, or quench the smallest hope, until he brings full justice with his final victory. (NLT)*

He actively encourages us by and through the work of his Holy Spirit to actively *"reason"* with him about life stuff, and to make a sincere effort and really *"try"* to please him in all that we do. He never demands his way with any of us—but he does perfect his love for us in our own weaknesses and failures. He accomplishes our salvation, and our sanctification, through the divine attributes of his amazing grace, and that grace alone. That is how he uniquely expresses that unconditional love of his on all of us. And, we are commanded by Jesus himself, to reciprocate, and to love God back with all of our hearts, our souls, our strength, and our minds.

However, Jesus also revealed the difficulty we all face in life, as we endeavor to put that love we have for God on display. He said that there will be obstacles for everyone who decides to follow after him. And, **the chief obstacle among many, happens to be our own selfishness.** One of the most insightful explanations of this obstacle, comes from one of my favorite

Christian authors, A.W. Tozer, and something he wrote that I quoted back in chapter 4—he said this: *"In every Christian's heart there is a cross and a throne, and the Christian is on the throne till he puts himself on the cross; if he refuses the cross, he remains on the throne."*

And, that's the rub isn't it? That's where the rubber meets the road—the dilemma of every Christian—the dilemma of facing difficult choices, that every believer is forced to contend with, as they travel down life's spiritual highway. We are free to choose, which way we will go—which path we will take. The bible is replete with insightful examples of people, in all walks of life, making good, beneficial, and godly choices—and, what wonderful results those choices can deliver in life. Those are the lifestyles that Jesus encourages all of us to emulate.

However, the bible is also replete with very candid examples of other people, even very prominent people, who have made incredibly sad and hurtful choices, leading to very destructive lifestyles. Those are the lifestyles that Jesus forewarns all of us to avoid, like the plague. So, godly wisdom will always lead us to pay heed to these examples of what to emulate in life, and what to avoid. The next several pages highlights a couple of specific examples of lifestyles to be avoided—that's where I want us to start. So, I encourage you to focus your attention on how that obstacle of selfishness, can raise its ugly head, in the lives of two very well known, but very different men, and their individual choices in life. There is a lot to learn from these guys....

FULFILLMENT – LOTS OF CHOICES
Throughout this book, I write about the following:

The cry of every human heart is to be loved, to be respected and to be accepted. And, in our attempt to fulfill that longing, our minds can be easily deceived into thinking that we can satisfy that very powerful pursuit for love, respect and acceptance by indulging in all kinds of destructive behavior. As a result, many Christians end up getting addicted to it.

So, the bible and this book both establish that all of mankind is looking for fulfillment, along those lines of the previous paragraph, from all kinds of sources they discover in life. However, God has wisely designed each and every human life to include a place within, that only our Heavenly Father, working through Jesus his Son, and by his Holy Spirit, can inhabit and fulfill—that's an unalterable fact.

That's precisely what Jesus is meaning in John 15 when he says, *"Apart from Me, you can do nothing."* The bible goes on to say, *"In him we live, breathe, and have our being."* Jesus becomes our identity in life—In search of fulfillment? Of course, you are, like all the rest of us, but, what kind of fulfillment? Where are you looking for that fulfillment? God says this to the alcoholic and drug addict:

> *Eph. 5:17-18 Therefore do not be foolish, but understand what the Lord's will is. Do not get drunk on wine, which leads to debauchery. Instead, be filled with the Spirit. (NIV)*

Be filled with the Spirit—we are to walk in and by the Spirit. When we do that effectively, the bible says we will not carry out the evil desires of our flesh. The bible is replete with examples and case histories of individuals and the life fulfillment choices they make; Both to experience extraordinary levels of highly valued spiritual freedom, and also to experience what happens when they make exceedingly terrible choices and end up running out of spiritual gas and ruining their lives.

Consider the legacy and history of two well-known men: King Solomon and Howard Hughes. One man knew and lived a part of his life for God's glory and the other man did not. Both men used knowledge and wisdom to build huge empires during their lifetime. Both men ended up looking for authentic, spiritual fulfillment in all the wrong places. King Solomon thought his wisdom and intellect would satisfy and fulfill the cry of his heart. Howard Hughes lusted after riches and wealth, and, he attained a financial empire, but, what did it get him?

However, and mark this well, neither man finished life successfully at all. The end season of life for both men was a dismal failure. The bible provides some keen insight into King Solomon's life that has been recorded into the bible that - **WE MAY LEARN** - just how critically important it is to acquire a strong spiritual foundation that in turn produces a life of spiritual freedom for oneself. Consider the following scriptures:

> **1Kings 4:29** *God gave Solomon wisdom and very great insight, and a breadth of understanding as measureless as the sand on the seashore.*
>
> **1Kings 10:23** *King Solomon was greater in riches and wisdom than all the other kings of the earth. (NIV)*

King Solomon starts his life out really well. God bestowed more wisdom upon him than any other man, arguably, in all of human history, other than Jesus Christ himself. Yet the following scripture reveals how King Solomon spent the last season of his life:

> **Neh. 13:26** *Was it not because of marriages like these that Solomon king of Israel sinned? Among the many nations there was no king like him. He was loved by his God, and God made him king over all Israel, but even he was led into sin by foreign women. (NIV)*

So, even though King Solomon possessed all that wisdom, he still suffered the domination of sin through the last season of his life. Why? <u>Because he lacked a strong spiritual foundation</u> that would have kept him from experiencing the besetting sin that produced such a destructive lifestyle; a lifestyle that ended up robbing him of finishing his life with robust spiritual freedom. Once again, that message God wants you to hear; *"God gives, but the devil takes away."* - That is, if you let him.

What are we to learn and take away from this?

Even if it were possible for you to acquire more knowledge and wisdom than all of the current leaders on the planet, you would still be exceedingly vulnerable to losing everything of value you might acquire in this lifetime.

You could, like King Sol, end up failing miserably in the last season of your life.

You can rightly conclude here, that a life-long pursuit of wisdom and knowledge forged from a superior intellect, will not, in and by itself, set you up to experience a fulfilling lifestyle. In fact, it can make you very vulnerable of becoming arrogant and prideful. The apostle Paul had to guard his heart diligently throughout his entire life to keep that from happening to him. And further, look what happened to King Solomon. He ended up like a dumb animal being led around with a ring in his nose lusting after sexual fulfillment. He lost his desire and first love of God. He lost his own dignity and majesty that God had provided him as King over Israel. He lost his perspective on the value of life and his unique contribution to make it better.

Over time, Solomon allowed his heart to become hardened, little by little, becoming a lover of pleasure, more than a lover of God. Over time, he failed to recognize the symptoms within himself, that he was becoming very selfish, very self-absorbed, and extremely self-centered. His godly conscience that once guided him so well became seared and useless.

And further yet—Don't think that this example of King Solomon being easily enticed to sin is a rare occurrence in the bible for godly leaders. Truth is, that this present generation we live in includes a multitude of church leaders who are also experiencing this issue of entrenched, besetting sin and are desperately trying to get free before their fear of exposure comes upon them. **The Barna Group and several other reputable Christian oriented research organizations cite 68% of Christian men and 50% of church pastors and leaders view porn on a regular basis.**

You and I, as well as church leaders, are just as vulnerable, and just as susceptible, as Solomon was, regarding sin. However, he possessed more wisdom than anyone else on earth at that time, yet, <u>he still ended up failing miserably in finishing strong in the last season of his life</u>. Dire straits indeed! All the intellect in the world won't cut it.

It really is, and always has been – ***ALL ABOUT JESUS!***

Therefore, what can you apply to your life that will cause you to avoid what happened to the mighty and wise King Solomon? That answer is not at all simple, it encompasses several layers and levels of spiritual knowledge—especially, the pragmatic kind.

In addition, it requires very consistent personal vigilance, godly resolve and godly discipline to be acquired and sustained over a lifetime. Those life-giving attributes of spiritual freedom will only come through a strong, viable and personal relationship with the person of Jesus, developed and sustained through and by, the Holy Spirit of God.

It's all about Jesus and acquiring his attitude isn't it?

That begins, as you know so well by now, when you choose to learn, adopt and apply the key principles and precepts of truth revealed in the following scripture references:

> **John 14:6** *Jesus answered, "I am the way and the truth and the life. No one comes to the Father except through me. (NIV)*

Jesus spoke the following words to the religious leaders of his day, the Pharisees and Scribes. Like Solomon, they put their trust in their knowledge of life and the scriptures and in their academic pursuits, thinking they would acquire a life of spiritual freedom and fulfillment.

> **John 5:39-40** *(Jesus speaking) You diligently study the Scriptures because you think that by them you possess eternal life. These are the Scriptures that testify about me, yet you refuse to come to me to have life. (NIV)*

But again, like Solomon at the end of his life, they were wrong—**they missed it.**

God sent them exactly what they needed to answer that cry of their heart, to provide that fulfillment of life that only God himself, through Christ, can complete. They refused to first humble themselves, and then come to the truthful understanding that every last one of us are actually in desperate need of a viable, fruitful and powerful relationship and consistent fellowship with the person of Jesus Christ. None of us can do spiritual life and freedom by ourselves! NONE..!

Now, what can we learn from the life experience of Howard Hughes? Let's take a look. The death of Howard Hughes was recorded on April 5, 1976. He attained 70 years of life on this planet. He was mostly known for his business empire. He definitely did not live his life for God, but, he had some knowledge of God even though his insight into God and his ways was very mistaken.

His mother had a significant influence upon his early, formative years, and instilled within him a paranoia about germs and a paranoia about health and sickness and other related issues that stayed with him throughout all of his life. This paranoia caused very significant fears to develop and run rampant, especially through the last years of his life. It became very difficult for him to develop meaningful and beneficial relationships. He just could not develop trust and get close to people. Because of his being motivated so heavily by so many fears in his life, he become a "recluse", and in fact, was well known for that.

During the latter years of his life, he employed, and relied upon, the advice and counsel of members of the Mormon Church. He never belonged to the Mormon Church, but, his reasoning was that they were the only ones he could trust. So, even though he amassed a fortune and a financial empire in his life, **he could not enjoy it at all.**

Functionally, all his fortune did was to provide him a significant number of options to reinforce his paranoia and fears about very normal things in life, turning him into a virtual recluse. The last season of his life produced a profound misery and mental derangement, ending in abject torment.

Not a life that anyone would want to replicate for themselves. This model of Howard Hughes life experience provides us a striking example of how the acquisition of even a massive financial empire does not guarantee the provision or production of happiness, security, freedom or any of the well-known benefits that are universally thought to be attached to financial success.

Therefore, the last season of life experienced by King Solomon and by Howard Hughes reveals some key principles of truth being revealed. Key principles that we can acquire and put into action, that will significantly help us attain and sustain authentic, spiritual fulfillment and that lifestyle of freedom we are all seeking. Very often, spiritual freedom can be acquired through learning **what to avoid in life,** as well as learning what to pursue. Many milestones in our lives can be traced back to learning a very valuable lesson regarding the belief about some truth or tactic that we have gained, adopted and put into operation that provides a great benefit in our life.

Other milestones come along that teach us to AVOID certain things that are sure to cause trouble, distress and regret if we pursue them—like what these two men ended up believing about life, and to a greater extent, what they put into operation. Those actions they ended up living with, provide significant warning to all of us of **"how not to live."** Jesus said it like this in his Gospel of Mark:

> ***Mark 8:36*** *(Jesus Speaking) "For what does it profit a man to gain the whole world, and forfeit his soul? (NASB)*
>
> ***Matt. 6:24*** *(Jesus Speaking) "No one can serve two masters; for either he will hate the one and love the other, or he will be devoted to one and despise the other. You cannot serve God and wealth. (NASB)*

FULFILLMENT – FROM KNOWLEDGE OR FAITH?

This quest for fulfillment and spiritual freedom for one's life is very often at odds with, and in competition with, the *control over our life that each of us want to exercise.* Human beings, by nature, do not want to give up that dominion of their life over to God. We are all rebellious by nature, and, apart from the grace of God, we would remain his enemy forever.

Our righteousness is as filthy rags. Remember that one? King Solomon and Howard Hughes had a sin problem, because they each had a heart problem. They both rebelled against God because they refused to accept and adopt how God wanted to fulfill their lives. They both refused to relinquish that level of control of their life over to God. **Why was that?**

A somewhat common question came up, many times, during a lot of my research over the years, that fits in context with this dilemma. A what-if kind of question. Goes something like this: *If only I would have known all the consequences that my addictive sin would have caused me* **beforehand***, then I never would have committed it in the first place.* Sound familiar to you? Heard something like that before? So, do you think that if King Solomon and Howard Hughes knew what their sinful lifestyles would end up costing them, that they would have refrained themselves from sinning against God like they did?

Let's evaluate that. God has challenged that conclusion in a number of ways. Let's start here – Jesus made this famous statement while experiencing his cruel death on the cross: *"Father forgive them, for they know not what they do."*

Let's unpack this statement with a little detail...
How about this; What if those Roman executioners really knew where the true consequences of their sinful actions of murdering Christ would lead them. Would they have chosen not to murder him? And further, regarding all the rest of us, what if each of us sinners saved by grace, really knew what the consequences of yielding to besetting sinful temptations would actually be— what if we really knew what price we would have to pay if we yielded to that sin. Would that knowledge be sufficient to refrain us or to stop us?

Have you ever thought about that?
Could it be that if we really knew that cost, then almost certainly, we never would have committed that sin in the first place. It would have been so costly that we would never have allowed it to gain a foothold in our life. What if Jesus was also meaning that?

What do you think? Let's make it personal:
If you had known the price you'd end up paying for all that trouble and distress experienced in your life, yielding yourself over and over to that besetting sin, that question is also valid for you. Could it be that if you really knew the cost that your current expression and experience of sin has cost you, then almost certainly, you also, never would have committed that sin in the first place. It would have been way too costly for you, as it was for them. You would not have allowed it to gain a foothold in your life...

Is that true for you? What do you think?
However, God, *in his wisdom, has already revealed what that cost is to you, me and all the rest of us.* He's done that prophetically, before any of us choose to rebel and sin against him. He also declared this truth in the book of Isaiah:

> **Is. 53:6** *We all, like sheep, have gone astray, each of us has turned to his own way; and the LORD has laid on him the iniquity of us all. (NIV)*

He knows the wickedness of the human heart, and that we are all easily enticed to rebel against him and sin. God in his mercy, and by his grace, wants each of us also to know what it can cost us. God has prophetically made these consequences of sin and rebellion known to us as a deterrent from every book of the bible. Want proof? God said this in the book of Romans:

> **Rom. 1:20** *For since the creation of the world God's invisible qualities—his eternal power and divine nature—have been clearly seen, being understood from what has been made, so that men are without excuse. (NIV)*

Therefore, God has clearly revealed that sin and rebellion against him comes from the wickedness of our hearts, and not because any of us have a lack of knowledge regarding the consequences of our sin. If a lack of knowledge was really our problem, we could resolve that. We could correct that by exercising our free will to acquire that missing knowledge. Gaining knowledge is a primary function of our will power to make those kind of beneficial choices—this is where our thinking, reasoning and intellect comes in.

Remember that free will scripture from previous chapters?

Here it is again as a reminder:

> *1 Cor. 6:12 "Everything is permissible for me"* **but not everything is beneficial***. Everything is permissible for me—but I will not be mastered by anything." (NIV)*

God has given us the limited sovereignty of choosing beneficial options in life as an exercise of free will. However, our willpower is wholly inadequate to change the condition of our hearts, no matter how desperate we become to do so. Changing the condition of the human heart, the seat of our will, the extent of our limited sovereignty, is the exclusive domain of Almighty God. That's why our trust in Jesus and his commands for our welfare and the fulfillment of our lives must be absolute.

Truth is, only God can truly cause our lifestyles to be fulfilled with joy, peace and spiritual blessings. Therefore, seeking various expressions of wealth as a part of our lifestyles can be of great benefit only when we place our trust in the Lord, putting him first in all that we highly value and pursue in life.

> ***Prov. 10:22*** *The blessing of the LORD brings wealth, and he adds no trouble to it. (NIV)*

So, what do we learn from these two radically different lives, that can help to motivate us and successfully move us forward toward a lifestyle of freedom? What did these guys miss in their lives that caused such a miserable ending? They were definitely not fulfilled with peace, joy and a fruitful legacy; However, **they could have been**—God did his part—He always does.

FULFILLMENT – IT'S PERSONAL WITH JESUS

I have documented this following scripture many times, by way of reminder, and through a significant amount of detail and explanation as you have pursued the principles, axioms and tactics you need to learn, acquire and put into action:

> *John 15:5 (Jesus speaking) "I am the vine; you are the branches. If a man remains in me and I in him, he will bear much fruit; **apart from me** you can do nothing. (NIV)*

Notice that Jesus did not say, *"apart from my teaching,"* or, *"apart from good intentions,"* or, *"apart from hard work,"* or, *"apart from wisdom and high intelligence,"* or *"apart from a vast knowledge of the bible"* – **You get the point...**

No, not at all. Jesus specifically and unequivocally said: **Apart from Me...**

That's very personal...!

God knows what the desire of your heart is, moment by moment, at all times, throughout your life. He knows what you want out of life and what you are seeking, including what it will take in your lifestyle to maximize the fulfillment you get out of life. God is not bothered by, or upset with us, whenever we desire more wisdom or financial wealth and other things in our life, however, he does teach us and he even warns us, to **never lust after any of those things**, like King Solomon and Howard Hughes did.

Those **"things"** can never fulfill our life like Jesus can...

Instead, Jesus teaches us how to develop a longer-term perspective and outlook on life through him that produces way more fulfillment compared to living life exclusively for ourselves, like King Solomon ended up doing, and Howard Hughes did. He teaches us to harness our lives in service to him, and, in that process, he sets us free and we become more thankful, contented and fulfilled in life than we could ever think possible.

Let's explore that and see if we can **ignite the flames of your faith again.**

Let's take a look at your spiritual condition the day before you were saved. The bible declares that you were *"at enmity with God"* – You were actually his enemy *(Rom. 8:7)* on that day. In addition, the bible states that *"you were dead in your sins"* on that day:

> *Eph. 2:1-2 As for you, **you were dead in your transgressions and sins**, in which you used to live when you followed the ways of this world and of the ruler of the kingdom of the air, the spirit who is now at work in those who are disobedient. (NIV)*

So, take a sobering look at this truth: Even when you were dead in your sins, God took notice of you in the fullness of his time, and he personally intervened in your life and saved you from the road to hell that you were on. He did not have to do that, but, he was very compelled to do that because of his tenacious love for you, others who care about you. Guess what? God hasn't changed how he feels about you—not in the slightest.

His enormous love for you is measured today with the same intensity as it was the very first day he personally intervened in your life, and saved you from your sin. *It's personal with Jesus—that's just how he rolls.* **Question is, do you believe that?**

That core biblical characteristic of spiritual freedom centers around where you focus your love, what you highly value in your life, and just how willing are you to deny yourself, pick up your cross daily and follow after Jesus.

It's that love of God, and love of people, that Jesus talked about so much— isn't that it? What do you think? There are way too many Christians, including a lot of church leaders, who think that word from Christ *"gets in the way"* of their enjoyment and fulfillment of life. So many think that they need something else—something additional in life. How about you? Remember way back in chapter one I posed the question centering on the intensity of your determination. So, after reading and studying 8 chapters here in my book, has that intensity increased in you? Has that list of who or what you cherish and highly value in your life changed a little bit? Has your outlook on life taken on a different perspective? I encourage you to go through this last chapter thinking about the words in this paragraph, and how they apply to you personally. **It's the most important thing—here's why:**

This next key is clearly intended to be one of those strategic axioms that you will always cherish and highly value:

> **Key #14** - *The true measure of your spiritual freedom amounts to the degree that you are willing and able to <u>love the Lord your God</u>, with all of your heart, soul, strength, and mind, and then to love your neighbor the same as you love yourself.*

Further, the evidence of that measure is how well you are personally able to consistently fulfill Heb. 12:1, and scriptures like it, over time. I started my book with this scripture reference, it is still in effect, and it always will be, throughout our entire lifetime, here on Earth.

Here it is again, FYR:

> **Heb. 12:1** - *Therefore, since we are surrounded by such a great cloud of witnesses, let us throw off everything that hinders and the sin that so easily entangles, and let us run with perseverance the race marked out for us. (NIV)*

Therefore, as you ponder this enigma posed from Hebrews 12, and many related scriptures in the bible and from this book, it begs another question for you to answer... *Are you ready to fight yet?* Even in the best of circumstances, God has injected struggle into every Christian life—it's that spiritual freedom thing that I've been writing about. Where does that sit in your brain about now? The Holy Spirit of God is likely challenging you here, if you let him... The same challenge he posed when he spoke to Cain eons ago: That conversation God had with Cain can be paraphrased to read something like this:

Here's God speaking to Cain: **"So Cain, do you love me and your brother Abel enough to humble yourself and repent of your ferocious anger, because if you don't, you'll end up killing him."** We know the rest of the story. Cain did not choose to love God, his brother Abel and himself with a high enough value, so, he had little to fight for. He chose not to fight and confront his deep anger, because he simply did not value the love he had for God and family sufficiently. Big mistake for him. He failed to "count the cost" and he lost his freedom. God had made available to him everything needed to overcome his anger, but, Cain allowed his adversary the devil, to take all that away from him. He foolishly gave the devil a *"foothold"* in his life *(Eph. 4:27)*. Always remember the fight; *"God gives, but the devil takes away."* - **That is, if you let him.** So, what can we take away from this? You've heard it before; Jesus said it like this:

> **John 14:15** *(Jesus Speaking)* *"If you love me, you will obey what I command. (NIV)*

And, like I paraphrased in earlier chapters:

If you love me, you will obey what I command - ***If you don't, you won't.***

Our Lord is looking for **EVIDENCE**. Jesus is saying here, in so many words, to you, me, and every other Christian. *"If you love me, prove-it—**let me see it.**"* The same thing he said to Cain, right? In so many words. He will not accept good intentions, lip-service, or hear-say when it comes to measuring your love for him, your neighbor and yourself. Check this out: He poses another question to probe the depth of your sincerity from Psalm 15: *"Who may dwell on my holy hill?"* Then, he answers with this:

He who speaks truth in his heart.

God always searches and plumbs what's going on in the depth of our hearts. ALWAYS! God cannot be conned, fooled or mocked by any of us. No one can shine God. God is appealing to all his kids here, as documented in Hebrews 12:1 and 2. It's as if he is saying:

> *"Therefore, if your current level, experience, quality and fulfillment of spiritual freedom is not sufficient, then here's what you can do about it. Identify all those obstacles, and the besetting sin(s) that hinder you from achieving that kind of fulfillment, throw that terrible yoke of bondage off of your life, then fix your eyes, heart and attention on Jesus and obey everything he tells you to do."*

Sounds simple enough, doesn't it? However, God also knows that struggle we all face in life trying to pull that off.

A paradox for sure—that's why God wants us to place such a high value on this core attribute of life, that is our spiritual freedom. He knows that our ability to love unselfishly is linked to that spiritual freedom. In addition, he also knows as that value in our hearts increases in intensity, at some point, we will indeed fight to hold on to it.

SPIRITUAL FREEDOM – A BALANCED LIFE
Recall A.W. Tozer's quote from chapter 4 again here: *"In every Christian's heart there is a cross and a throne, and the Christian is on the throne till he puts himself on the cross; if he refuses the cross, he remains on the throne."*

So, in light of this quote, how does a Christian navigate life in such a way as to not refuse the cross, when life challenges the believer with strong temptations to throw off the yoke of Christ and do exactly that?

Here's a few advanced tactics you can activate:
1. Balance two, very key aspects of spiritual freedom, without violating either of them—works like this:
   First – learn to be content in all things, like Paul documented in this scripture:

   > **Phil. 4:12** *I know what it is to be in need, and I know what it is to have plenty.* **I have learned the secret of being content** *in any and every situation... (NIV)*

   This is a mind-set—don't set yourself up for debilitating stress and anxiety with unrealistic expectations, by getting out over your skis. Don't get ahead of Gods moment-by-moment leading in your life—thinking that you can, or thinking that you should, be able to do the next thing... Be exceedingly realistic about your faith and your capabilities—be sensitive to that still small voice of the Holy Spirit, so you don't inadvertently violate his immediate plan for your life. (**read:** *the very next thought or action <u>he wants you to take</u>—it just might be that he wants you to rest).* Cherish the peace of God that comes from being content—refuse to gamble with it—it's just too valuable to risk losing.

Second – learn when to apply grit (read; intense determination) to whatever God is leading you to think or do. Grit works exceedingly well every time you do this:

> **Phil. 2:5** *Your attitude should be the same as that of Christ Jesus:...* (NIV)

That's a mind-set also—the bible says that Christ, set-his-face-like-flint towards Jerusalem—towards the cross. He would not be deterred from the appointed mission his Heavenly Father had given him—***nor should you.***

2. In concert with that, when you are challenged with either taking an action, or avoiding one, you apply this scripture to your thinking—to your mind-set:

> **Rom. 12:3** For by the grace given me I say to every one of you: ***Do not think of yourself more highly than you ought***, but rather think of yourself with sober judgment, in accordance with the measure of faith God has given you. (NIV)

3. Having done that, you are ready to realistically assess what your actual status is, in regards to the next action you think that you need to take. You ask yourself this question: Can I do this right now, is my faith strong enough—can I really pull this off? Especially, if you know in your heart that you are likely not yet ready, willing or able to do it—Here's why:

> **Rom. 7:19** *For what I do is not the good I want to do; no, the evil I do not want to do—this I keep on doing.* (NIV)

The Apostle Paul wrote these words in the book of Romans some 20 years after his salvation. It took around 14 years for God to dismantle, and then rebuild, the spiritual foundation for Paul, getting him ready for ministry.

He wrote Romans 7 as a practicing Christian—for practicing Christians. Accounting for the blunt truth of this scripture, you ask yourself the following question: Am I really able to obey the good that I know I should do here? If you think you have a good shot at doing so, apply items 1 & 2 above, and go for it. Don't blow it off because you might have failed many times before. However, the following two reasons are almost always in play, and prevalent, when you know that you are about to hop onto the Yo-Yo again for another miserable ride:

You are either **unwilling** to do the good you know you should do—your heart is still too hard and your mind needs more renewing. Or, you are addicted, and therefore **unable at the time,** to do the good you know you should be doing. The Apostle Paul had to find that balance of being content, and at peace with his God and himself, and then knowing, at the same time, when to apply his tenacious grit and intellect to something he knew that Jesus wanted him to do—and that my friend, is not easy or quick to achieve—even if you had at your disposal, such an amazing theological genius, like the Apostle Paul. It wasn't easy or quick for him—it won't be for you and me. So, give God all the time he wants to enable and activate his plan for your life.

So, you can see the tension set-up in your mind of becoming very contented in your lifestyle and, at the same time, being ready to apply your tenacious, spiritual GRIT to the very next thing God wants you to give him—what he wants you to do.

MORE THAN CONQUERORS – THROUGH THE GOSPEL
Hopefully, you are beginning to believe and apply the sheer goodness of God and the power of his Gospel into your current spiritual condition. So, keep thinking about that with your eyes fixed on Jesus and check out this next key principle taken from Romans 8:37 – we are more than conquerors through him who loved us.

> **Key #15** - *We are enabled and empowered by the Holy Spirit within each of us to be... not just adequate, but actually to be made into **spiritual warriors that are more than conquerors**, as we increase in the unsearchable riches of the knowledge of Christ as He develops, establishes and sustains our personal spiritual freedom.*

Christ has done for each of us what none of us could possibly do for ourselves. He has truly defeated and absolutely obliterated the power of sin and death that used to hang over every human being like the Sword of Damocles!

> *1 Cor. 15:56 The sting of death is sin, and the power of sin is the law. (NIV)*
>
> *Rom. 8:2 because through Christ Jesus the law of the Spirit of life set me free from the law of sin and death. (NIV)*

Therefore, by the sheer Grace of God, through the Gospel of Christ, and, through the person of Jesus, by his Holy Spirit, He gives us grace and truth which in turn provides each of us, his followers, with the **opportunity** of acquiring spiritual freedom—that freedom is not given to us outright, but, the opportunity to seek it with all of our heart, is. However, to take advantage of that opportunity, each one of us has to figure out and learn for ourselves *(Each and every one of us, through the indwelling Holy Spirit)*, exactly how the Gospel of Jesus Christ actually works—how it functions pragmatically.

Each of us needs to learn, put into operation and consistently practice applying the Gospel of Christ until it literally becomes a very functional part of our life—this strategic member of our comfort-zone. **We Need to OWN it.** And, very specifically, what part of the Gospel we are directly responsible to God for, and what part God himself fulfills. The freedom that comes from grace does not happen in a vacuum—acquiring that distinctive spiritual freedom requires action.

There is a *"transaction"* between the Christian who has just committed a sin, Jesus our Savior, and the Holy Spirit of God. The bible clearly explains and documents the terms of this transaction here, in the book of first John:

> **1 John 1:9** *If we [freely] admit that we have sinned and confess our sins, He is faithful and just (true to His own nature and promises) and will forgive our sins [dismiss our lawlessness] and [continuously] cleanse us from all unrighteousness [everything not in conformity to His will in purpose, thought, and action]. (AMP)*

The moment this transaction happens in accordance with the grace and truth provided to each Christian from Jesus, something incredibly wonderful and miraculous transpires. At that very moment, in accordance with our faith, we experience the freedom that comes through grace. Literally, you will never be freer than you are at that very moment. Simply put, that's how the Gospel of Christ works—learn it, practice it, own it.

You jump off the Yo-Yo - *you humble yourself and sincerely submit yourself to God* by confessing and repenting of your sin according to 1 John 1:9 above, then you can rejoice and praise the Lord for your freedom. It comes to you through the mercy and grace of Almighty God, just like your first day of salvation. You'll never earn it, or better yet, be required to earn it. Jesus did that for you.

NO ONE CAN "OUT-SIN" THE GRACE OF GOD
Now, be encouraged with this—that even in the midst of the most grievous sin you commit or omit, the grace that Jesus has provided you is still very active and working to get you free and put you back on the path of life. Check this out:

> **2 Cor. 9:8** *And **God is able to make all grace abound to you**, that always having all sufficiency in everything, you may have an abundance for every good deed; (NIV)*

The bible documents many scriptures about grace; check out another one:

> **Rom. 5:20** *And the Law came in that the transgression might increase; but **where sin increased, grace abounded all the more…** (NASB)*

What about even deliberate, pre-meditated, disobedient and rebellious sin committed against God, all because you corrupted your mind, over and over for years, to the point of becoming addicted to it—even that level of sin. Can God's grace account for that? Does God's grace cover that? ***Absolutely, unequivocally yes..!*** You want some proof? *Check this out again:*

"When you were dead in your sins… God forgave all of your sins, making you alive with Christ" *(2Cor. 2:13-14)*. Therefore, being completely dead in your sins is exponentially worse than being disobedient and rebellious in your sins, yes? In addition, when you were dead in your sins, when you had not yet believed in Jesus, <u>you were actually God's enemy</u>, according to the bible. His enemy! Think of that; And, even in that condition, his grace was made available to you because of his love, and he forgave all your sins. So, even if you think you have sinned so much, so many times, over and over, with multiple repetition and unbelievable consistency, that Almighty God could never forgive you—even then; and remember as well, this axiom of spiritual truth always:

> **Matt. 18:21, 22** *Then Peter came and said to Him, "Lord, **how often shall my brother sin against me and I forgive him? Up to seven times?"** Jesus said to him, "I do not say to you, up to seven times, but **up to seventy times seven**." (NASB)*

If Jesus directs Peter to forgive his brother 490 times *(70 X 7)*, then how much more will your Heavenly Father forgive you through his forbearance, mercy, grace and loving kindness? Do the math—apply the logic here, whether Jesus is speaking literally, or not. **At least 490 times in a day!** So, do you actually believe that?

Is God really that good?
Is his Gospel really that powerful?

The moral and empirical context of this is truly profound and exceedingly wonderful! The fact is that none of us can sin so often or so grievously that we put ourselves in a place where God's grace cannot find us, forgive us, rescue us, deliver us, heal us and restore us. *We simply cannot out-sin the grace of God.* It is virtually impossible. Our sin cannot take us to a place where God's grace is not available any more. That will never happen!! *Never forget that!!*

Therefore, knowing and believing this truth, the very minute that you humble yourself, then sincerely confess and repent of your sin and turn from your wicked ways, then all the destructive lifecycle issues listed in previous chapters are immediately stopped in their tracks, halt their adverse consequences, and your life begins to be abundant, and begins to thrive again. All because God really is that good and his Gospel really is that powerful.

Here's the Gospel summary one more time:

> *2 Chr. 7:14 If my people, who are called by my name, will humble themselves and pray and seek my face and turn from their wicked ways, then will I hear from heaven and will forgive their sin and will heal their land. (NIV)*

Once again, this scripture clearly documents the pragmatic results of this transaction, previously described, between the Christian who has just committed a sin, and the Holy Spirit of God—and, it happens every time that the Christian believes and acts upon the Gospel of the Lord Jesus Christ. Did you get that? **EVERY TIME!**

So, at this point in the life cycle, you're free again. You've humbled yourself, sincerely confessed your sin to God, repented and made pertinent restitution (if needed), and you believe that you are now completely forgiven. You now are understanding and believing that you no longer bear any guilt whatsoever for that sin, you also understand and believe that God now sees you just like he sees Jesus – No imperfections, no sin, no blemish – Made perfect through the atoning work of Christ on the cross on your behalf – _your debt is fully paid_ – _you owe nothing._

Okay, let's validate... Do you believe all this? Do you believe that the Gospel of the Lord Jesus Christ is really true? Do you believe that it is really this powerful, efficacious and strong? Do you believe that Almighty God is really this good to you **personally**, knowing that you do not, and never will, deserve this goodness from him? Do you believe that Almighty God loves you personally so much, and that he wants his relationship with you restored so completely, that he actually intervened in the course and annals of human history and sent his son Jesus to receive the full penalty for your sins? Do you really believe all that? *It is really essential that you do...!*

FREEDOM STRATEGY – ARE YOU READY?
First things first—before you plan and act, YOU THINK and YOU PRAY. Every great and effective Freedom Strategy that ends up activating, empowering, and putting into motion a great and effective Life-Action-Plan, starts out in the mind, as a thought. However, the freedom strategy that you want and need to develop and put into operation for yourself, *doesn't begin in your mind. It begins in the mind of Christ.* Want some proof?

"*For I know the plans I have for you, declares the Lord.*" Remember that one?

So, let's unpack that powerful perspective with a little detail to get us started. First things first, you fix your eyes, and focus your mind on Jesus to acquire his attitude. Right? Jesus lays it out in scripture for you like this:

First, you Prepare....... You just get your mind ready:

> *1 Pet. 1:13 Therefore,* **prepare your minds for action***; be self-controlled; set your hope fully on the grace to be given you when Jesus Christ is revealed.* (NIV)*

* *Remember that Jesus is not only revealed physically at the time of his second coming, but, he also reveals himself to you spiritually on a daily basis in fulfillment of Rev. 3:20, as he stands at your door and knocks. All you need to do is to open that door, and, keep that door open all day long.*

Next, you Deny Yourself...... Put on weaponized humility:

> **Luke 9:23** *(Jesus speaking) Then he said to them all: "If anyone would come after me,* **he must deny himself*** *and take up his cross daily and follow me. (NIV)*

* *Jesus set the example for all of us from the Garden of Gethsemane when he said these words: "My Father, not as I will, but as you will"*

Then, you Submit to God...... Put that humility into action:

> **James 4:7 Submit yourselves,*** *then, to God. Resist the devil, and he will flee from you. (NIV)*

* *Remember how much the highly detailed process involved in fulfilling this scripture was documented from the last chapter? That is why, and, this is where, it fits into your freedom strategy, every day.*

Finally, you Take Dominion...... display strength and act:

> **Gen. 1:28** *And God blessed them and said to them, be fruitful, multiply, and fill the earth, and subdue it** *(using all its vast resources in the service of God and man); and* **have dominion*** *over the fish of the sea, the birds of the air, and* **over every living creature*** *that moves upon the earth. (AMP)*

* *This would involve the members of your body, including the focusing of your own mind....*

Okay, let's put this process of integrating these four passages of scripture into a workable perspective: They combine together within your mind, thereby enabling you to fulfill the following well known scriptural mandate:

> **Dan. 11:32** *the people who **know their God** display strength and take action.* (NIV)*

* *Over and over, I have deliberately put this scripture in your face—this is where the rubber meets the road!*

Got all this down? Now you're on first base—you're actually running and competing in the race, laid out for you in Heb. 12:1, remember that?

So, what's next?

All the chapters in this book have been leading and preparing you to develop a formidable freedom strategy that will culminate into a highly effective, rewarding and valuable life-action-plan. The last 3 chapters, in particular, have focused on developing perspective, some advanced tactics, and a longer-term outlook on your life, just like Christ, with Christ, and through Christ.

In addition, we can never *"pay God back"* for what we owe him—he knows that. God initiated the love he has for each one of us and he primarily wants us to learn, and then to dedicate, loving him with all of our heart, our minds, our souls and our strength. We are created in his image and he wants us to be a loving people, serving him with a loving heart and attitude. God calls that **"our reasonable and spiritual service of worship."**

> **Rom. 12:1** *Therefore I urge you, brethren, by the mercies of God, to present your bodies a living and holy sacrifice, acceptable to God, which is your spiritual service of worship. (NASB)*

God considers this to be his *"normal and reasonable lifestyle"* for Christian living. For that purpose, he sent Jesus to establish and become the mediator of a "New Covenant," documented in Heb. 12:24. Further, our Heavenly Father determined that the Gospel of Jesus Christ, would function as the spiritual engine of his new covenant, powering all of us through to the end of this age. Again, we can never pay God back for the debt we all owe him, but we can certainly **"service that debt."** And, we do that by **"offering ourselves in service"** as the Holy Spirit leads us to follow Christ daily, building his church.

Therefore, if there is one, specific scripture that accurately encapsulates and captures a powerful and effective freedom strategy for you to plug into your mind and adopt for your own life...

It may very well be this one:

> **Rom. 6:12-14** *Therefore do not let sin reign in your mortal body so that you obey its evil desires. Do not offer the parts of your body to sin, as instruments of wickedness, but rather **offer yourselves to God**, as those who have been brought from death to life; and offer the parts of your body to him as instruments of righteousness. **For sin shall not be your master, because you are not under law, but under grace.*** (NIV)

To the degree that you are enabled to consistently, and faithfully, fulfill this scriptural mandate from God in your life, you will be experiencing true, spiritual freedom. So, first things first, you'll need to **think** your way into fulfilling this mandate for your life by loading and weaponizing those four steps I just documented into your brain. That process, consistently practiced over time, will develop into a formidable and effective freedom strategy—you craft this into a life groove that becomes a highly effective habit driving your new comfort-zone.

An old biblical idiom says to: *"set your face like flint"* toward the object you are seeking to acquire. This means to take on a very aggressive attitude that you will succeed where you may have failed, or come up short, many times before—<u>but not this time!</u> Jesus himself modeled the right attitude we should all embrace: *"And it came about, when the days were approaching for His ascension, that He resolutely set His face to go to Jerusalem" (Luke 9:51).* Jesus resolutely **"set his face like flint"** toward the cross. He definitely was not going to be denied or even deterred from his appointed mission to redeem humanity from sin. Jesus had the right attitude formed because he was purpose-driven in his mission.

*This is what **GRIT** looks like put on display...*

> ***1 Pet. 4:1*** *Therefore, since Christ suffered in his body, arm yourselves also with the same attitude, because he who has suffered in his body is done with sin. (NIV)*

You should approach your mission to acquire and achieve personal freedom for yourself with the exact same attitude as Christ Jesus had regarding his mission!

A formidable, and purpose-driven freedom strategy for you, will plan on committing to him all the time, energy and resources that you possibly can, in context with loving and caring for your family, ministry, job, etc. Intentionally put God first and his response to you will literally provide the greatest, highest and most valuable fulfillment, that is possible for you to ever experience in your lifetime. Start out small if you need to, as I have detailed throughout this book. But *give God something more than what you have been doing*. And, especially, give him something of yourself. Something he can work with, bless, and reward - **Give, and it will be given to you** - You'll never regret it..!

Okay, we have a strategy—so, what do we do with it?

LIFE ACTION PLAN - *Where the Rubber Meets the Road*
It is God's unique plan *(Jer. 29:11)* here that becomes your Life Action Plan; they are one and the same. Further, it is within this plan that you lovingly submit your life of service to him in his kingdom, following and obeying Jesus as he builds his church. It is this particular service from you that fulfills the mandate from Jesus - **that you bear much fruit** - from John 15. That is precisely how you service that eternal debt that you, me, and all the rest of us, owe to God. Okay, having determined the thought process and freedom strategy behind your plan, we need to develop and activate the initial *"what, when, and how"* aspects of putting your life action plan into operation. Looks like this:

What to Do...... *(First, always connect with Jesus through prayer and bible study)*
  1. You already have a *"Comfort-Zone"* made up of a series of habits, both good and bad, beneficial and destructive, that are a part of your

life. So, first make a list of your habits that you believe are good and beneficial for you and another list of those habits that you believe are harmful and bad for you. Write this list down to program your brain.

2. Figure out what you believe will improve and increase the effectiveness of all of your good habits, thereby making them even more beneficial, and put that into operation.

3. Figure out what you believe will make each of your good habits *easier to perform,* and *will be more joyful* as you do them, then make that happen.

4. Figure out what will result in the most fulfilling and valuable reward that you can think of receiving upon completing each of these good habits, then put that into motion.

5. It has been effectively established over the years that it is exceedingly difficult to just delete, or eliminate a bad habit. However, it has also been established that a bad habit can successfully be REPLACED WITH A GOOD ONE. So, target those bad habits that you know need to be replaced with good ones; think through and determine each of those good habits, and how they will replace the bad ones—see that actually happening in your mind's eye. And especially, what it will feel like overcoming and replacing each bad habit with a good one.

6. Figure out what tactics you can employ to *make it much more difficult* for you to perform each of your bad habits. Make it really hard for you to do that. Resist the devil and the wickedness of your own human nature......!

When to Do......

1. Jesus said, *"Do not worry about tomorrow... and that each day has enough trouble of its own."* In addition, there is ample commentary in scripture that God directs us to focus the attention and planning of our life - **one day at a time.**

2. Further, most successful leaders break down a day's activities into at least 3 separate parts; Morning, Afternoon and Evening. Therefore, make your To-Do list as specific as needed to fit your lifestyle.

3. So, in the context of acquiring freedom, especially from a destructive lifestyle, plan your To-Do list activities *(Your Good Works - Eph. 2:10)* for each day of the week, and rarely plan good works, other than appointments, beyond a week.

4. Set up an efficient monitoring system to evaluate your new comfort-zone once a week. Document each day of freedom from destructive behavior that you experience on a calendar.

5. Look back over the week and assess how effective you were, making your good habits easier to do, and making your bad habits much harder to do. Adjust as needed over time as Jesus leads you. And remember that Jesus said this for you: *"My yoke is easy and my burden is light."* **Enjoy your life..!**

How to Do......

1. First things first, set up a specific prayer time to ask God to impart a spirit of love, a sound mind and discipline in you. Next, ask and pray that he would impart supernatural favor, blessing, words of knowledge and vision in you – and further, that he would lead, guide, bless and anoint the work of your hands and your mind. Then to make you very aware of each good work he has prepared for you to do that day from Eph. 2:10, that will fulfill the plan he has for your life from Jer. 11:29.

2. For each day, consider a maximum of 10 activities, including personal, family and work stuff, that you would like to get done. From that list, prioritize the 3 activities that you consider would provide you the highest return, all things considered. From that short list, develop a habit to pray and ask God which of all those activities that **HE would consider to be the most important, have the highest**

value, and represent the timeliest to get working on first. That good work is where you want to start. This process gives you the assurance that if all you are able to accomplish, is the first activity for that day, you'll know that's the one God wanted you to do before any others.

Okay, remember this following statement from a little while ago......?

This is a spiritual warfare check point for you. Here's another one:

The only way that you will know for certain that you have gotten off to a really good start at fulfilling your freedom strategy for the day, is when you actually initiate and begin to accomplish the first good work you and God have scheduled. That is, **"when you actually put your hand on the plow and get to work."** You actually display strength and take that action. You take dominion. When that actually happens, you will know that you have wisely and successfully made the choice to deny yourself and proclaim God, his will and his plan to be the winner for that day. At least to begin that day.

Always remember that hopes, dreams, good intentions, excuses and lip service, will not suffice. This is the time for proof—for evidence. It truly is a measure, that is, a *"snapshot in time,"* of where your faith, your heart, and your love of Jesus, currently is at. It is truth. It is where you place your value. It is where the rubber meets the road, on this particular day, and at this particular time. **Do this consistently, and that truth will set you free.** However, what if the following **shocker** comes your way...? Be prepared—develop this plan:

In Case of Emergencies....... *Use your "Spiritual Fire Extinguisher"*
1. **Do This:** After applying all that you can from your new Life-Action-Plan, should you find that your spiritual strength is just not sufficient to resist that nemesis of sin—to put out the fire of temptation, burning within you... Do what Joseph did when the devil attacked him through Potiphar's wife... ***"BOLT – Get the hell out of there"***

2. **Or This:** Immediately fix your attention on Jesus, and the presence of his Holy Spirit... You'll need some help—one of the most effective

methods of doing that consistently, is to set apart several sections of this book, to be used *"In case of spiritual warfare emergencies."* Here's what I mean—As you read through, and study the pages of this book, you'll encounter sections of 3 or more pages at a time, where you sense the presence of God, to be very close at hand. When that happens to you, mark the beginning page for each of those particular sections. There will be many. Know where each of these sections start, so you can quickly turn, and begin prayerfully to read through that section. Do this at any time you find yourself really struggling to resist the *"sin that so easily entangles you."* Here's why:

> *2 Cor. 3:17 Now the Lord is the Spirit, and **where the Spirit of the Lord is, there is freedom.** (NIV)*

This is the irrefutable word of God—said another way, *"where the Spirit of the Lord is, there can be NO SIN present."* That's the place you want to be whenever you find yourself under horrific temptation to sin in some way. Do what Jesus did in the desert when the devil tempted him to sin...He cited the word of God, saying: *"IT IS WRITTEN."* The Spirit of the Lord showed up—the devil had to flee... *He had no choice....*

Want more proof? Christian counselors, therapists, and psychologists who specialize in treating addiction, cite and use the following fact about the inner workings of the human brain. Almost all temptations to sin, **have a finite time frame of intensity.** That's some very strategic, and some very good news—especially for a believer struggling to fend off a barrage of temptation coming their way.

Here's why—It has been scientifically, and clinically proven, that the intensity, and the ferocity, of most temptations begin to dissipate significantly after a time frame of 2 to 5 minutes. So, knowing this, the wise believer being besieged by an intensive bout of temptation, can apply this **spiritual fire extinguisher-by reading a key section of this book,** to quench that fire. That's how it works...
So, hang in there—wait it out—it will blow away.....

However, be forewarned—these 2 tactics should not be used in an impulsive way. So, *be sure to plan your way into this*, in advance. Forebear with yourself by making this decision, to take this action, well in advance of the spiritual attack—know that this is the action you have predetermined to take in the event of a spiritual warfare emergency. Write it down as a part of your freedom strategy and life action plan— **make these 2 tactics to be your "spiritual fire insurance policy."**

And, always remember this about Gods' grace... If and when you experience a *"clash of wills"* between you and God, and, for whatever reason, you determine that you either cannot, or will not, submit yourself to God that day, well then... You will likely end up jumping on the Yo-Yo again for another ride - *And, you know that drill by now.*

Then again, for every day that you are enabled and empowered by the grace of God to faithfully **bear much fruit,** you can expect God to reward you with that **well done witness of good work—you'll be rejoicing...**

So, every time that happens, you should receive his supernatural favor and blessing, give him abundant praise, and then, do it again tomorrow and the next day, and the day after that, and every day thereafter... **Hallelujah..!**

THIS BOOK IS NOW FINISHED... *SO, WHERE DO WE GO FROM HERE?*
What's Book 2 All About—A different kind of freedom......

Book 1 – *Freedom through grace*.... Begins and ends with increasing the unsearchable riches of your knowledge of Jesus, and then learning and increasing your understanding of how the Gospel of Christ functions, and how you put it into effective operation on a daily basis. Acquiring that attitude of Jesus, and then consistently thinking more, and acting more, like him in your lifestyle.

Book 2 – *Freedom through obedience*.... The next book on acquiring freedom is all about applying what has been learned from book 1, to effectively work out your salvation with fear and trembling. Learning and understanding how you cooperate with the Holy Spirit more effectively, as he sanctifies you on a daily basis. Developing and establishing *a deep, rigorous life-groove* of surrendering and submitting your will to Jesus, more effectively, thereby *making him the Lord and Master of your life* as well as being your Savior, Teacher and Coach.

> *Phil. 2:12-13 Therefore, my dear friends, as you have always obeyed—not only in my presence, but now much more in my absence—***continue to work*** out your salvation with fear and trembling, for it is God who works in you to will and to act **according to his good purpose.** (NIV)*

Three words that can change your life in ways that you can only imagine, or hope for. *"**His Good Purpose."*** Your Freedom Strategy and Life Action Plan from this book 1 are deliberately designed to lead and develop your unique place in God's Kingdom. He created you and put you here on earth for good reason. Jesus wants to express, and to magnify his incredible love for you, by preparing you, and then giving you, the keys that will unlock the highest fulfillment of your life. Expressed and documented here from a couple versions of scripture:

> *Titus 2:14 He gave his life to free us from every kind of sin, to cleanse us, and to make us his very own people, totally committed to doing good deeds. [good works] - (NLT)*
>
> *Titus 2:14 Who gave Himself on our behalf that He might redeem us (purchase our freedom) from all iniquity and purify for Himself a people (to be peculiarly His own, people who are) eager and enthusiastic about (living a life that is good and filled with) beneficial deeds. (AMP)*

Three words that can change your life in ways that you can only imagine, or even hope for... *"**His Good Purpose."*** Book 1 has been designed to develop a highly effective spiritual foundation within you in preparation to take on the lifestyle challenges I've written in Book 2.

Remember these two statements from earlier chapters:

Find out what God wants from you and **give it to him**
Find out what spiritual freedom will cost you and **pay that cost**

In each case, you will be challenged, and those challenges will be revealed as you pursue the unique expression of spiritual freedom that you can only develop through obedience to the commands of Christ. God has a unique "Calling" for you—*His Good Purpose for your life*, in service to his kingdom:

> **Eph. 4:11-13** *It was he who gave some to be apostles, some to be prophets, some to be evangelists, and some to be pastors and teachers,* **to prepare God's people for works of service,** *so that the body of Christ may be built up until we all reach unity in the faith and in the knowledge of the Son of God and become mature, attaining to the whole measure of the fullness of Christ. (NIV)*

Applying that attitude of Christ, that you develop in Book 1:

> **Eph. 4:1-2** *(Jesus speaking here through Paul) I want you to get out there and walk—better yet, run! - on the road* **God called you** *to travel. I don't want any of you sitting around on your hands. I don't want anyone strolling off, down some path that goes nowhere. And mark that you do this with humility and discipline—not in fits and starts, but steadily, pouring yourselves out for each other in acts of love, (Message)*

So, book 2 is designed to get you to the next level, and the next experience of true, authentic, spiritual freedom—remember, it's a life journey. I document more research results to help answer compelling questions from ordinary Christians who are being hammered by various expressions of destructive lifestyles. Here's a few:

1. How successful is the *"Cold-Turkey"* method of getting free from various addictions—especially for a Christian?

2. When is it prudent to seek medical and/or professional help?
3. What's going on in my brain that makes it so difficult to renew my mind?
4. Why do so many Christians end up relapsing so often after having been rescued or delivered from besetting sins and addictions?

Book 2 will explore more forward-looking spiritual warfare tactics of how ordinary Christians have been very successful prevailing over besetting sins and addictions that have tripped them up for years—common patterns of thought and behavior that trigger those besetting sins that can easily entice you, and, how to effectively combat them. God's calling on your life;

His Purpose—Your Freedom..!

And now, I want to really thank each one of you for your dedication and commitment to read and study what I have written. I sincerely hope that you enjoyed it and that these words of mine have given you a number of life changing things to think about. Wishing you the very best as you now begin to put all you've studied through the pages of this book, into effective and rewarding operation.....

GODSPEED TO EVERY ONE OF YOU!

BIBLIOGRAPHY *(A Partial Reference List By Relevance)*

THE BONDAGE BREAKER – Break the Chains Holding You Back -
Jan. 1, 1993 - by Neil T. Anderson *(Publisher: Harvest House)*
BATTLEFIELD OF THE MIND - Winning the Battle in your Mind –
April 13, 2011 - by Joyce Meyer *(Publisher: Faithwords)*
THREE STEPS FORWARD TWO STEPS BACK – Persevering
July 1, 1980 - by Charles R. Swindoll *(Publisher: Thomas Nelson Inc)*
FLY INTO THE WIND - How to Harness Faith and Fearlessness –
November 17, 2020 - by Lt. Col. Dan Rooney *(Publisher: Harper Collins)*
THE WHISPER OF GOD - The Voice that Speaks Freedom –
October 24, 2017 - by Mark Batterson *(Publisher: Multnomah)*
TAKE BACK YOUR LIFE - Fight to Take your Life Back –
August 4, 2020 - by Levi Lusko *(Publisher: Thomas Nelson)*
CAPTURE – Unraveling the Mystery of Mental Suffering –
April 12, 2016 - by David A. Kessler M.D. *(Publisher: Harper Wave)*
SWITCH ON YOUR BRAIN – The Thought Life –
September 1, 2013 - by Dr. Caroline Leaf *(Publisher: Baker Books)*
THE END OF ANXIETY - A Biblical Perspective—Overcoming Fear
July 21, 2020 - by Josh Weidmann *(Publisher: Salem Books)*
OVERCOMING ADDICTION - A Biblical Path Towards Freedom –
August 1, 2018 - by Elizabeth A. Shartle
(Publisher: Life Sentencing Publishing, Inc.)
CRUSH YOUR FEARS - Powerful Promises to Overcome Anxiety –
November 18, 2019 - by Daniel B. Lancaster
(Publisher: Lightkeeper Books)
GOLIATH MUST FALL - Winning the Battle Against Your Giants–
May 16, 2017 - by Louie Giglio *(Publisher: Thomas Nelson)*
I WANT TO CHANGE MY LIFE - How to Overcome Addiction –
March 1, 2010 - by Steven M. Melemis MD PhD
(Publisher: Modern Therapies)
BECOMING A THREAT TO ADDICTION - How to Eliminate Relapse–
July 16, 2019 - by Mark Winslett *(Publisher: Indy)*

SHAKEN - Discovering your True Identity in Life's Storms –
October 25, 2016 - by Tim Tebow (Publisher: Waterbook)
CHOSEN BY GOD - The Sovereignty of God and Free Will –
1986 - by R. C. Sproul (Publisher: Tyndale House Publishers)
RENEWING YOUR MIND - God's Thoughts and Ways Are Higher –
1973-'82-'98 - by R. C. Sproul (Publisher: Baker Books)
GRACE AWAKENING – Grace and Truth To Live By
1990 - by Charles R. Swindoll (Publisher: Word Press)
THE POWER OF THE SUBCONSCIOUS MIND – Unlocking This Key
2007 - by Joseph Murphy (Publisher: Wilder Publications, LLC)
WINNING THE WAR IN YOUR MIND – Thinking & Life Changes
2021 - by Craig Groeschel (Publisher: Zondervan Books)
BEYOND THE COSMOS – Knowing God in a Relational Way
2010 -'17 - by Hugh Ross (Publisher: NavPress)
RESPECTABLE SINS – Confronting the Sins We Tolerate
2007 - by Jerry Bridges (Publisher: NavPress)
DESTINED FOR THE CROSS – Spiritual Warfare
1982 - by Paul E. Billheimer (Publisher: Tyndale House Publishers)
REVEALING THE MYSTERIES OF HEAVEN – Knowing God
2019 - by David Jeremiah (Publisher: Thomas Nelson)
THE BOOK OF SIGNS – End Times Prophecy
2019 - by David Jeremiah (Publisher: Thomas Nelson)
REVELATION—THE NEXT DIMENSION – Prophecy and Christian Life
2014 - by Greg Laurie (Publisher: Keygma Publishing)
GOD – As He Longs For You To See Him
2004 - by Chip Ingram (Publisher: Baker Books)
THE MIRACLE OF LIFE CHANGE – Spiritual Metamorphasis
2003 - by Chip Ingram (Publisher: Baker Books)
THE PLEASURE OF HIS COMPANY– Intimate Friendship with God
2014 - by Dutch Sheets (Publisher: Bethany House)
LEADERSHIP BY THE BOOK– Tools To Transform Your Workplace
1999 - by Ken Blanchard - Bill Hybels - Phil Hodges
(Publisher: Waterbrook Press)
LIFE FORCE – Quality of Life via New Technological Breakthroughs
2022 - by Tony Robbins (Publisher: Simon & Schuster)

www.ingramcontent.com/pod-product-compliance
Lightning Source LLC
Chambersburg PA
CBHW042013060526
44119CB00123B/440/J